HISTORIC
GARDENS
of DORSET

HISTORIC GARDENS *of* DORSET

Timothy Mowl

TEMPUS

For Michael Liversidge

Front cover: Mapperton, Beaminster
By kind permission of Lady Caroline Sandwich
Back cover: 1767 painting by William Tomkins of Plumber Manor
By kind permission of Richard Prideaux-Brune
Frontispiece: The Large Globe, Durlston Park, Swanage
By kind permission of Howard Eaglestone & The New Arcadian Journal

First published 2003

PUBLISHED IN THE UNITED KINGDOM BY:
Tempus Publishing Ltd
The Mill, Brimscombe Port
Stroud, Gloucestershire GL5 2QG

PUBLISHED IN THE UNITED STATES OF AMERICA BY:
Tempus Publishing Inc.
2 Cumberland Street
Charleston, SC 29401

British Library Cataloguing in Publication Data.
A catalogue record for this book is available from the British Library.

ISBN 0 7524 2535 8

Typesetting and origination by Tempus Publishing.
Printed in Great Britain by Midway Colour Print, Wiltshire.

Contents

Foreword

Dorset is one of the most rural counties of England. With no main industry, no drive-through motorways and no large city (unless you count Bournemouth on its eastern edge), Dorset retains a timeless air of sleepy isolation. It has a beautiful and varied countryside, redolent with Hardy-esque pastoral mystery. However, with comparatively few great landowners – although those there are have lasted through the centuries – but with a plethora of smaller manor houses, the county has always been touched by national events, not least in the changing fashions of garden style.

The county's gardens, intimately part of the landscape, have long awaited a perceptive review. Their exploration by Timothy Mowl is masterful; it is stimulating, educational and provocative. His great strength, besides elegant prose, is his deep knowledge of garden history which makes it possible for him to see each garden in its wider contemporary context, whether the garden accompanies an Elizabethan mansion or a modern conversion. He produces some surprises. Some of the Dorset garden layouts of great historical importance have been his discovery both through persistent archival research and through actual identification on the spot. Which of us knew that the seventeenth-century gardens surrounding Lulworth Castle were as grand a concept as those of Wilton House and executed at least twelve years earlier? Throughout his book he illuminates influences, traces gardening ancestry, and opens up gardening vistas into the past and future. It is rare to find a scholar with the spirit of an explorer. The book makes inspirational reading, not least because of his forceful personal opinions which put both old and new garden makers firmly in their place. Alexander Pope and 'Capability' Brown, both generally considered icons of the eighteenth-century garden world, daringly get short shrift at least as far as their influence in Dorset is concerned. Above all, far from the book being a list of facts and dates, the writer walks the reader through garden scenes, sensing theatrical drama, anticipating surprises and disappointments and communicates the meaning of the garden. In interpreting the 'genius loci' Timothy Mowl follows, even if perhaps unwillingly, in Pope's footsteps.

Penelope Hobhouse

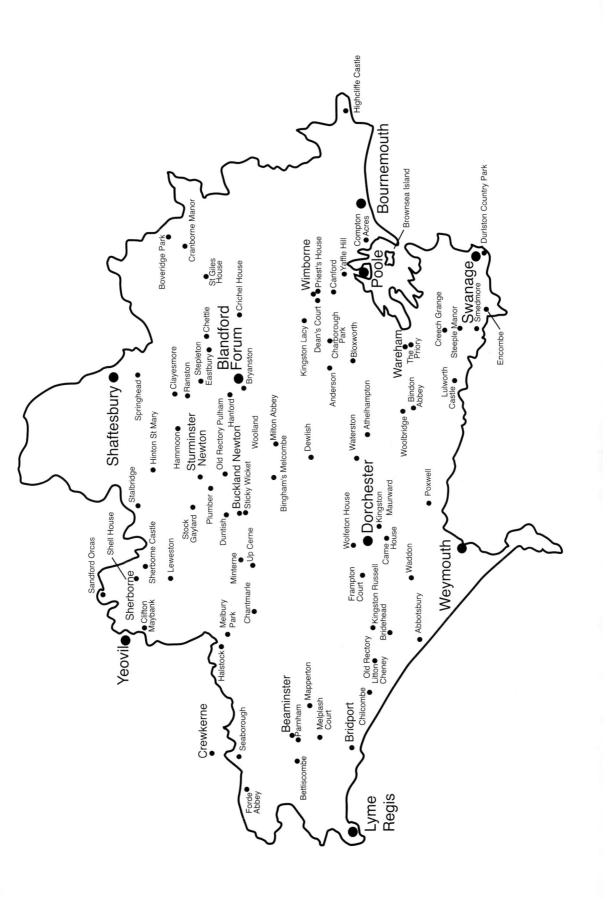

Acknowledgements

My first thanks go most warmly to the committee members of the Dorset Gardens Trust who have made the researching and writing of this book possible with their generous support and advice. The Trust Chairman, William Gueterbock, made the initial approach during one of my public lectures in Sudeley Castle and has busily projected lectures, publicity and the forthcoming launch; Sarah Fitzgerald shared much valuable information on the sites and their owners; Graham Davies has read the manuscript and offered sound and scholarly advice; Penelope Hobhouse has written a thoughtful and enthusiastic foreword, in addition to giving me a most memorable tour around her own garden at Bettiscombe.

The Dorset Record Office has been a most valuable resource for documentation on the gardens and I would like to thank all the staff for their enthusiastic help and efficiency. Then there are close friends and academic colleagues who have been ready to answer my queries; these include John Harris, Nigel Temple, Michael Liversidge, Stephen Bann, Michael Richardson and Hannah Lowery, David Lambert, Kate Feluś, Anthony Beeson, Dawn Dyer, Patrick Eyres, Howard Eaglestone, Judith Roberts, Hal Moggridge, Anne Andrews, Val Hurlston-Gardiner, Ann Smith, and my MA students, Christine Stones, Stephen Parker, Trish Gibson, Stephanie Macdonald, Angela Nutbrown and Steve Coffin.

Almost all the owners I have met or contacted have been ready to allow me to roam at will in their gardens and parks and have been helpful with both information and enthusiasm, as have their archivists and gardeners. I should like to make especial mention of the following: Lord Shaftesbury, Lady Cranborne, the Honourable Mrs Townshend, Lord Digby, James Weld, Sir Philip Williams, Lady Caroline Sandwich, John Wingfield Digby, Nigel Thimbleby, Anthony Pitt-Rivers, Viscount James and Jemima Fitzharris, Andy Poore, Dilly Hobson, Rupert Scott, Robin Harcourt Williams, Denis and Patricia Moriarty, Carol Hammick and Adam Tindall, Martin Lane-Fox, Selina Gibson-Fleming, Mrs Jaffé, Jennifer and Derek Coombs, Nigel Davis, Hazel Garrick, Jill Howes, Jim Farquharson, Norman Hayward, Suzy and John Lewis, Geoff Adams, Alison Smith, John D'Arcy, Steve Teuber, Trevor Toogood, Dave Austin, James and

Sarah Gordon Wild, Charles Chaffyn-Grove, Janie Martin, Peter and Gwen Holguette, Roy Portch, John and Betty Langham, Pam and Peter Lewis, Mark and Sue Douglass, Gillian Elliott, Mrs Mackenzie-Johnston, Simon McDonagh, Rosalind Richards, the late Colonel Yeatman, Sue Frampton, Adam and Susanna Laurie, Simon and Alison Tremewan, Olivia Eliot, Mr and Mrs Timothy Lewis, Lucinda de Moubray, Hugh and Carol Lindsay, Peggy and Robert Lazenby, Jeremy and Rosemary Isaac, Will Isaac, Mr and Mrs Howard Carter, Joanna Parker, Simon Bonvoisin and Sir Mervyn Medlycott.

Richard Prideaux-Brune kindly let me take down his Tomkins painting of Plumber Manor for the back cover picture and Stephen Morris photographed it and undertook archival photography for me in his usual professional and expert way. Ann Pethers of the Bristol University Arts Faculty Photographic Unit developed all my films with quiet efficiency and has produced the prints that illustrate the book.

I should like to thank my good friend and co-researcher, Brian Earnshaw, for his intellectually rigorous approach to the garden sites and for his map reading and companionship on those seemingly interminable car journeys from Bristol to Dorset. My agent, Sara Menguc, has been as encouraging as ever, and Peter Kemmis Betty, Tim Clarke and Michelle Burns have produced the book with their usual efficiency and enthusiasm. Finally, I should like to record my debt of gratitude to my wife, Sarah, my son, Adam, and my daughter, Olivia, who have weathered my every intellectual storm and cheerfully shared my firm commitment to this exciting project of producing studies of the historic gardens of the counties in England; Wiltshire next.

Timothy Mowl
Bristol
Winter 2002

Introduction

Towards the real garden history

A good case could be made for Dorset being the most stable county – socially speaking – in Britain; stable being a polite word for conservative, and conservative being a cautious euphemism for feudal. Consider the great county families of the past – Howards, Cecils, Ashley-Coopers, Wingfield-Digbys, Fox-Strangways and Welds – except for the Howards, who left in 1641, every one of those families still sits comfortably in house, garden, park and generous land holdings, rallying points of confidence around which the lesser gentry have gathered, models for wealthy newcomers to imitate. Dorset's fortune has been that the Industrial Revolution passed it by. If its chalk streams had been reliable enough to power woollen mills or if Kimmeridge shales had proved usable substitutes for coal, events might have been different. But it was no accident that Trade Unionism found its martyrs at Tolpuddle.

Then, as a park and garden factor, there was the county's remarkably consistent topographical profile. With no broad river valleys, no coastal plain, and with Somerset taking over to the north almost as soon as the contours levelled out, the Dorset landscape is one of mildly dramatic, though never threatening, hilly irregularities. Every mile the vistas switch bewitchingly, change and recompose. Parks on the boring, handsome model of Capability Brown virtually shaped themselves. From a landscape designer's point of view the only disadvantages were the intermittent nature of the winterbournes, the need for heavy clay puddling in most areas if a lake was required, and the poor sandy soil of the heaths, where deciduous trees grew warped and stunted.

A great county then for gardens, and so for me 2002 has been my wonderful Dorset year. Writers like James Lees-Milne and Bevis Hillier, John Betjeman's biographer, build up a picture of a forlorn aristocracy hanging on in crumbling mansions and ruined gardens, so they can never have spent much time in Dorset. Between January and October I visited eighty-seven gardens in the county and inevitably missed many more. It was a most memorable ten months. Not every day was easy; one owner set security staff on alert to check that I did not step off the one right-of-way across a frankly rather dull park. Another held a Rottweiler on a short leash while I stood in the drive, pleading in vain for a glimpse of the pleasure grounds. But I am grateful to the other eighty-five civilized and hospitable landowners, not a bad proportion, who made most of my Dorset gardens hugely enjoyable and immensely rewarding.

I am not claiming for a moment that this is a definitive survey. Nikolaus Pevsner's *Buildings of England* architectural volumes went rapidly out of date and are now being brilliantly revised. Pevsner travelled around his early counties in a few weeks hard labour during the academic holidays, so my ten months' researching and visiting seems positively leisurely and potentially rather more comprehensive in its coverage. I have interpreted 'historic' to mean significant, irrespective of date. Even with the generously offered and invaluable support of the case files prepared by the Dorset Gardens Trust's determined team of researchers, I must have missed vital features and telling evidence in several gardens. Dorset is wonderfully garden-rich and I am happy to admit that there are minerals still to be mined.

In defensive mood let me mention three, not discoveries, because they have always been there and someone knew about them, but one complete layout and two fascinating garden buildings whose national importance is being aired for the first time in these chapters. At Bindon Abbey, Dorset has the only complete Tudor water garden in England (**1**). There is no need to scrabble around dry earthworks or speculate on television about what might have been. It is a garden of haunting melancholy whose shadowy waters are deep and wide enough to row a boat along, as Paul Hentzner rowed his in 1598 on the canals of Lord Burghley's Theobalds. Thanks to the wise conservatism of a great Dorset landed family, the recusant Welds, it is all still there, yet a recent issue of the Garden History Society's journal on Tudor gardens gave it merely one line.[1]

Then there is that so-called 'Summerhouse' in a dark wood at Castle Hill, or Duntish Court, Sir William Chambers' severe 1764 villa, which was demolished in the uncaring 1960s (**2**). The Summerhouse was a joke, or should I say a rictus on the face of Sir William, an intensely correct classical architect. It was cluttered up with wood and workmen's garden gear when I saw it, appropriately so as Chambers never intended this gloomy bothy as a summerhouse; it was later described as the 'Carpenter's Shop'.[2] He was suffering from a recent Scottish experience with a classical fanatic, and he designed it to be constructed from flints and bricks, with window relics salvaged from the earlier house. Then, to amuse or instruct his patron, Fitz Foy, timbers were tacked onto its walls to represent pediments, columns and entablatures, and so to mock the theories of the trendy Abbé Laugier who had claimed in his *Essai sur l'architecture* that the origins of classicism lay in the post-and-lintel structure of the primaeval wooden hut and that, therefore, to use these merely as decorative motifs was a sin. Not one expert has spotted the significance of this building. All the inspectors from the Royal Commission on Historic Monuments could do was to analyse the mouldings of the re-used Tudor windows, when under their noses was the bitter humour of a great, frustrated classicist, a witty protest against pedantry from an architect who was himself often something of a pedant.

1 *A corner of the Elizabethan island garden at Bindon Abbey with the Gothick Lodge of 1798 as prelude to the Retreat House and Chapel*

2 *The Summerhouse or 'Carpenter's Shop' at Duntish Court, Sir William Chambers' mockery of the Abbé Laugier's theory of the origin of classical architecture from the primitive hut*

With the last of my chosen three let me underline the beauty and again the national importance of the Shell House in the grounds of Harper House, Sherborne. It is a Rococo temple of refined sophistication that has languished unsung in the garden of a public school boarding house. No conglomeration of Jamaican sea shells like the Grotto at St Giles House, it must have been the considered creation of a London craftsman, and it gives a new slant to England's reception of that alien, inventive Rococo style that so nearly rescued us from the predictabilities of the Palladian interior.

The real garden history of this country has yet to be written; and it is still too early. Academics began writing the history of gardens and designed landscapes much too soon, under the influence of literary studies rather than of the first-hand, hard walking experience of many hundreds of actual gardens. For an academic there was always the temptation to pick up some obscure sevenneenth- or eighteenth-century poem, so boring and badly written that others had ignored it, and then to construct a learned exegesis of its implications for garden design of its period. It would make an acceptable article for a journal and then, later, it could be cobbled together with a few more of the same in an allusively titled book creating a new academic discipline – Garden History as the scholarly world understood the term. Throughout the whole process there was never any need to scrape the mud off walking boots.

The distraction and the danger lay in following two over-worked circuits. One was the circuit of iconic, celebrated gardens that every writer referred to like so many safe stepping-stones across a marsh. The list writes itself: Hampton Court,

Wilton, Castle Howard, Stowe, Rousham, Stourhead and so on. The other was
a circuit of source books, by Isaac de Caus, Stephen Switzer, Alexander Pope,
Horace (the Great Deceiver) Walpole, Joseph Spence, Humphry Repton, all so
helpful and quotable, but all making their own biased cases.

I have recently written on the seventeenth-century gardens of just one county,
Hertfordshire, and found that the gentry there were introducing Arcadian layouts
in their modest gardens long before the much trumpeted Wray Wood at Castle
Howard that always gets the credit for the innovation simply because Switzer
focused our attention on it. Another distraction has been those collections of
letters and plans that were spirited away across the Atlantic by Anglophile million-
aires in the 1960s when they were going cheap and we needed the foreign
currency. They are so much easier to handle than the massive treasure of accu-
mulated documentation, part catalogued and waiting to be unravelled, in just
about every County Record Office of England and Wales. Extrapolating from
magpie resources in Washington, Toronto or Boston had the advantage of making
American and Canadian readers feel part of the action and, of course, it swelled
book sales. But it rarely amounts to more than half-supported generalisations.
What is needed is to spread out the net of knowledge much wider, to all gardens,
county by county, to sub-districts if necessary, walking and then writing with an
open mind, not in the expectation of certain patterns. Our Wray Woods need to
be put into their real national garden context.

Read on for so much else, for at least a rough profile of the real gardens of
Dorset: for Jacobean gardens still carefully tended in the mid-eighteenth
century, for Capability Brown most improbably anticipating Kew, for the
twentieth-century idealism of Sticky Wicket and for the ebullient confidence
of recreated Bloxworth, umbrella pines and all. Lastly my unashamed gratitude
to the gentry of both sexes, the upper and upper middle class garden owners
of Dorset, for making a naturally beautiful county far more varied and
delightful than it was when God had it to himself. That, after all, seems to be
what we are here for.

1

A Renaissance garden for a Howard, a Medieval garden for a Queen of Spain

The oldest complete garden in Dorset surviving in its original form, though not with its original planting, may have been begun soon after 1544, in the last years of Henry VIII's reign, by Thomas Howard, second son of Thomas, the 3rd Duke of Norfolk, in what had been the grounds of the Cistercian Abbey of Bindon in the parish of Wool. Thomas was a cousin of Elizabeth Tudor who, when she became Queen, made him 1st Viscount Bindon in 1559. He died in 1582, by which time it is reasonable to suppose his gardens were in their prime. It could be argued that they are the most complete Tudor gardens anywhere in England, but the scholarly Royal Commission on Historical Monuments volume for south-east Dorset, after devoting three pages of detailed description of the ugly and fragmentary ruins of the Abbey, dismissed Lord Bindon's creation in its final paragraph with: 'Ice house, in mound surrounded by wet ditches', a reminder of how recent is the intense national interest in gardens and garden history.[1]

What makes Bindon so fascinating is not only its melancholy beauty, but the possibility that Lord Bindon was following a much earlier pattern of monastic hydraulics when he laid out his own watery grounds. The Cistercians had settled at Bindon in 1172 for the potential of its water. The Frome flows through a flat and, scenically speaking, rather dull area of the county, where it can be channelled, sluiced and controlled to water a wide fertile area. Their monastic church, a modest structure, lay within sound of the roar of two mill weirs, one mill, now lost, was for fulling cloth (3). The other is a grist mill whose almost impossibly picturesque atmospheric mill house, like something painted by George Morland, still stands, smothered in old roses, but deserted because of recent floods. Even in a dry summer the flow of the river over its weir is frighteningly strong and the Abbey buildings actually lie well below the Frome's level above the weir. Bindon is a place where the river has to be handled firmly and skilfully, otherwise the fields would revert to marshland, like that tangled stretch of waste land on the other side of the Piddle from Athelhampton.

Thomas Howard was the river tamer whom the site needed, but he was not the man who first received the Abbey property after the monks were expelled

3 *The ruins of Bindon Abbey with a water channel, mill house and river beyond from Hutchins'* Dorset of *1774.* Bristol Reference Library: Central Library

in 1539. That was Sir Thomas Poynings who bought the site in 1540 and he, nervous perhaps of all that water, shunned the complex site. Instead he began its enduring relationship with Lulworth by using material from the Abbey to build a hunting lodge, Mount Poynings, a mile to the west of present-day Lulworth Castle.[2] Poynings died in 1544 and Howard, his brother-in-law, bought Bindon from Poynings' brother and settled down there, turning the domestic ranges of the Abbey into a 'fair house'.[3] Henry Pollard was doing exactly the same thing at the same time in the west of the county at Forde Abbey; but there the union of monastic buildings and domestic residence has endured in a stimulating stylistic complexity.

The buildings which Thomas Howard had bought lay in a square about a cloister to the south of the Abbey church, all serviced by a hydraulic system of sluices and channels. A stream drawn off the Frome up-river entered this square of monastic structures at its south-western point, by the dormitory of the *conversi*, the semi-religious workers of the community. It then ran along the south range, turned due north to service the lavatoriums on the east range, after which it was fed on east to rejoin the river. Presumably in 1544, only five years after the Dissolution, there would still have been some of the nine monks, who had been pensioned off, or skilled *conversi* in Wool village who understood the system of sluices that kept these waters flowing. Using their labour and expertise Howard expanded the waterworks boldly, digging out two large moated squares of garden, the lesser to the south-west of his courtyard house, the larger, with its big garden mount, immediately to the east (**4**). In both of these ambitious new gardens the flow of water along their canals was kept moving by an extension of the same system of sluices that the monks had been using for the past three centuries.

That is a simplification of the garden canals at Bindon. In addition to these two broad, square moats of water and the Frome itself there is another fast moving channel, which was cut in the nineteenth century, possibly as a trout stream for Cardinal Weld, who loved fishing. This flows over gravel between the river and the larger moated square of garden. A much older, slower channel runs between the two squares and the road. These two moated gardens with their canals make up a Tudor water garden on a grand scale, one befitting the house of a cousin of the Queen. So to hydraulic engineering Lord Bindon added wit in the form of conceits, one to each garden within its moats. In the centre of the smaller garden is a little lozenge-shaped pond with a lozenge-shaped inner island. The larger garden has its inner horseshoe-shaped moat curled around a viewing mount.

The 3rd Lord Bindon, the first Lord's second son, Thomas, who inherited the estates in 1600 after the death of his older brother Henry, was another builder. Previously, in 1586 at Waterston Manor, he had added a rich classical frontispiece to the vernacular fabric, and in 1608 he was adding a new gallery

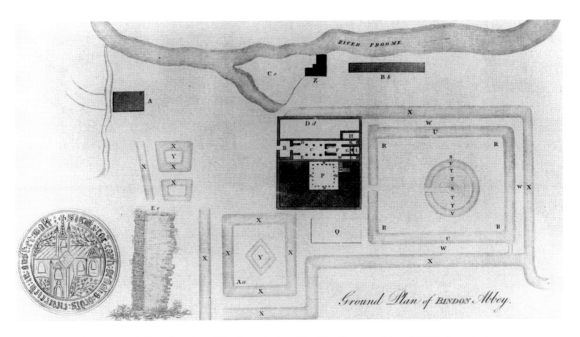

4 *This conjectural plan of Bindon Abbey from the later Hutchins* Dorset *edition of 1861 shows the two water gardens largely as they survive today, but assumes that they were of monastic origin.* Bristol University Special Collections

to the monastic buildings at Bindon.[4] But it was this 3rd Lord Bindon, ultimately, who would be responsible for the decline and fall of the Abbey. In 1605, using the Abbey stones and materials from Mount Poynings, he began to build that quintessential Jacobean conceit, Lulworth Castle. Perhaps he had tired of Bindon's damps and floods, but he was also intent on luring King James to stay at an impressive hunting lodge out on Purbeck.

After his death in 1611 his cousin and successor, the extravagantly corrupt old sea dog Thomas Howard, 1st Earl of Suffolk, succeeded in doing just that. Lulworth Castle was launched socially by the royal visit in 1615 and Bindon fell into neglect. When the 2nd Earl of Suffolk, Theophilus, ruined by his larger-than-life father, became strapped for cash in 1641, he sold both Bindon and Lulworth to a wealthy London merchant, Humphrey Weld. The epic Dorset story of its most remarkable county family, the staunchly Roman Catholic Welds, was thereby inaugurated at the worst possible time for such recusants, only a year before the Civil Wars broke out with the triumphs of militant Protestantism. During the course of the wars' marching and counter-marching Bindon's 'fair house' was demolished in 1644, but its gardens have lingered on, virtually unchanged in benign neglect, one of Dorset's rarest and least noted treasures.

Today, from the East Stoke to Wool road, nothing is visible except a low line of concealing woodland; though at the corner beyond Bindon Farm the road crosses one of the feeder channels that still keep the gardens alive, and all these water meadows are dotted with sluice gates which a determined Wellington boot wearer can explore. This is that land, 'a green trough of sappiness and humidity', which Thomas Hardy uses as the setting for some of the most nightmarish episodes in his *Tess of the D'Urbervilles*. This is his 'Vale of the Great Dairies' where the Frome runs clear and rapid, 'with pebbly shallows that prattled to the sky all day long'.

At a break in the woods where a drive comes out from Bindon, a passing motorist can get a glimpse of the improbable fantasy world of the gardens. Two airily amateur buildings, the Lodge and the Retreat House, stand one behind the other, styled in that appealing Gothick of the late eighteenth century which preceded Pugin's scholarly muscularity. They are tempting but unfortunately entry is forbidden unless the Weld estate office at Lulworth has given permission and the tenants have agreed to conduct a visit. Nearest to the road is the Lodge, a turreted three-bay carriage shelter with cramped accommodation above (**5**). Now much decayed, it is still an engaging garden building in faded pastel colours, oxblood, blue and ochre, embattled and pinnacled. Its wooden gates have cusped and traceried panels like a page from some contemporary antiquarian pattern book explaining the growth of Gothic architecture from the Romanesque.[5] This and the Retreat House are Gothick intruders and belong to a later Weldian episode of the grounds, one more connected to the ruined Abbey than to the Tudor gardens.

5 *The rear view of the Lodge at Bindon. It has rooms over the arch as well as on each side. The gates are carved with Gothic and Romanesque motifs like a page from an architectural pattern book*

Immediately behind the Lodge lie the canals of the smaller garden kept, by the wise stewardship of Denis and Patricia Moriarty, dredged but not disciplined, as a wild water garden of yellow water lilies, reeds and bulrushes (**6**). The moated island garden itself is quite flat and covered in rough grass and meadow flowers. At its centre is the lozenge-shaped pond with its small lozenge-shaped inner island, a retreat within a retreat, access to which is via a plank bridge over the slowly moving, lily covered waters.

Here, better than anywhere else, not just in the county but the country, it is possible to evoke the spirit of that great garden which William Cecil, Lord Burghley, created between 1575 and 1585 at Theobalds in Hertfordshire. Theobalds was primarily laid out to entertain Queen Elizabeth, but it was automatically an assertion of Burghley's prestige, and its gardens impressed both the English and visiting foreigners. Its Great Garden was described in 1598 by the German, Paul Hentzner:

> From the place one goes into the garden encompassed with a moat full of water, large enough for me to have the pleasure of going in a boat and rowing between the shrubs. Here are great variety of trees and plants, labyrinths made with a great deal of labour.[6]

James I liked it so much that he pressured the Cecils to exchange their Theobalds for the old, run-down royal palace of Hatfield. And at Hatfield,

6 *The lozenge-shaped island in the middle of Bindon's Elizabethan water gardens, probably the earliest surviving example in England complete and still watered*

between 1607 and 1612, Robert Cecil, soon to be Earl of Salisbury, contrived another garden feature almost identical to the lesser garden at Bindon.

In the middle of Hatfield's artificial lake, composed of four canals, was a lozenge-shaped island, and that was quartered by streams with a central pavilion built over their meeting point.[7] 'You have', a French visitor reported of Hatfield, 'where the River enters into and comes out of the Parterre, open Sort of Boxes, with Seats round, where you may see a vast Number of Fish pass to and fro in the Water.'[8] Fish, by their mere presence, were considered an entertainment and, while the water features at Bindon tend to be described as ornamental canals, it is inconceivable that this maze of rectangular pools, still trout filled and kept moving by at least eleven sluices linked to the water meadows, would not have served as larders for Fridays as well as for the fashionable gentry sport of fly fishing.

Bindon was laid out much earlier than Hatfield, but both gardens gave pride of place to a lozenge-shaped island. It is only possible to speculate as to the nature of the wooden pleasaunce or seat which must have occupied Bindon's island, but its planting may have been similar to that at Theobalds. Cecil's Great Garden had nine frets: fences enclosing a square and twined about with fruit espaliers and rose bushes. So the outer raised walk around Bindon's first square island, or the shore of its inner island may have had similar screening frets. They would have given a purpose to the second and larger moated garden because its high mount would have overlooked the other's privacy.

This second presents an entirely different experience to the first garden. A wide plank bridge, in its original Tudor position, leads into a solemn world of dark trees over wide, shadowed waters. Beeches, alders, sycamore and ash have taken over the whole square island including the steep mount that rises by two stages in its centre. There are two raised walks: one around the island's shore and a parallel, longer walk around the outside of the moat. Either would have given the ladies of the house their exercise for the day. The atmosphere here is almost Arthurian, a quiet green gloom of short vistas, its silence broken only by the occasional splash of a brown trout rising in the moat. Everything is enclosed: a world of leaves and water with no sky.

This is the magical melancholy of the second garden today, but in its original concept it must have been very different. An early postcard view shows the mount quite bare of trees and bushes (**7**). Pattern rather than flower colour was the essence of Tudor gardening. Low hedges or 'pallisadoes'[9] of juniper, whitethorn, sweet briar and osier, set around with strawberries, primroses and violets, were staple features bordering turfed or gravel paths. The mount is partly surrounded by a horseshoe-shaped moat and it had a circling terrace halfway up for viewing the patterns of these hedges. On the top would have been a wooden pavilion from which all the geometric knots and frets of the neighbouring island garden could have been enjoyed. Theobalds had a similar feature, which is described in 1613: 'There is also a little wood nearby. At the end you come to a small round hill built

7 *An Edwardian view, before the trees grew up, of the Mount and its much later Grotto in Bindon's larger water garden.* W. Pouncy; Private Collection

of earth with a labyrinth around. [It] is called the Venusberg.'[10] This is in accord with the larger garden at Bindon, which may well have had a maze on the inner island, with the central mount as a tribute to Elizabeth as the Goddess of Love. The garden would have been sunny and extroverted where now it has become a mood creator for gloom and introversion.

Quite what the Welds made of it all is uncertain, but later they pierced the mount with a tunnel that leads into the most depressingly dank, brick-vaulted garden room in Dorset. It was certainly never an ice house, as the RCHM supposes, because it has three Gothick-arched niches for candles, but who, even on the warmest day, would have stayed long within it for pleasure? On the top of the mount are the foundations of a square building with a projecting porch or portico, perhaps an eighteenth-century classical temple as a counter to the Gothick Grotto below.[11]

The 1st and 3rd Lord Bindon's reactions to the remains of the Abbey have not been recorded, but they were Howards and the Howards were a conservative family, faithful in most of their generations to the old Catholic order.[12] The first Weld, Humphrey, was a convert to Catholicism by marriage, and while the Arundels and Norfolks, as premier peers of England, tended to brush off the disadvantages accruing to a persecuted faith, the Welds clasped their sufferings from anti-Catholic mobs and predatory tax collectors to their bosoms, revelling in minor martyrdoms and intensifying their transmontane allegiances. Their activities at Lulworth belong to later chapters, but it would be illogical to delay an account of their building at Bindon between 1793 and 1798 to another chapter as it was the ruins of the Abbey that kept drawing them back to the seat which they had lost in 1644, and it was the Abbey that gave a unique character to their garden buildings.

Bindon Abbey haunted the consciences of the Welds in almost every generation. As ardent, persecuted yet still influential landed gentry they must always have dreamed of a Bindon restored to the monks. The brief reign of James II would have given them an equally brief charge of hope. Otherwise they lay low, paying their additional, punitive taxes, sending their sons to universities in Flanders for a Catholic education and marrying their children off to the children of fellow recusant gentry. Half of a yellowing plan survives among the Weld papers.[13] The date is ripped off, but it was prepared for one of the two mid-eighteenth-century Edward Welds and is a careful, reasonably accurate reconstruction of one half of Bindon Abbey as it would have stood before the disaster of 1539. Another, dated 1806, and drawn for Thomas Weld ('the Builder' as the family called him), again shows the Abbey complete with Thomas' arms in one corner.[14] Then there are five other reconstructions of the site, nineteenth-century in style, but undated and roughly drawn. So the site was something of an obsession, a challenge, a pious duty shirked.

There had always been a private family chapel in Lulworth Castle. Thomas the Builder, who ruled from 1775 to 1810, rebuilt and redecorated this room, but then, having charmed George III on a visit when the Weld children sang an anthem to 'Great George', he received royal permission to build a proper Catholic church. Designed by John Tasker, this went up near the Castle between 1786 and 1787: an elegant domed structure like the Roman Pantheon as conceived by James Wyatt (**colour plate 12**). Thomas Weld then turned his mind to crumbling Bindon. His Account Books for the various years prove that in 1793 he was learning to think Gothic instead of classical and paid for his agent John Hunt to make notes on Gothic churches during his several journeys about the country.[15] On 5 September 1793 money was given 'To Hunt to pay journeys spent in seeing Cathedrals £3.17.6 & £21'. On 18 October in York, Thomas seems to have studied that cathedral personally. The note for the day reads: 'Seeing the Cathedral 2.6'; and on the next day: 'For cloaths at York making in all £4.10.6', which indicates that the visit was multi-purposed.

Then on 2 December Thomas seems to have moved decisively with: 'to Cox [his contractor] for mending the road to Bindon 12.6', followed on 23 December by the mysterious: 'Paid ye two old men at Bindon up to this day inclusively £2.1.0.' The illustration of the site in Hutchins' *Dorset* shows a small cottage behind the ruins, so possibly the two old men were caretaker-gardeners. After that the Bindon payments to carpenters and labourers multiply, culminating on 29 June in: 'To Cox for cleaning ponds at Bindon.' So the gardens were being restored while the new Gothick structures were going up. An entry of 6 July in 1796 of '£500 to Mr Tasker pd reemander of the principle' suggests, though does not prove, that John Tasker was the architect, moving from the classical dome of his Lulworth church to an elegantly spiny but quite unscholarly essay in the Gothick style. The mason was Mr Towsey, paid £55.11.0 on 11 August 1794, an advance on the £500 he would be owed. A final costing 'For ye Abby House & premises £1850 Total £1913.5.0' was made, presumably for both buildings, the Retreat House and the Lodge, on 27 July 1798.

The scholarly problem at Bindon is how to describe the 'Abby House', for it is like no other garden building in England. In its original form it had four modest rooms on the ground floor with a much taller single room, the Chapel, on the first floor. As recorded in the 1972 Newman and Pevsner's *Buildings of England* volume for Dorset, when this was still consecrated, it had three large windows with simple 'Y' tracery and a plaster groin vault supported on groups of emaciated Early English Gothic shafts with an altar on the blind east end. Pevsner described it aptly as 'innocent unarchaeological Gothic'.[16] Thomas Weld may have taken the lean Gothic shafts from the chapter house at York Minster. It was a building of much charm and great significance for the Catholic community. While not registered as a place of worship until 1885, it clearly functioned as one from 1798 onwards. At the same time that it was built the Grotto was hollowed out of the Tudor garden mount, so there was some concept in Thomas Weld's mind of devotion and pleasure being combined in one garden: a retreat house with humble accommodation below and a chapel above. The revived Tudor gardens and the ruins of the real Abbey would have acted as reminders of a lost age of faith.

It is not easy to see where the Bindon Abbey gardens' future lies now that the whole building has become a comfortable dwelling with the chapel turned into an exotic drawing room. There is the awful possibility that an 'authentic' garden of Tudor knots will eventually be replanted as part of some heritage scheme in a 'Thomas Hardy Theme Park'. Our best hope is that the traditional piety and historic awareness of the Weld family will be a defence against that fate. It is, however, impossible to leave this extraordinary site without mentioning the use which Hardy made of it in *Tess of the D'Urbervilles*, that glorious piece of bodice-ripping writing which has rather improbably established itself in English literature as a classic of authentic rural tragedy.

Woolbridge Manor, upstream from Bindon, was where Angel Clare and Tess came for their ill-fated honeymoon and he discovered with horror that she had lost her innocence some years earlier to the unscrupulous Alec. In an improbable piece of writing the distressed Angel sleepwalks out of the house with Tess in his arms, carries her across the Frome on a narrow plank bridge and, coming to the ruined choir of the Abbey church, lays the frightened girl in 'the empty stone coffin of an abbot, without a lid' (**8**). Still fast asleep he kisses her twice on the lips, 'when he immediately fell into the deep dead slumber of exhaustion'. Tess managed to raise him up, without waking him, and guided him back, still implausibly fast asleep, this time over the stone road bridge, to bed again. Hardy has brushed the Welds' Retreat House out of the chapter. The empty stone coffin, apparently that of Richard de Maners of about 1310, still lies in the east range of the ruins, and all the other features of Hardy's melodrama survive, waiting to be turned into a popular adventure trail. So Bindon deserves to be protected by the strictest possible preservation order.

At this point in a survey of early historic Dorset gardens it should be remembered that there must have been many gardens in the county far older than Bindon. The Bishops of Salisbury, in the twelfth century, had a substantial garden in the precincts of their castle-palace at Sherborne, but no one is certain in which area of the walls and there is no relic of its layout surviving. Ralph Cresswell's 1586 plan of Corfe Castle indicates a garden in the south-west corner of the inner bailey, but there is no record of what it might have looked like.[17] Woodsford Castle, Overmoigne Court and Godlingston Manor, Swanage are all medieval houses which might be expected to offer medieval garden traces. Their problem is that they have all been in continuous occupation. Occupants must eat, so they bring their gardens up-to-date. Bindon's distinction is that, while the parent house died early, in 1644 when its gardens were barely a century old, the grounds lived on for sentimental reasons in the casual guardianship of the conservative Weld family.

One other candidate for extreme garden antiquity does deserve to be mentioned. At their very earliest the Bindon canals could have been laid out

8 *In Thomas Hardy's* Tess of the
D'Urbervilles *the sleep walker Angel
Clare lays the terrified Tess in this
medieval stone coffin at Bindon*

in the last years of Henry VIII, though more probably they are Marian, or early
Elizabethan. It was Elizabeth who in 1559 created Thomas Viscount Bindon,
which suggests that his house and grounds had achieved viscount status during
her reign. But there is one fortified manor in this socially remote and retiring
county which did actually entertain, presumably in its gardens, a Queen of
Spain and her husband, the Archduke of Austria, back in 1506 when Henry
VII was on the throne. This was Wolfeton House outside Charminster, today
a forlorn fang of a manor house as atmospheric and textured as any manoir in
the rural depths of Poitou. It lies on the headwaters of the same river as
Bindon, the Frome, but in a less intimate relationship with its floods. While
Bindon's house disappeared completely when Lulworth took over the estates,
Wolfeton only lost, early in the seventeenth century, its aristocratic owners, the
Trenchards. Tenant farmers were installed, several ranges of the house and its
chapel crumbled away or were demolished, particularly between 1822 and
1828, but elements at least of its gardens remained until more appreciative
owners, first William Weston then, after 1875, Albert Bankes, took possession
and gardened more positively.

Even so there is very little in Wolfeton's grounds that pre-dates Bindon's
watery enclosures. Still, a Queen of Spain, even if it was only poor Joanna
the Mad, mother of the Emperor Charles V, is quite a catch for any garden,
so Wolfeton does merit for its rough charm at least a prolonged footnote in

this chapter. The Queen's visit was apparently inadvertent. Her ship had suffered storm damage and taken refuge in Weymouth harbour, or so it was claimed. The situation was in reality, diplomatically delicate. Joanna was not really Queen of all the Spains. She was the elder daughter of Los Reyes Catolicos. Her mother, Isabella, Queen of Castile, Leon and the Asturias, had just died, but her father, Ferdinand, King of Aragon, was still alive and ruling. Joanna, who was on her way from Flanders to claim her thrones, was the sister of Catherine of Aragon who was living in England in uneasy widowhood, her husband, Arthur, Prince of Wales, having died in 1502. Catherine was hoping to marry Arthur's brother Henry, which indeed she did when he succeeded his father in 1509. Joanna's 'accidental' arrival at Portland may well have been a deliberate move to gain support for her claims in Spain or her sister's cause in England.

This explains why Sir Thomas Trenchard was so eager to entertain the royal couple in Wolfeton while posting news of their arrival to the King in London. But what, if anything, in Wolfeton's present-day gardens could Queen Joanna have enjoyed? Not the great Riding School, which is the oldest in the country, a ravaged but gauntly handsome stone barn, buttressed and patterned with blocked mullioned windows. That dates from 1610 and stands beside the ill-surfaced track that links Wolfeton with Charminster. Wolfeton is open to the public and has a number of interesting and beautiful features: doorheads, overmantels and chimneypieces within, but this track must discourage the average country house enthusiast. In the woodland to the right of it there is a lake and an icehouse, but they do not connect with the main gardens south of the house, though there is a shrubbery walk around the lake and it is crossed by a sluice bridge.

The track becomes a drive, dips under low trees and emerges before what is left of Wolfeton's much restored northern entrance front. A three-tiered fountain splashes noisily in this informal space. Behind it is a clump of golden yews, euonymus, golden privet and battered yew trees, sprawled over by an enormous vine and some honeysuckles. Straight ahead is a gatehouse; its irregular twin drum towers have conical roof caps and are quite outrageously quaint, but even these Joanna cannot have seen, because they are dated 1534. Through these gates lies a nondescript area of rough grass and trees. On the 1839 Charminster tithe map this, not the lawn south of the house, is marked as 'The Bowling Green'.[18] A 1774 engraving of the house in its garden from Hutchins' *Dorset* confirms this, showing the Bowling Green well kept and surrounded by a low wall (**9**). Round the corner of the house from this is a broad expanse of mown grass overlooked by the wildly picturesque south front, which has an early sixteenth-century tower, a garderobe and late sixteenth-century rooms of state. This lawn is confined on its west side by Wolfeton's only authentic early garden feature, a long, embattled Tudor wall. The Hutchins view shows that it had a matching twin wall to the east. The two, linked by an ornamental fence with white posts topped by urns, enclosed a

9 *Hutchins' 1774 view of Wolfeton House shows the Bowling Green on the right, the Ladies' Garden behind a paling, and the battlemented wall of the Kitchen Garden: a typical Tudor layout.*
Bristol Reference Library: Central Library

pleasaunce with rose bushes climbing the walls. Beyond that, as now, was the Kitchen Garden with its espaliered apple trees.

So the areas of the gardens which could have been admired by the mad Queen of Castile and her husband, Philip Hapsburg, are limited to these three units: the Bowling Green, the Pleasaunce and the Kitchen Garden. An impressively scholarly survey of the grounds conducted for the Dorset Gardens Trust casts doubt even on these, urging that the wall, with its white wisteria and pink climbing roses, dates only from Sir George Trenchard's rebuilding operations of the 1580s.[19] It is also questionable whether a pleasaunce would have been sited immediately below the principal garderobe or lavatory of the house as seems to have been the case. Visitors are unlikely to have been impressed by such a conjunction.

The point that Wolfeton makes is that the gardens of most of Dorset's medieval manor houses were no more ambitious than this: an area for games, an area for walking which would be reasonably dry under the ladies' feet, and a garden for fruit and vegetables and herbs, simple walled enclosures for shelter and privacy. Bindon represented an entirely different garden concept. It was semi-royal, a garden of the Renaissance, open to French and even Italian influences. Thomas Howard had set out to create conscious patterned paradises, islands within islands, and a viewpoint from which to look down upon it all. Years after those unexpected royal visitors, Trenchard would still be adding, in 1534, a fortified gatehouse to Wolfeton. Ten years later Bindon, on the other hand, was completely undefended, its gardens were not walled; everything was for display and pleasure. It belonged to a different age and a far more ambitious garden aesthetic.

2

Jacobean enclosures and a Baroque precursor

It has become a cliché of English garden histories that the true precursor of the formal gardens of the post-1660 period was a great Franco-Italian design laid out at Wilton House, Wiltshire, by the 3rd Earl of Pembroke in the 1630s (**10**).[1] Inigo Jones and Isaac de Caus were its designers; it was created specifically to please King Charles I, who often visited the house, and it had the good fortune to be illustrated in detail in a book entitled *Wilton Garden* or *Le Jardin de Vuilton*, with plates probably engraved by the celebrated Jacques Callot. Nicholas Stone carved statues for it, John Aubrey wrote about it in his usual gossipy inaccurate style and John Evelyn, when in his Puritan phase, described it disdainfully. Wilton has, therefore, found a firm niche in the accepted sequence of garden influences.

The garden at Lulworth Castle, laid out in the preceding reign of James I by the 1st and 2nd Earls of Suffolk, was equally grand in scale and planned on much the same Franco-Italian axial layout (**11**). Being some ten or even twenty years earlier than the Wilton garden it should have been recognised by garden historians as a style setter of national importance, one visited often by King James, who introduced the Italian classicism of Andrea Palladio to England by commissioning in 1619 Inigo Jones to build the great Banqueting House at Whitehall Palace.

Unfortunately, the Lulworth garden labours under a number of handicaps which have prevented it, right up to the present day, from being given its true place in English garden history. It is not associated with a famous name like Inigo Jones and no contemporary wrote about it except Lieutenant Hammond who, in his 1635 *A Relation of a Short Survey of the Westerne Counties* only writes of 'large and goodly Parkes'.[2] Most damagingly, it was not illustrated until 1721, shortly before its almost complete destruction, and then only by an amateur; it was 'delineated by the Lady of ye Seat', Mrs Margaret Weld. Other circumstances have conspired to obscure its fame as compared with that of Wilton. Lulworth was deserted by the Suffolks in 1641 and, gutted by a fire in 1929, it is now a mere shell of bare walls. Wilton has remained the seat of the Pembroke earls, splendid within and without and still surrounded by gardens, though only one displaced and rebuilt architectural fragment of the original

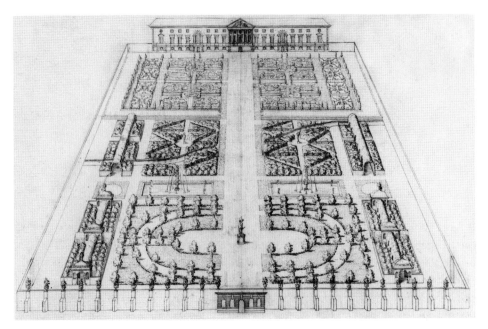

10 *The 1630s proposals by Inigo Jones and Isaac de Caus for the gardens of Wilton House, Wiltshire. The Franco-Italian sequence of parterres, wilderness, orchard and garden house follows, in some features, that of the earlier grounds of Lulworth Castle.* The Provost and Fellows of Worcester College, Oxford

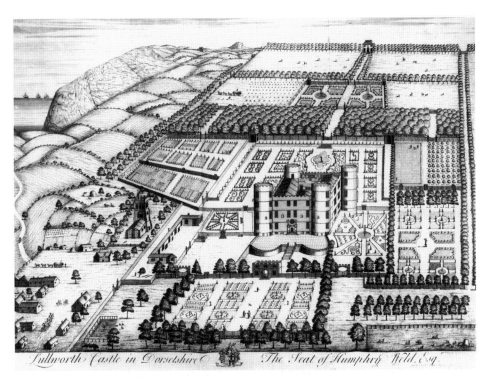

Lulworth Castle in Dorsetshire   The Seat of Humphry Weld Esq.

11 *The gardens of Lulworth drawn in 1721, just before the Stuart layout by the 1st and 2nd Lords Suffolk was swept away. The gardens to left and right of the main axis and in the foreground were additions by Theophilus, the 2nd Earl.* John Harris

Jones-de Caus garden has survived.[3] This chapter will try to set straight the record of innovation, authorship and chronology.

It was during the twenty-two-year reign of James I (1603-25) that Dorset became, for that short time, the favoured county of the most influential Court aristocracy and a perfect hunting ground for their master the King. As early as 1594 Sir Walter Raleigh had begun building his outrageous fantasy Castle at Sherborne, but Raleigh was not a man with whom the new King ever felt at ease, until he had him executed in 1610. Robert Cecil and Thomas Howard were different. They belonged to that powerful group of aristocrats who had engineered James' unopposed accession to the throne, adding the crowns of England and Ireland to that of Scotland. In a return of favours James made Cecil Viscount Cranborne, after the old royal hunting lodge of Cranborne which, together with the Rangership of the 250,000 prime hunting acres of Cranborne Chase, Cecil had bought or been granted in the closing years of Elizabeth's reign. As chief minister of the Crown, Cecil became the second most powerful man in the kingdom. In the same year, 1603, the King created Thomas Howard, Earl of Suffolk; in 1614 he would make him Lord High Treasurer of England. In the meantime the new Earl began to buy up land in Dorset close to the existing estates of his cousin, the other Thomas Howard, 3rd Lord Bindon.[4] It was understood that Suffolk was to be Lord Bindon's heir and both Suffolk and Cecil encouraged Bindon to speed up the building of a hunting 'castle' at Lulworth, so ambitious as to seem more a country seat than a mere sporting box. Cecil wrote: 'For that which you mean to do in your park, the rather upon my wishes I am very glad to hear it, because it may give the greater contentment to those towards whom you are a second parent to live in these parts.'[5] Lord Bindon had no children.

The King is the key to all this emphasis on hunting. For his ministers to retain his friendship and influence his decisions it was essential to keep him entertained. He loved the theatre, masques with music and dancing, and he enjoyed the company of good-looking young men; but most of all he loved the full panoply of a royal hunt, with hounds, trumpets, bloodshed and well-presented refreshments. An active man by nature, he had weak legs, which he sometimes thrust into the gutted bellies of newly slain stags to benefit, as he believed, by their vital energies. On horseback he was secure, but off the horse he liked to sit comfortably in a convenient pavilion refreshing himself with soft fruits, cherries for preference. Also he enjoyed his privacy and never became used to the eager curiosity of the English into every detail of the royal lifestyle. To satisfy this need for comfort, refreshments and seclusion, Robert Cecil built the remarkable total of sixteen little pavilions, or 'banqueting houses' as they were usually described, around the gardens and deer park of his principal seat at Hatfield in Hertfordshire.

Lord Bindon died in 1611. By that time the Castle, begun in 1608, was partly habitable, but it is unlikely that any start had been made on the grounds. Yet by the time an inventory of the Castle was made in 1678 the gardens had acquired eight 'Banketting houses' in addition to a castellated 'Porters Loge', a 'green house', a 'keepers loge' and 'ye doggs house'.[6] At some point then in the sixty-seven-year interlude the lavish grounds bespattered with little pavilions that Margaret Weld would draw in 1721 had been laid out. The inventory lists not only the 'Banketting houses', but also their contents offering a rare and valuable insight into the nature and function of these exotic buildings. There were:

> In ye 2 rooms ouver green house (bedsteads bolsters foot stools)
> In ye 2 Banketting houses in ye terrace walks in ye garden (2 stone tables 26 wooden chairs 2 garden ladders)
> In ye 2 Banketting houses at ye upper end of ye viniard (2 long forms with Backs)
> In ye 2 Banketting houses in ye new garden (8 forms with Beds & 11 wooden chairs)
> In ye Banketting hous under pidgeon House (1 stone tabell 16 wooden chairs 6 large poclows 1 plaster hodd)
> In ye Banketting house in ye Bowly greene 4 double Boxes of wood for Booles wth 3 Barks too each of them 1 stone Table 6 wooden Chairs 12 pairs of Brazile Bowls 2 Jacks

The list gives the impression of slightly down-at-heel store rooms which have long ceased to function as places of light entertainment. But the actual dating of their construction can be narrowed down further by study of the financial circumstances of the several owners, the 1st and 2nd Lords Suffolk, Thomas and Theophilus his son, James, the 3rd Earl, who inherited in 1640 and sold the Castle in 1641, and the unfortunate Humphrey Weld, who bought it and hung on, in often highly adverse conditions, until his death in 1685.

The 1st Earl Thomas was made Lord High Treasurer in 1614, three years after he inherited Lulworth. He was high in royal favour and wildly corrupt, draining the Treasury for his own building ventures at Audley End in Essex and, presumably, at Lulworth. In 1615 he was entertaining the King there, 'to disporte himselfe in the Parke, as alsoe in the Island of Purbecke neare adjoineing'.[7] This would indicate that the deer park and the pleasure grounds near the Castle had already been prepared with a full tally of 'Banketting houses'.

In 1618 Suffolk's corrupt dealings were discovered. He was fined the crippling sum of £50,000 and dismissed from his high office. But he was not just a Howard; he was a national hero, a bluff, hearty rogue who had fought bravely back in 1588 against the Spanish Armada, and a garden expert whose advice Robert Cecil had taken in April 1607 on the planning of the grounds at Hatfield.[8] Such was the King's affectionate regard for him that he reduced the fine to £7,000 and soon restored him to favour. Suffolk would have known Cecil's gardener, Mountain Jennings, and his architects, Simon Basil and Inigo

Jones. He lived on in reduced circumstances, but by 1619 he was £50,000 in debt and unlikely to have been indulging in lavish garden extensions, which again seems to limit the period of his Lulworth gardens to 1611-18. The old King died in 1625 and Suffolk a year later in 1626.

His son Theophilus, 2nd Earl Suffolk, a vice-admiral and Lord Lieutenant of Dorset in the same hearty, lordly manner of his father, was similarly addicted to high living, unwise expenditure and gardening. In 1636, when King Charles was preparing to seize his goods as payment for debt, he had just laid out 'a fayre garden and Orchard walled about at Lulworth'.[9] This, with its bowling green, is shown on the 1721 engraving to the right of the Castle and that main axis of the grounds which his father had laid down twenty years earlier. Then there is 'Payment for glass for his Lordship's new summerhouse at Lulworth',[10] which proves that at least one of the 'Banketting houses' in the 1678 inventory was a building by a Howard and pre-1636.

After pawning jewels and plate, Theophilus died, still owing £26,000, in 1640. His son James' first action was to rid himself of the Castle. With King Charles uninterested in hunting it had long ago lost its usefulness to the Suffolks. Humphrey Weld, a recent but sincere convert to Roman Catholicism, bought the twin estates of Lulworth and Bindon in 1641 in the confident expectation of a continuance of royal favour from Charles' Catholic Queen, Henrietta Maria.[11] Even so it took him two years to scrape the money together and by that time the Civil War was imminent; 1642 was not a good time to be a Catholic landowner. Parliament seized the castle, burnt Bindon, sequestered most of Weld's property and was still, in 1651, refusing him entry into Lulworth, his own house, so these were certainly not years for gardening.

In 1660 the Restoration brought a change. Weld was made Governor of Portland and used as a royal emissary to the court of Louis XIV. Furniture was bought and the rooms of the Castle repaired. That inventory of 1678 appears to have been part of a restoration programme and an assessment made after the years of persecution. The obvious conclusion about those eight 'Banketting houses' is that they were built for the 1st and 2nd Earl between 1611 and 1636; so in 1721 Margaret Weld was drawing a formal layout, the bones of which had been set down in the latter years of James I and the early years of Charles I. The peaked roofs of the pavilions in the 1721 engraving and the Artisan Mannerist fenestration of the 'keepers loge' or Deer House tend to confirm a dating to the first two Stuarts. The original garden at Lulworth pre-dates Wilton and is, therefore, of real significance in garden history.

If this conclusion is accepted then there are interesting similarities in overall planning between the Lulworth and Wilton gardens. Both are three-part gardens with a large area of parterres immediately behind the house, over-looked by raised terraces. Then comes a formal band of wilderness followed by a second, smaller parterre enclosure with two fountains. All three areas in both gardens are laid out on long axial avenues terminating, at Wilton, with an arcaded grotto house, at Lulworth with a two-storey Deer House, 'ye keepers loge in my deere parke', described in the 1678 inventory. This last was an area of twin paddocks into which the deer were allowed to come, from the wider park outside the enclosing tree belts, for feeding in winter. Watching the deer feed was a typical garden pleasure of the time.

In addition to these three areas dating back to pre-1618, the 1721 engraving shows a large, walled vegetable garden to the left of the Castle and, balancing it on the right, is the 2nd Earl's 1636 Bowling Green and orchard 'walled about'. That 'new garden' mentioned in the 1678 inventory could be any one of three sections to the right or centre of Margaret Weld's careful bird's eye view: a forecourt garden,[12] a fountain garden or a statue garden. The cost of tending all these areas must have been prohibitive and in 1686 Humphrey Weld's widow, Clare, was appealing to William Weld, his heir and nephew, to 'allow a salarie for reparations of the gardens, orchards, bowling greene and Castle, wch was readdy to dropp downe'.[13] When, quite soon after the engraving was published in 1726,[14] garden fashions turned against these formal layouts, the impecunious Welds were among the first to sweep theirs all away. On the Buck engraving which was drawn in 1733, Lulworth Castle stands in an almost bare landscape.[15] The efforts of the Welds to compensate for this vandalism will be considered in a later chapter. What must be stressed at this point is that it was the 1st Earl Suffolk who laid out England's first Franco-Italian formal garden on a long axial plan in Dorset in the years 1611-18, and not the 3rd Earl Pembroke in Wiltshire in 1635. At Wilton, Inigo Jones and Isaac de Caus were following a Dorset precedent, the authorship of which remains a mystery as the Lulworth garden is not in the style of Mountain Jennings.

After these long lost complexities of Lulworth it is a garden pleasure of the first order to turn to the wonderfully preserved poetic simplicities of Cranborne Manor's exactly contemporary garden. One senses that Robert Cecil, having done his utmost with the pleasure grounds of Hatfield to satisfy the exacting requirements of the King, turned with some relief to please his own more austere tastes in the reshaped gardens of Cranborne Manor.

These gain much by the contrast between the hidden rook-loud hollow in which they lie and the surrounding windswept bareness of the Chase. That old royal hunting ground may once have been a lovely wilderness, but time and modern farming have left it poor in trees and, compared with west Dorset, featureless and uninteresting. I was there on a grey, still February afternoon. The road drops down, large beech trees close in above walled, attractive private places and there is a big village, a small town by seventeenth-century standards, with handsome gentry houses and homely cottages. The Manor is sited behind the church and protecting brick enclosures, above the shallow valley of the Crane, a typical Dorset winterbourne (**12**). Entrance is through a succession of walled nursery gardens and, when the last door opens, there can be just the slightest sense of anticlimax. Accounts of the place build up an expectation of a garden

12 *Cranborne Manor from the south. Robert Cecil's three-arched classical porch is a first nervous step towards the lifestyle of sunshine and garden leisure*

with an Italian feel to it and a house quaintly southern in aspiration: the Jacobean notion of a classical villa in those years before Inigo Jones demonstrated the real thing at Greenwich. Instead there is a gentle slope of grass with an uncertain scatter of anemone and aconite, a few leafless trees and a large Elizabeth Frink head with a Monty Python air to it. It could hardly be more English.

Then the absurd charm of the place takes over. How could the Manor look other than English when it is only a recladding, post-1608, by William Arnold, of a hunting lodge of 1207 built for King John? Arnold learnt his loggias at Montacute and then went on to design Wadham College, Oxford, so Cranborne is somewhere in between. The gardens went through a similar process of Anglicizing.

There are two maps,[16] one more of a bird's eye view of Cranborne drawn attractively on vellum as a wall hanging. This shows the gardens as their reserved, orderly owner, Robert Cecil, King James' 'Little Beagle', the Earl of Essex's 'wry neck, crooked back, splay foot', intended them to develop (**13**).[17] It was drawn by John Norden, Cecil's surveyor, probably in 1610. The other, larger, rougher and more of a plan than a cartographer's map, was scribbled out by an anonymous clerk. It shows how the gardens really ended up when English gardeners shaped them, possibly during one of Cecil's longer absences. For a garden historian it is fascinating to see how many features of that larger plan still survive on the site. Late winter, when only the bones of the garden are visible, was the perfect time.

On Norden's map the Manor is approached along a north-south axis, through a fenced pound for tethering horses, across the canalised Crane by a massive causeway, then through two ornately pinnacled gateways to a four-arched loggia.[18] On the left of these gateways is the Kitchen Garden with its private path to the kitchens. Above this is a complex formal octagon of flower beds with a raised viewing terrace to the south. This has a private path into the south forecourt with its embattled wall and twin lozenge-plan lodges of superior brickwork. On the west side of the manor is the Italianate feature of four broad terraces descending down towards the Crane, though cut off from it by a wall.[19] Geometry and reserve characterise the design. It would have been a very severe garden, had it ever been laid out.

Utility has shaped the larger second plan (**14**). The north-south axis remains, but now a wide avenue of trees marches right up to the first forecourt wall with no canal, just a stable yard and horse pond on one side, a fish pond on the other. In place of the four Italian-style terraces is a large square garden quartered with simple grass parterres and next to it, a long rectangular garden with an oval pattern of beds. These are both enclosed by thick hedges giving that typical Elizabethan sense of privacy. Above and below these two gardens are lines of orchard trees. On the other, east side of the house the 'Kitchin Garden' has shrunk and a 'wood court' takes over most of its area. The octagon garden has been redesigned. It is now quartered with grass plats and at the centre of each is a circular area with a statue or urn. The central space with its diminishing circles is likely to be a viewing mount, the staple feature of Elizabethan gardens, topped by a statue. The south forecourt is similarly quartered with further statues or urns, symmetrically arranged. It is interesting to note that straight tree avenues are shown striding off south, west and north as gestures of territorial inclusion; this was long before John Evelyn published his 1664 *Sylva*, the book often considered to have set a fashion for such avenues.

The present planting of the garden represents a twentieth-century interpretation of how a 'Jacobethan' garden should have looked rather than how the Cranborne garden actually looked in Cecil's time as recorded by the maps. It is the survival of the garden buildings that persuades visitors that this is the real thing. Those twin forecourt lodges with their active angularity are perfectly scaled to flatter the height of the Manor behind, and the two loggias are again invitingly human in scale. That on the south front with its stone seats is an early sun-trap, and the two zodiacal roundels above it are high art in miniature. But otherwise so much has been changed. Those lines of orchard trees, a homely touch, have disappeared; that square of grass parterres on the west side is now plain lawn and all the orchestration of yew hedge, yew columns and flower beds has been applied to the oval which now has a central mount and is called the Sundial Garden. That east garden, octagon or quartered, is plain grass and open; the Kitchen Garden has been reduced. On the two maps there is no trace of funereal yews, but now they have taken over as the garden's punctua-

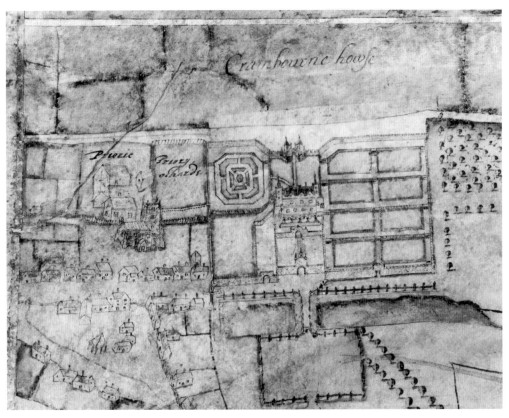

13 *John Norden's plan of Cranborne from the north was a 1610 proposal which should be compared with the later, anonymous plan of what was actually realized.* National Monuments Record; Marquess of Salisbury

tion and articulation and, it must be admitted, very handsomely they handle it. There are two yew arbours, one with a stone shepherdess, and the west garden, where Robert Cecil intended four terraces, is sliced across with a dramatic double yew allée which contrives to produce a terraced effect.

I was enjoying the gloom and the antiquity of it all down in the winter-bourne garden when, from the other side of the Manor, what was clearly a very big dog barked, or rather bayed, threateningly, quietening even the rooks. The deep barking drew nearer, a quite disturbing Baskerville effect, and then, through a gap in the yews, an enormous, soot black and entirely amiable Newfoundland dog, with a dim white spaniel and Hannah Cranborne in tow, burst into sight. The dog registered my presence then plunged excitedly, exactly as Newfoundlands are supposed to plunge, into the icy waters of the Crane. It was a very Dorset moment; my Dorset gardens have all been full of dogs.

The restoration of the gardens was begun by Lady Salisbury and they have continued to develop horticulturally and aesthetically under her daughter-in-law, Lady Cranborne. That Frink head dominates the grove of trees in the

14 *On this anonymously drawn plan of Cranborne from the south the triumphal arches for a northern ceremonial approach have been abandoned, an oval garden mount has been added to the western terraces and there are not one but three areas of formal parterres.* National Monuments Record; Marquess of Salisbury

upper west garden, a disturbing presence over several acres of ground, floodlit at night it must be true garden theatre, and it was Lady Cranborne's choice. A convoluted metal sculpture, designed by Angela Connor, was about to be put in place in the south forecourt; by now it must have transformed, enlivened or devastated that atmospheric space. It is satisfying to find major art works in a garden instead of the big pots that garden designers often fall back upon. Most engaging of all is the 'Mollusc' Mirror by David Booth, set within the bottom yew hedge (**colour plate 28**). This is a conceit in the mischievous Jacobean spirit of Burton's *Anatomy of Melancholy*. A narrow plank bridge crosses the Crane with no handrail for support. Then, when halfway across and nervously balanced, you look up and your unprepared and unflattering image is caught in that round mirror's reflection. You are the sculpture; again, like the Frink, it is garden theatre, reminiscent of those water jets that squirted Celia Fiennes in Wilton's seventeenth-century grotto house.[20]

The layout at Stalbridge Park, on the other hand, is far from interactive, not so much the preserved memory of a great garden as its fossil. Chronologically it comes naturally after Cranborne, being more Caroline than Jacobean in date. All the stony parts of its grounds are intact. The house has gone, so have most of the trees; mounds and edging stones suggest the outline of its flower beds. Its Old Park of fifty acres was enclosed in 1620 by Mervyn, Lord Audley, executed for unnatural practices in 1631. Its next owner, the Earl of Cork, was the elaborator of its gardens, though it is unlikely that the 'plott, for contriving my new intended buylding', drawn for him by Inigo Jones' occasional clerk of works, Isaac de Caus, was ever realised.[21] That structure, to be built 'over the great sellar' at Stalbridge is, in any case, unlikely to have been a garden building.[22]

In 1638 the Earl made an agreement with Walter Hyde, mason of Sherborne:

> . . . to make sufficient Rayles, bases, Balusters and peddistalls as will serve between my outward gate and my hall-door, and the Tarass before my hall-door, from wall to wall being in all that is rayled in about 300 feet . . . The Ballusters to be sett so near and close together that a dog cannot creep between them.[23]

and Gregory Brimsmead had to pave 'the Tarass before my house with Ranger pavies of Freestone'.[24] This suggests that the drive from the road to the house and the terrace in front of the house anticipated some of the formal stonework of one of Charles Barry's nineteenth-century palazzi, like Cliveden. Not a 'Balluster' and only a very few 'Ranger pavies' survive, and an 1813 engraving of Lord Audley's house, made shortly before its demolition, shows it standing in a featureless green wilderness for sheep, so the Capability Brown revolution had already swept the park clean.[25]

The loss of these elaborate terraced works is particularly to be regretted as they formed the quiet rural academy where, from 1643 to 1650, the Earl's seventh son, Robert, studied and puzzled over the problems of mathematics and natural sciences. In the next reign Robert Boyle would become the celebrated proposer of Boyle's Law and the equal, in the scientific ranks of the Royal Society, of Newton. It is related by Hutchins that 'for almost forty years he laboured under great feebleness of body . . . tall and slender, his countenance pale and emaciated'.[26] By his personal application of the laws of physics he had 'different sorts of clothes to put on according to the temperature of the air and the thermometer . . . but the simplicity and regularity of his diet supported his existence'.[27] It was while he was living here at Stalbridge in the summer of 1648 that Boyle wrote *Seraphic Love*, published in 1658, contrasting the love of women with the sublimity of the angels' love of God.

The most impressive relics of the gardens in which he meditated on such diverse topics are the massive gatepiers, the Earl's 'outward gate'. Crudely vermiculated in a primitive seventeenth-century imitation of their suave Italian models, they are capped by the Boyle lions and stand in the ten-feet-high walls of elegantly constructed limestone, all built in 1750 without mortar, that stretch away for more than a mile on either side, still in remarkable preservation. The drive into the park is straight and lined with limes and a guttering of Gregory Brimsmead's flat stones. Near the nineteenth-century farm building there are the platforms of that formal 'Tarass', destroyed in the landscaping of 1745. A little to the south-west is a flat area where 'a noseless man named Thomas Ford' made the Earl of Cork a bowling green.[28] From their prevalence in this and most other counties it appears that the game of bowls was as popular and perhaps even as prominent in the gentry's psyche as soccer is today.[29] Most evocative of all are the eight-foot-high stone walls around half an acre of sheltered garden. These lie across the drive from the farm, south of where the original house stood. One half of the walled area is now laid out to lawn, the other in a cruciform bed of flowers and vegetables with espaliers and wisteria. There are traces of old paths lined by stones. It was here that, despite 'lowness of spirits and weakness in his eyes',[30] Robert Boyle brooded over both the nature of angels and the expansion of natural gases: a very metaphysical, seventeenth-century combination.

There are likely to have been a number of 'metaphysical' elements — conceits with a philosophical or spiritual connotation — in Sir Walter Raleigh's gardens at Sherborne Castle.[31] That curious pulpit-like construction now called Raleigh's Seat suggests by its placing that it was rather more than a retreat for the original pipe smoker. It looks out over what was, in the early seventeenth century, a roadway, so it had the usual gazebo function. But it would have looked back, the direction in which its seating is aligned, at what would then have been a rural valley threaded by a stream with the antique ruins, much more picturesque in Raleigh's time before their Civil War slighting, of the Bishop's palace-castle. Was there already a cult of the Gothic, a pleasure in romantic decay, old towers and fine trees, long before the Picturesque cult of the later eighteenth century became a fashion and a cliché? The Raleigh of 'Give me my Scallop shell of quiet/My staffe of Faith to walke upon',[32] was a not inconsiderable poet, as Alexander Pope recognised when he was staying, a century later, in Raleigh's New Castle, but sharing, as he supposed, the same Gothic and Romantic reactions to the scene.

Dorset is not rich in seventeenth-century garden houses of the gazebo type. Perhaps an introspective, effete and idle persona was required before a fanciful two-storey roadside pavilion would be built at some distance from the parent house simply to act as a spying position upon the activities of one's neighbours. Were Dorset squires too happily bucolic and Dorset wives too busy making pickles and jams, or were Dorset roads too empty to make gazebos worth building? There is something in that last point because the only ambitious and richly crafted gazebo in the county stands at Poxwell Manor on the road from Weymouth to Poole and London, and it was built by the Hennings, a family of Poole merchants who could have had a legitimate interest in what passed along their main road (**15**). Completed in 1634, the gatehouse-gazebo is

15 *Dorset's earliest true Gazebo and Garden Pavilion of Poxwell Manor is an Artisan Mannerist structure of 1634 overlooking the road to Poole on one side and a walled garden on the other. Its thimble finials are an attempt at classical detail*

hexagonal, round-arched, pyramidal-roofed and has absurd bobble tops on its six pinnacles. The room over its arch is reached by an outside stair and the impudent little building is the sole feature of any note in the brick walled garden. Stylistically it is illiterate with no single classical detail to equal the gallant show of Flemish orders that had been applied to Cranborne a full twenty years earlier.

Melbury had two garden turrets of this period overlooking its walled garden.[33] One of these has survived possibly, as at Sherborne, because it also commanded a wide view over a valley. Inwardly and outwardly, however, it was transformed into a Batty Langley Gothick icon of the 1740s, and so belongs to another chapter.

There is a danger at this point of offending many of the county's gardeners whose grounds include stone or brick walled enclosures of some age and who have filled these garden spaces with perfect lawns and resonant herbaceous borders. Their gardens are beautiful and thoughtful, but old walls and a fine show of roses and peonies do not make an historic garden, so they cannot all be named and praised, even though those walls are attested Jacobean in date.

A county pattern for the period emerges which a few random examples will illustrate in their range, charm and lack of significant historic interest. Hammoon Manor, the enticingly thatched, is basic in its garden features. Undated, but of the early 1600s, it has a meagre, low-walled front garden, a token space to separate it from an exceptionally muddy side road. Its rear area is entirely a farmyard, implying that its brick-walled garden across the lane was an afterthought as living standards improved. Inside that walled garden, wires for peaches, vines and soft fruit hang empty on the walls; a tunnel of apple and pear trees cuts the enclosure in half: lawn and flowers near the single entrance gate, vegetables on the far side. But is that arrangement traditional and, therefore, historic? There can be no satisfactory answer. Occasional inundations from the Stour have kept this irresistible house in a bucolic roughness.[34] It is an ill flood that does no historic complex any good. Floods from the Frome may have done Woolbridge Manor the same conserving service. It has a low-walled, plain front garden, a mere frame to its Caroline brick façade.

Clifton Maybank, a much grander house, has been so much looted architecturally by other houses, notably Montacute and Hinton St George, that it is unfair to criticise its grounds. There was certainly a very ugly Jacobean gatehouse, maliciously attributed to Inigo Jones. What survives is that typical feature of the period, a bowling green, double-sized and flanked on two sides by raised earth terraces for spectators. Next to it, on its north side within stone walls for protection, is the equally standard Kitchen Garden.

The list of unhistorical Jacobean gardens can end worthily at Sandford Orcas Manor which has everything architecturally – gatehouse, heraldic porch, long double ranges of bay windows flaunting pinnacles, and stables almost as handsome as the house – but very little in the way of garden history. What it can claim is that it has been gloriously planted up on the cottage garden option by Sir Mervyn Medlicott, the fortunate owner.

After the gatehouse and the stable court there lies, on the right, an east garden stretching uphill from the main porch. It is only confined by a wall on the stable side, ending, after lawns and flowers, unsatisfactorily with rough pasture. There are orchards and the south garden on its open unwalled side, but this south garden has to fight the Ham Hill stone of the hall and great chamber. It was doing that on my visit with an excitingly conflicting rage of dahlias. Across the lawns the truculent pink of the hydrangeas was varied by one bush which had been ingeniously coaxed to flower in two distinct shades of blue.

None of this, of course, was remotely Jacobean, except the 1616 porch. The yew hedge of complex castellations was planted by Mr Peyman in 1910 and this compliments the bays and irregularities of the house. Beyond it are the almost inevitable twin grass terrace walks overlooking the level ground of a bowling green. In so far as there was a Jacobean garden pattern for the average Dorset manor house, this was it: one or two walled areas and a Bowling Green with grass terraces. That was what made Lulworth a garden in a completely different register and an innovatory breakthrough into the next formal age of garden design, thirty years before the rest of England.

3

Luxury and intolerable expense –
the brief reign of the Baroque

Dorset can claim the earliest Baroque garden layout at Lulworth Castle, which was kept up from 1612 to 1725, and one of the very last, Eastbury, maintained from 1728 to 1780. In between these two giants the county's formal gardens were modest in scale and generally rather late in construction. It may not have done much for the popularity of such grand garden gestures that the spreading grounds and many pavilions of Lulworth would have been associated in the minds of the county's gentry with the Welds, who were recusants and, after the scares of the Popish Plot of 1678, suspect in their patriotism.

When Leonard Knyff and John Kip brought out their *Britannia Illustrata* in 1707, with eighty meticulously drawn bird's eye views of the most impressive house and garden combinations in England, one of their aims was to demonstrate that Great Britain was not behind Continental countries like France in the scale, ambition and order of its formal gardens.[1] Significantly, only one of their eighty plates, that of Bryanston, which was pushed to the end of the book at plate number seventy-seven, is from Dorset (**16**). The gardens at Bryanston were very modest efforts, which must have scraped into the pages of the book rather to fill them up than to enrich them. A close study of plate seventy-seven exposes the homely realities of Dorset's Baroque. The house of Henry Portman, who was a mere 'gentilhomme' among the many 'ducs', 'comtes' and 'mylords' of the book's 'Table Alphabetique'[2], was a commonplace Tudor vernacular range with a small classical wing and a Commonwealth block to the rear. The only Baroque feature of the grounds is a large carriage sweep with a fountain at its centre and a flower bed around it. Everything else is a sham. To the left of the view there is a large vegetable garden with fruit trees and bushes, all set out in regular lines to look like formal gardens. Raised up at house level is a square garden quartered by four plain lawns. Three terraces have been cut very recently into the bank behind this and planted with young trees or shrubs. And that is all. Up on the right of the house behind outbuildings and more vegetable patches is that standard Jacobean feature, the bowling green, with a pergola-shelter. The only garden buildings are two shelters for fishermen on the banks of the Stour and a plain pavilion on the quartered lawn. Only Henry Portman's subscription to the book can have secured the inclusion of the plate.[3]

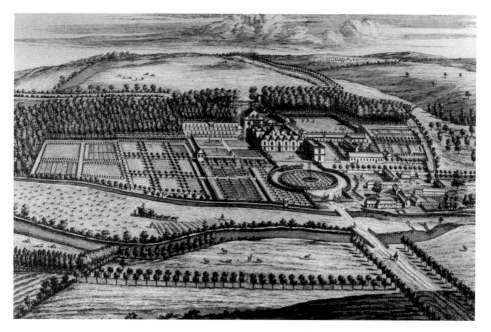

16 *Kip's 1707 view of Bryanston illustrates a homely manor house pretending to formal grandeur in its gardens by laying out vegetable patches and orchards geometrically. It has four lawns, fishing boxes, one fountain and a bowling green.* Bristol University Special Collections

A full-blooded Baroque garden, such as survives after expensive restoration in the late twentieth century at Hampton Court, offers order on an impressive scale: a grand design of canals, terraces, fountains and statues, with the flowers and topiary marshalled into patterns like guardsmen trooping the colour. Such a garden is an acquired taste; in the last half of the seventeenth century, and for a few decades into the eighteenth, it was a demonstration of landed power, of the ability to control and reshape nature. The cost of this upkeep was enormous and a Baroque garden did not age well, which explains why so few survive intact today. The Arcadian and Rococo parks which succeeded them age gracefully because they were designed from the beginning to work along with their particular topography. An overgrown temple has romantic appeal, an overgrown parterre has very little. If a rectangular canal fills up with rushes it looks untidy; if a lake with natural outlines grows rushy it looks more natural. Were the National Trust to abandon Stourhead for thirty years the place would become a wonderful tangle of azaleas and beech trees around the Temple of Hercules and the Temple of Apollo. Leave Hampton Court with no gardeners for the same length of time and it would be a weed-grown tip around unkempt yew trees. Significantly, not a single pavilion or terrace of Lulworth's vast layout survives today.[4]

The same is true of the formal landscape that Sir Ralph Bankes created to dramatise Kingston Hall, the house he had commissioned from Roger Pratt in 1663 at Kingston Lacy. Kingston Hall was closely modelled on Inigo Jones'

Coleshill in Berkshire, where Pratt had been clerk of works, but unlike Coleshill it was built of brick rather than stone. The shell of the house with its viewing cupola commanding the park was up by 1665, and the interior furnishings were completed by 1667. During the next ten years Sir Ralph initiated the planting of an impressive Franco-Dutch formal garden at Kingston. He was heavily in debt on his death in 1677 and the house was subsequently let to raise money. It was not until 1693 that John Bankes the Elder, Sir Ralph's son, could return to the family home. He and his wife Margaret, who kept meticulous records of expenditure, set about works in the park and gardens to restore Sir Ralph's schemes. The landscape survived well into the eighteenth century and is recorded in an estate plan of 1774-5, drawn by William Woodward.[5]

To the south of the house Sir Ralph planted a walled Parterre Garden with four grass quadrants centred by statues. This was flanked by two smaller enclosures planted with evergreens, fruit trees and flowers. At the south end of these formal areas was a terraced cross-walk giving onto a walled exedra set with statues and urns. To the rear of this wall, double avenues of trees radiated out into the Upper Park in a *patte d'oie*; there was a repeating pattern of avenues on the north side into Court Close. On the edge of the formal gardens Sir Ralph built a raised belvedere, usually referred to as the 'banqueting house', for views out to the park; it was demolished in 1721.

The avenues in the Upper Park were devastated by the 'Great Storm' of November 1703 and one of the clearance gangs spent six weeks 'raising of trees in the walks blown down with the violent wind'.[6] When John had raised enough money in 1713, restoration began in Sir Ralph's formal gardens. Walls were repaired and gilded lead planters were set out for exotics. A Bowling Green was made on the east side and to the north, 146 elms were planted in Court Close in 1716-17. Minor alterations were made to the landscape in 1733-5, but Sir Ralph's formal garden remained virtually intact until the 1780s when new minimalist fashions swept it all away.

In Dorset the most sensibly scaled layout of the seventeenth century, formal like Kingston rather than technically Baroque, for it had none of Lulworth's spreading arms and movement, was at Charborough Park (**17**). General Thomas Erle was its creator. He was a local hero of the Glorious Revolution of 1688 and it was in a grotto of his garden that he and some like-minded Dorset gentry, 'in the year MDCLXXXVI', according to the inscription on that much restored structure, plotted their course of action.[7] Erle's successor, Henry Drax, a secretary to Frederick Louis, Prince of Wales, admired the garden of his great-uncle by marriage so much that, between 1740 and 1745, he had it painted twice.[8] An ogee-domed garden pavilion appears only in one of the two paintings, presumably the later, done after the Prince's visit in 1741.

At that time the main approach to the house was from the north-east, from Poole, via a stable court and a carriage sweep. West of the house, where the

17 *In the 1740s Charborough Park still retained two formal areas: a curvaceous parterre and a statue garden overlooked by the 'Conspiracy' Grotto whose finials are just visible between two urns on the right.* National Monuments Record

main entrance now lies, were two distinct twin gardens. Both were overlooked on the west from a terrace set with six great urns, and it was within the side of this terrace that the 'Conspiracy' Grotto had been excavated, which proves an early, pre-1686 date for the whole layout. The more southerly of the two gardens, the one with the Grotto, has two grass squares, lined with low topiary hedges and surrounded by gravel paths. In the centre of each lawn is a tall statue. The other garden is laid out ambitiously with a grand parterre of four swirling patterns in a box; and it was on the north-west corner of this that the new pavilion stood. Hidden in trees to the south are the church of St Mary and a short, straight drive leading to a two-storey triumphal arch. An avenue of young trees has already been planted leading up to the hill where, after 1790, a Gothic folly tower would be built (**18**). So some earlier garden building is likely to have preceded the tower.

It was an attractive, relatively manageable layout. What made the upkeep of these formal gardens tiresome and expensive were the parterres. Baroque gardens were geometrical and straight-lined in their broad outlines, but fluidly patterned in the detail of their parterres. The English compromise was usually to cut out a graceful pattern in turf and fill the gaps with coloured gravel. At Charborough the more laborious outlining in low box hedges had been chosen. It is interesting that Henry Drax should have been so proud of his, by then, old-fashioned garden, because his employer, Prince Frederick, is often referred to as the 'Rococo

18 *The Gothick Tower at Charborough was built in two stages after 1790, but occupies the site of an earlier building, the focus of a pre-1740 formal avenue.* National Monuments Record

Prince' and considered a patron of the new style of informal garden-parks set out with casually eclectic garden buildings in the Gothick, classical, Turkish or Chinese styles. When the paintings were made, ordinary hedged fields still covered the adjacent hillsides and there was no park outside these two gardens. By the time Hutchins illustrated Charborough in 1774 the dismal Brownian landscape fashion would have swept everything away except the Grotto.

When a survey of the gardens of a particular, not necessarily rich or fashion conscious county like Dorset is made, Baroque formalism emerges as far more flexible in its application to gardens than the plates of Kip and Knyff suggest. Waddon Manor at Portesham has a complete and compact formal, terraced garden that was improvised by Harry Chaffyn and his wife, who was the widow of the previous owner, Bullen Reymes, after the fire of 1704 had destroyed the main, south-facing section of the house.[9] This had left them with their newly built wing of silvery white Ridgeway stone running from the roadway to butt, end-on, into the steep, dry hillside behind the house. Westward this new wing faced the confined site of the lost main building; eastward it faced a narrow yard of service buildings; southwards, where it had few windows, was one of the finest views in the county, over a wide valley to glimpses of the sea.

Formalism had the answer to the problem of reshaping the site with three terraces, one above the other, running west, but facing out south, and each presenting wider and wider views the higher they mount up the hill (**19**). To dignify this unusual arrangement Chaffyn used a punctuation of austerely grand gatepiers with very deep v-jointed rustication and massive ball finials. The lowest of the three terraces is very narrow, a mere three yards wide; the middle one is as wide as the house that faces along it; the uppermost, reached up a bold flight of steps, is between the other two in width. On the east side of the house, beyond the service area, is a pyramidal-roofed pavilion on the same level as the upper terrace. It would be pleasant to describe it as Chaffyn's garden house, but the terrace has not been extended to reach it and, as it stands above the narrow Kitchen Garden, it was almost certainly a stately privy.

After the Chaffyns, for two whole centuries, Waddon was a farmhouse. Then Mr B.O. Corbett bought the place in 1928 and, in an inspired act of gentrification, raised the status of the lowest set of gatepiers, those from the bottom terrace to the road, by giving them ball finials and rustication to match the stately pair above them.[10] The effect is almost one of stage scenery and in

19 *The enchanting miniature grounds of Waddon Manor demonstrate how easily a formal layout could be adapted to a difficult natural site with the help of a few gatepiers*

their modest grandeur Waddon's terraces are among the most covetable gardens in the county. All three are laid to lawn, and when I was there the lowest was lined with fuchsias ending in a salvo of red hot pokers against dark bushes. The borders of the wide middle terrace were disciplined by low box hedges and its two Irish yews had grown sentinel tall. Pink lilies dominated the herbaceous borders of the top terrace which ends in a flourishing bay tree. A perfectly functioning sun-trap, Waddon demonstrates how well the Baroque works on a steep site.

Whereas Waddon is a nearly perfect formal survival of minor gentry Baroque, the formal gardens of Frampton Court, just outside Dorchester, were lost in the division of the grounds which followed the demolition in 1931 of the undistinguished Baroque house of 1704. A handsome arched stable block remains and two detailed plans which present something of a stylistic puzzle as to how far a formal garden could go before it became Arcadian or even Rococo.[11] In a large leafed sketchbook of fine paper William Jennings Junior, Land Surveyor of Evershot, has drawn and painted in delicate precision, on facing pages, two beautiful plans of Frampton Court and its grounds (**colour plates 9** & **10**). Captions describe the first plan as 'Previous to the alterations of 1778', the second as 'Frampton and Demesne Grounds 1818-1836'.

Apart from their precision and fine colouring, the two plans deserve to be better known. Richard Brinsley Sheridan, a grandson of the playwright, inherited Frampton by marriage to Marcia Maria Grant in 1835, and he must have commissioned the two plans as a deliberate historical record of the aesthetic changes in landscape gardening that had taken place between the two dates, 1778 and 1836. That in itself reveals a remarkable topographical awareness. It would be interesting to know whether Sheridan thought the later condition of his grounds, softened and simplified in outline by the Brownian fashion in landscape, was an improvement on the former.

What, however, is revealing for this chapter is the extent to which the garden and park in the first plan have already seen their formal elements modified by a movement towards informality. It is characteristic of the Baroque that the gardens and the park should have been entirely separate, and the park at Frampton was still strictly formal. It had a coppice at each of its four corners and it was cut in half by a straight canal running from the Frome to the driveway with a square basin at its centre point. The gardens filled an irregularly shaped area behind the house and its offices and between the river and another drive. Dominating this area was the long, walled rectangle of the Kitchen Garden which Jennings has painted in careful detail with all its intricate vegetable patches, a world of domestic self-sufficiency which would, by Sheridan's time, be cut to half the size.

East of this Kitchen Garden is a long straight walk; south of it is a large rectangle of orchard bounded by another long straight walk. To the west of it the harsh formal geometry continues with a rectangular pleasure garden. The central feature of this is a long canal and there are two other round ponds. At one end of the canal is a 'Summer House and Bath', while at the far southern end of the pleasure garden is a 'Temple'. So already, in this otherwise Baroque layout, the garden buildings which will later, after 1730 perhaps, begin to define a naturalistic Arcadian park, are beginning to take their place as essential garden features, though here at Frampton they are sited strictly geometrically.

There remains, to the north of the Kitchen Garden, an entirely different area: the Wilderness. As early as 1651 there was a wilderness in Anthony Ashley Cooper's garden at Wimborne St Giles, but that was an exact square divided into quarters.[12] There was another wilderness, planned in 1723 though possibly never planted, at Lulworth.[13] That also was strictly geometrical, two rectangles side by side. But Frampton's Wilderness was conceived in an entirely different spirit. Deliberately winding walks led through it, in the 'Artinatural' style of Batty Langley, to a clearing, and a stream or canal is shown passing through it on an easy course.[14] To the north-west the Wilderness is bounded by a curious winged water and, at its northern tip, by a widening of the Frome into a regular lake.

The implication of the plan is that the formal and informal elements of this garden at Frampton were conceived as whole, probably at the time the house was built in 1704. It is frustrating to have no views of either the Summer House or the Temple. Lulworth, where Edward Weld ruled from 1722 to 1761, had lost its grand Baroque gardens by 1733 and Weld was toying with the idea of building a Greenhouse. Nothing came of it, but a design survives of an outrageously provincial domed structure with a façade of giant Corinthian pilasters, long windows and a deeply recessed centre.[15] Something of this kind, on a more modest scale, may well have been erected in the pleasure garden at Frampton as a 'Summer House and Bath'.

It is most noticeable that whoever designed Frampton had no interest in parterres. Edward Weld at Lulworth, in his indecisive fashion, had commissioned, presumably at the same date as that 'wilderness', two designs, each for eight beds of parterres from 'Wise and London', the celebrated owners of the great nursery gardens at Brompton Park.[16] Henry Wise was the sedentary member of the partnership, and for his name to appear before that of the travelling partner, George London, suggests a design sent by the post and not one resulting from a site visit by London.

One, of all those many features shown on the first plan of Frampton, has survived behind a high brick wall: the long rectangular canal. This typical feature of the Baroque garden has tended to be retained in the county and made a feature of later, more relaxed layouts. At Creech Grange, where Denis Bond reshaped the grounds in the 1730s and early 1740s, the ornamental water in front of the house is a straight canal while ponds further into the woods are natural in their outlines, and Bond's general aim seems to have been Arcadian. Dean's Court in Wimborne Minster turned its monastic fishponds into a broad rectangular canal, presumably in 1725 when, according to Hutchins, the dull Baroque house was built for Sir William Hanham. It is safe to presume that such a geometrical water feature would have had accompanying formal bedding, but in the locust years towards the end of the century the aesthetics of economising set in as usual and the grounds of this urban jewel among Dorset's gardens reverted to rough grass and specimen trees. But what specimens! In addition to false nutmeg with late summer flowers of a dull red, medlars with creamy white blossom in May, ginkgo, a tulip tree with dark red fruit and the inevitable mulberries, Dean's Court has a glorious swamp cypress which is not only the second largest in the country, but which has easily the most distinguished pedigree. Its seed is believed to have been given to the Hanhams to nourish by the Tradescants, the great plant hunters and botanists of Charles I's reign, at the end of their voyage back from Virginia. They were on their way to Cranborne to present the cream of their fruits to the Cecils, but the Hanhams got this one exotic cast-off.

The other prodigy of this rare garden is the formal Kitchen Garden behind its crinkle-crankle wall, which family lore records as having been built by French prisoners of war. Which war is not stated, but it has a delightful rhythm and must have been very expensive to construct. The ruling Hanhams are not simply organic gardeners, but imaginative and experimental ones. They have filled many of the crinkles with obscure crab apple trees, built a new, tightly enclosed rose garden with a water feature to celebrate the Golden Jubilee Year, and virtually every bed of their vast potager mixes flowers with vegetables and is enclosed in a neat collar of low box hedge. These hedges alone must take a week each year to clip. On its occasional open days Dean's Court serves cream teas with home made jams and is certainly one of the county's five star gardens, deviously structured and intensely full of character; a great survivor.

Gatepiers are also survivors. At Mappowder a bizarre group of four piers has endured, two of them topped with the busts of negroes dressed in Roman garments. The crest of the Coker family was 'a More's head side faced wreathed Argent and Gules', which explains the blackamoors' imperial robes.[17] They were probably erected by Robert Coker who 'engaged on the parliament side' and lived long enough to see the Whigs back in power again in 1688.[18] When the Cokers sold off their estates in 1745 one set of gatepiers found themselves leading into a farmyard while the Moors add a Baroque dignity to a very modest farmhouse.

At Clifton Maybank a rather sober Baroque Garden House was built at one end of the Jacobean terrace overlooking the double Bowling Green (**20**). It is possible that when it was put up, the green had been turned over to parterres in the Franco-Dutch mood. The name of Sir James Thornhill comes naturally to mind as the architect of the Garden House,[19] but nothing has been proven. Another architect, one far more committed to the theatrical swirls of the Baroque, was living only a mile or two over the Hampshire border at Hale Park from 1715 to his death in 1743. This was Thomas Archer and, since he was almost certainly the architect of the suavely Baroque Chettle House, built after

20 *Sober, unimaginative and classical only in its symmetrical proportions, this late Baroque Garden House on the earlier terrace of Clifton Maybank is a possible design by Sir James Thornhill who was living nearby*

1711, he should have had some influence on Dorset's formal gardens. Archer's design career was, however, one of irresolution and stumbles. Nothing reflects his bad luck better than his little semi-circular Garden Seat hollowed out from a bulge in the outside wall of Bingham's Melcombe.[20] The Seat should face east-west over the vast green sea of the bowling green towards the best Tudor face of the house, but since it was built a modest boundary hedge of yew has grown into a Brobdignagian monster (**colour plate 1**), supposedly the most enormous hedge in Britain, a mountain range of undulant greenery, and Archer's Seat stares straight into its black bowels.

Topiary work can, like growing monster leeks and marrows, become a noble obsession. No one seems to have noticed it, but Sydling Court at Sydling St Nicholas has a hedge that rivals Bingham's in height and cubic content and totally outpoints it in length. It also suggests that giant topiary may have been a Victorian rather than a Georgian or Tudor fixation. A view of the court published in 1815 shows bare Brownian grounds and the unrelieved walls of a vast Kitchen Garden.[21] But in the 1860s Sir William Marriott bought the place, 'Gothicised' the house and planted topiary around the outside of the Kitchen Garden walls, some golden yews, some dark green (**colour plate 2**). This, either by accident or design, has grown into irregular enormities of colour creating by mere serendipity a sheltered garden between the stone, brick and flint wall and the switchback of the yews. The walk around this is a surprise succession of spaces produced by the surges of the hedge as lawn succeeds to herbaceous border, all sunny south and west facing. The Court's new owners, Viscount and Lady Fitzharris, have cut a gap in that wall and have plans for a lively development of the Kitchen Garden, but there is very little anyone can ever do to the Great Hedge at Bingham's Melcombe except relax and enjoy it.

Blinding Archer's Garden Seat was a small disaster in a great garden, Geoffrey Jellicoe's Dorset orchestration of dry Tudor bones into a twentieth-century symphony of restraint.[22] Using a round stone dovecote as a base he planted two more long straight yew hedges parallel to the existing yew mountain, accentuating the positive. Between them run three long lawns, green upon green, with just an armillary sphere sundial for relief. Behind the dovecote were two small Tudor gardens. These he cleared of clutter, leaving a vine arbour in the Bar Garden and subdued flowers within a box parterre in the Ladies Garden. Both are happily human in scale and the ladies have an open stair down to the wine cellar. North of these firm geometries is a Wild Garden down by the Devil's Brook, but Bingham's real floral indulgence is in the Kitchen Garden below the Bowling Green. There high tents of runner beans vie with equally high tents of sweet peas in a box-disciplined potager. Only here, in this immaculately enclosed, introverted garden, are outside Dorset and the west winds allowed into the sheltered enclosures.

No one would accuse Archer's Horton Tower of being upstaged by a yew hedge, but neither would anyone seriously describe that menacing brick hexagon in a rounded triangle as a garden building.[23] A typical Archer exercise in volumes, it was built as an observatory and has met with the well-deserved fate of conversion into a transmitter for mobile phones. Chettle continues the saga of Archer accidents. It retains the keyhole-shaped terraced earthworks of its original Baroque, east entrance front. This is now the garden front and laid to lawn. Its west front, originally the garden but now the entrance, faces uphill to the wreck of an avenue which once cut through parkland to a cresting line of woods that was the focus of its vistas. That same line of beech trees serves, on the other side of the same hill, to focus the views of that great beast among all Dorset's Baroque gardens: the vast lozenge of land that Sir John Vanbrugh and Charles Bridgeman managed between them to impose on the rolling downland around Eastbury.

Fair warning needs to be given that what remains of Eastbury is for the dedicated garden detective. Armed with permission from the owner of the land and a copy of the plan of the grounds in their prime, Eastbury can still give an enthusiast at least two hours of interesting exploration, but expect no conventional garden attractions except, initially, at the main gates. Where the lane up from Tarrant Hinton reaches the first cottages of Tarrant Gunville there is a duck pond filled by a brisk, clear stream that comes tumbling down alongside Eastbury's low, brick park wall. Vanbrugh staged his principal entrance to the park over this stream with a curiously homely pomp. His drive crosses it on a rusticated arch far too grand for the cheerful little winter-bourne, and a row of massive stone markers has been half-buried to dignify its bank. Four ball-topped pylons of alternate blocked rustication stand about the drive gate like the first four notes of a trumpet with no following fanfare. They seem inadequate as an entrance to a palace that was not much smaller than Blenheim or Castle Howard: it is Vanbrugh in an unusual village register. There were originally lodges where the dark grove of trees stands, but they were demolished in the nineteenth century, possibly because their architect had put pomp before practicality. The drive climbs steeply up a bare slope that was once shaped into a wooded amphitheatre by two embracing arms of trees. At the top of the climb, on a broad shelf of level land are the ungainly remains of the house, its surviving north service wing.

Eastbury had a difficult launch. George Dodington, one of the Lords of the Admiralty, bought a farm here in 1709 and commissioned in 1716 the first of thirteen designs for an ambitious house from the still fashionable Sir John. Dodington died in 1720 when only the wings and the forecourt were in place. Then his nephew and heir, George Bubb Dodington, a plump, ingratiating diplomat, politician and dandy, did very little until 1724, even though his uncle had left ample funds. Two years later Vanbrugh died, but Charles Bridgeman still had twelve years left, so the garden design should be attributed chiefly to him.

A water-colour plan in the Bodleian Library (**colour plate 3**)[24] indicates what Bridgeman intended to lay out, but monochrome illustrations in volume three of *Vitruvius Britannicus* (1725) record the modifications made when he was actually supervising the planting (**21**). Any survey of what remains will be more rewarding if an attempt is made to judge how far Bridgeman was responding to the actual lie of the land and how far he was just making a paper imposition. Those years of the 1720s and 1730s saw a revolution gathering in the garden world and Bridgeman is often considered, by his gardens at Stowe and Rousham, to have been an initiator of that new developing Arcadian informality which William Kent went on to perfect. Are there any indications of this at Eastbury?

The Bodleian plan proposes a lozenge of gardens lying entirely on the eastern, uphill side of the house. This is to be enclosed, in its turn, by a huge irregular octagon of geometrically planted tree belts. This octagon is broken immediately in front of the house, possibly to allow the main rooms an uninterrupted view of Dorset nature at its best, a broad landscape with no note of artifice, but framed by the trees of the amphitheatre. When Bishop Pococke, a great fancier of fashionable Rococo gardens, came here in October 1754, he wrote at rapturous length about the interiors of Eastbury, but dismissed the grounds in three lines: 'The gardens are well laid out, lawns, clumps, and some walks of trees in the old way, and there is an open pavilion at the further end of the garden, with a pediment in front supported by columns', which was faint praise.[25]

When George Bubb Dodington died in 1762, Eastbury passed, by the terms of his uncle's will, to Earl Temple of Stowe and he, finding no one willing to live there, blew it all up, both the main house and the Temple. The garden has been reverting to nature ever since. It is worth taking, as a starting point, the proposition that Bridgeman's formal design – that outer octagon of trees blocking out most of the vistas, together with the regimented squares of woodland marching out south and the double row of mounds, tree-crowned, marching out north –

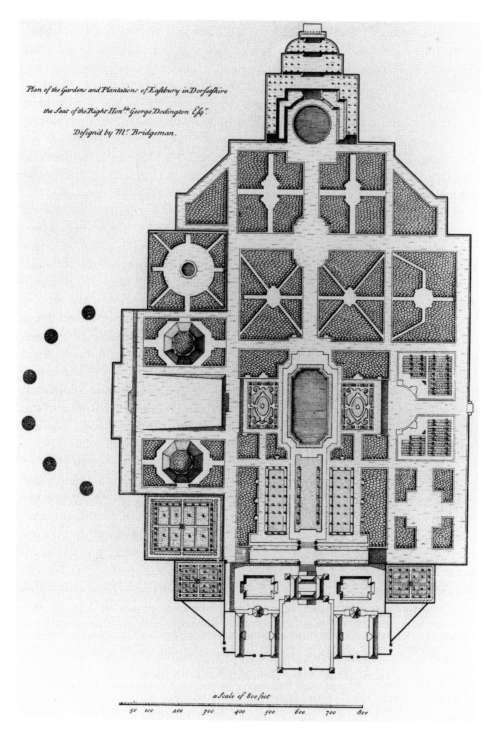

Plan of the Gardens and Plantations of Eastbury in Dorsetshire
the Seat of the Right Hon.ble George Dodington Esq.r.
Design'd by M.r Bridgeman.

a Scale of 800 feet

50   100   200   300   400   500   600   700   800

21 *Charles Bridgeman's elaborately geometrical lozenge of gardens and plantations which he, together with Sir John Vanbrugh, imposed upon the downs behind Eastbury House, is compelling evidence that neither man had much feeling for informality of garden design.* Bristol University Special Collections was an insensitive response to a potentially rewarding tract of high downland. Vanbrugh had proposed two giant garden buildings. The Bagnio on the south side was never built; the Corinthian Temple, Pococke's 'open pavilion', was built, a splendidly sited structure halfway up the hill to the east, under that crest of beech trees. But Vanbrugh never grasped the Arcadian or Rococo garden ideal: that ornamental garden buildings should have their own modest scale and not try to equal the dimensions of their parent houses. The portico of the Temple was thirty-feet high, almost as tall as that of the church of St Martin-in-the-Fields in Trafalgar Square. Eastbury may have been a necessary learning experience for English garden designers, but not very much more.

On arrival at the old forecourt it is essential to consider the scale of the surviving north service wing and pay respects to that oddity, a giant bonsai, two Scots pine trees growing out of the top of an arch, designed in Vanbrugh's usual thrusting manner of muscular overstatement. It is rewarding to walk the entire north side of the big garden lozenge where much of his arched and round-windowed containing walls still survive in attractive decay. They give way to walled orchards, marked clearly on Bridgeman's plan, and to the two twenty-foot viewing mounts. These present Bridgeman's aesthetics at their most worrying. Overgrown now with trees, they were once octagonal and still, through the tangled branches, look out to the north over a flat field with a row of fourteen mounds like prehistoric tumuli drawn up for inspection. They pointed to a rare gap in that outer octagonal belt of trees, but there is no significant vista in that direction to justify the emphasis. The fourteen mounds could work only in a bird's eye view, which must explain these twin viewing platforms.

Bridgeman made the usual rectangular canal the inner garden's central feature, with four geometrical box parterres uphill. These have all now returned to rough grass, but the walk which ran around them is still traceable. Further to the east along this north side of the lozenge is a large walled garden. On Bridgeman's Bodleian plan this was the Wilderness. It had, like that at Frampton Court, a few winding walks and it was Eastbury's only escape from geometry but, unlike the Frampton Wilderness, its outline was square and unromantic. Nevertheless one of Bubb Dodington's favourite house guests, the poet James Thomson, author of 'The Seasons', could write, in response to this insistent geometry:

Oh, lose me in the green delightful walks
Of, Dodington, thy seat, serene, and plain;
Where simple Nature reigns; and every view,
Diffusive, spreads the pure Dorsetian downs,
In boundless prospect; yonder shagged with wood,
Here rich with harvest, and there white with flocks![26]

A recitation of those lines in this strange angular wilderness will bring home the gap between the Baroque idea of 'Nature' and our own.

After the Wilderness the relics of Eastbury grow thin on the ground. As the downland rises steeply and the level shelf of the old garden ends, there should be a substantial round pond with the Corinthian Temple rising in exact symmetry behind it. Nothing remains of either, not even a fold in the chalky soil of the broad wheat field. This is, however, a good vantage point from which to look down at the rough field between the two lines of trees. At least the outline of the garden remains, but centring the view there should be the palatial hulk of the house itself on its terrace, climbing in that memorable perversion of classical order that Vanbrugh made his own distinctive style.

All the way back down the south side of the lozenge to the forecourt it is possible to trace every angle of the Vanbrugh-Bridgeman brick-walled ha-ha. Halfway along it the footings can be made out of the gate which should have led out of the lozenge to what Bridgeman had intended as another big viewing mount, matching the two on the north side opposite. Vanbrugh thought nothing of the idea, the view in this direction being distinctly nondescript. He wanted to build a bath house (the Bagnio) on the same scale as the Corinthian Temple. In the event Bubb Dodington vetoed both schemes. The straight avenue through the wood, which should have led to the Bagnio, can still be made out, and within the woods the topiary parterre of box bushes that Bridgeman planted has gone wild and turned into a thicket.

A tour of Eastbury is not likely to raise the spirits or to present the Baroque garden in a positive way. Forde Abbey, near Chard, whose garden was recently declared Christie's Garden of the Year, should set the record straight. Forde is not, by any means, purely Baroque, but it is fair to say that the bones of the garden are Baroque and largely account for the brilliant combination of order and happy visual confusion that make a visit to Forde so memorable. No attempt will be made to separate Forde's Franco-Dutch elements from earlier or later work and Melbury will be given the same unified treatment. Gardens like these are unities that have grown historically and need to be treated as such.

If Iris Murdoch had invented Forde Abbey as a setting for one of her early novels, such as *The Bell*, critics would have said her imagination had run too far ahead of her. Early Pointed Gothic, late, exuberant Perpendicular lapsing over into François Premier French Renaissance, and Commonwealth's club-footed classicism should not go together in one house, but at Forde Abbey they do. Its gardens are an equally bizarre stylistic mix of the centuries.

The Franco-Dutch waters that hold the grounds together so romantically were channelled from the profuse local springs by Cistercian abbots in the twelfth century to make fish ponds and to drive a corn mill. The Gwyn family, who inherited Forde in 1702, are credited with creating the Abbey's formal gardens, though the giant yew hedges and soaring spires of yew that the antiquary Edmund Prideaux drew on his visit in September 1727 look to be much older than a mere twenty-five years (**22**).[27] The Gwyns gave way in the nineteenth century to a succession of owners who endowed the garden slopes

22 *When Edmund Prideaux made his drawings of Forde Abbey in 1727 a conventional formal punctuation was still applied to its south-western gardens.* John Harris

south of the house with specimen trees: redwoods, Douglas fir and Cedar of Lebanon, that have still not been assimilated into the Gardenesque. It is the Ropers in the late twentieth century who have brought the Baroque of the Gwyns back to life again, in an imaginative union of order and disorder, and given the lie to an earlier claim in this chapter that the formal does not age gracefully. Set unkempt woodlands beside tumbling cataracts, sharp-edged pools and walks of perfect grass; for parterres substitute, as the Ropers have done, herbaceous borders of brimming virtuosity, and the Baroque will live as gloriously in England as in Italy, though with a distinct insular charm.

There are at least nine distinct regions in this most generous of Dorset gardens. On several of them the Roper magic has yet to be worked, but criticism fades beside what has been achieved in the Baroque areas. Entry is by an intensely productive north garden of rich, black soil. This should be monastic, but dates in fact to a nineteenth-century Bristol merchant, a Mr Miles. Around the corner of the monks' austere living quarters the grounds begin to come to life, with a wall of wisteria and a lime avenue reaching away into bucolic Dorset. At the next corner, by the Chapter House, inspiration flags and an undulating yew hedge climbs the steep slope to hide an ordinary flower garden and an under-flowered rockery. Higher up are the alien shapes of the arboretum.

The Ropers have, perhaps to avoid competition with Abbot Chard's lichened gatehouse, left vacant at this point a green enormity of lawn. When Prideaux was here this was one of Forde's two Baroque axes. Enclosed on either side by yew hedges the lawn itself was geometrically alive with alternate round and spired topiary. Then, beyond a wrought iron fence, the hillside rose to a *patte*

23 *A multi-coloured soup of waterweed enlivens the Long Pond at Forde Abbey, a survival of the formal layout recorded by Prideaux. On its far side is the most ambitious herbaceous border in the county*

d'oie or goose-foot of three avenues cut through woodland. All that is lost, but now the Ropers have compensated abundantly by restoring the Long Pond of dark clear water, with a flattering green weed mottling half its surface (**23**). In 1998 Elizabeth Roper raised the Temple rotunda at its far end for her husband Mark (**24**). 'Amor vincit omnia' runs around its entablature; there is a healthy smell of horses blowing in from the stables and, where Prideaux drew only one cataract descending in two stages from the woods behind, the Ropers have created three cataracts, crossed on stepping stones, while a fourth spring wells up from the Temple's own basin to fall into the Long Pond. Not many Italian gardens equal its charm.

Parallel with the Long Pond, the Long Walk sweeps up between Dorset's two finest herbaceous borders, a bold claim in this county, past the weather worn statue of a naked blacksmith to a wrought iron *claire-voie* on the skyline. Prideaux drew this Long Walk trapped on either side, in the Italian fashion, by towering yew hedges, which screened off the enchantingly discordant façades of the house. When I was there at the height of summer, a white explosion of flowers on a *Hoheria Sexstylosa* competed memorably with the architecture.

This should be enough, but the Baroque waters have only just begun their sequence of set-piece pools. To reach the others requires a scramble up the Mount. This is not an Elizabethan relic, but the dam that the monks built to hold back the streams. First of the surprises is the Mermaid Pond, reached without warning and first seen at eye level because of the slope. Leda and the Swan is by Enzo Platzotta. There are few flowers, just grass, water, trees and a pergola of old columns from the Abbey leading into deeper shade. Next is the Gwyns' Canal Pond with another noisy waterfall tumbling into it from the Great Pond up above on an even steeper slope. That is almost the top. The climb beside the waterfall leads out onto the bank of the Pond where the Beech House, a bird-watching hide of pleached hedges, stands. The countryside is closing in, with a forest of reeds on the left. To the right, where the Great Pond has silted up, a bog garden of unhealthy vegetable shapes is flourishing. There is a route back by yet another herbaceous area or, by keeping to the contour level, through the arboretum where a pair of nineteenth-century statues of nymphs can be viewed. Far better to experience the Baroque waters again and return the same way.

Except at Eastbury, Dorset has usually contrived to confuse the stylistic boundaries of the formal era with devious variations. At Forde the medieval works alongside the Baroque. At Melbury, another of the county's great and highly complex parks, the Baroque garden phased by retardataire degrees into those half-formal 'artinatural' gardens advocated in Stephen Switzer's 1718 *Ichnographia Rustica* and Batty Langley's 1728 *New Principles of Gardening*. Some convoluted Strangways family history explains why the 'artinatural' was still being practised at Melbury in the 1740s, a decade after its sell-by date.

Sir Thomas Strangways, who ruled at Melbury from 1673 to 1713, added in 1692 a wing to the rambling Tudor house in a maladroit artisan Baroque by a local builder called Watson. Sir Thomas then built an entirely unnecessary six-arched bridge to carry a new drive over the streamlet below the house (**25**). One small arch would have served, but at the same time Vanbrugh was constructing an equally unnecessary imperial viaduct across the diminutive Glyme at Blenheim, and Sir Thomas had strong connections with the Marlboroughs of Blenheim. His son, another Thomas, was a colonel in the Duke of Marlborough's army and one of Sir Thomas' two daughters, Susannah, was a

24 *The Rotunda at Forde was set up in 1998 by Elizabeth Roper as a tribute to her husband Mark. It is not a seat but a springhead, the waters flowing down into the Long Pond*

close friend of the Duchess Sarah.[28] Vanbrugh, or Charles Bridgeman, planted a wood at Blenheim with a star of radiating avenues, and Sir Thomas may have intended the same for Melbury, but in 1713 he died, after marrying Susannah off badly to the fourth youngest son of the Horners of Mells in Somerset. By a remarkable number of fatalities Susannah's own brother and older sister died, as did her three Horner brothers-in-law and her Horner husband, who had kept her, financially, on a tight rein. Released by his death and now a great landowner she began in 1742 to carry out at Melbury the kind of garden improvements that would have seemed fashionable thirty years earlier.

Estate accounts for 1743 record that a star of eight avenues radiating out from a circle on a hilltop north-west of the house was being cut out from the Great High Wood (**colour plate 4**).[29] Susannah Horner may have been copying the Spring Wood, a forest garden that Bridgeman laid out in 1727 for the Duke of Bolton at Hackwood Park in Hampshire. It is just possible that she was using an old Bridgeman plan passed down from her father. Whatever the inspiration she created what Horace Walpole described in 1762 as: 'a charming wood of 200 acres, cut into wild walks, with a natural Water, & two beautifull Cascades. It rises to a very large circular field, round which is an Etoile of six walks, commanding rich Views'.[30] The Fox-Strangways estate, in a rolling programme of environmentally sensitive restoration initiated by the Estate Steward, Andrew Poore, which should be a model for the whole country, has recently brought

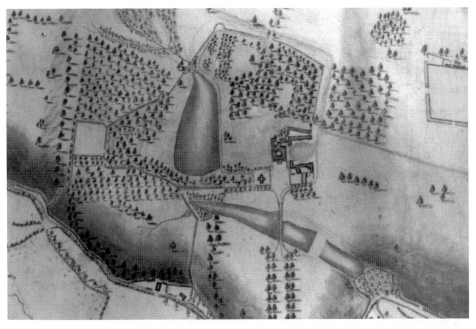

25 *A section of the superb estate map of Melbury, showing the grounds near the house. While the bridge built by Sir Thomas Strangways is still in place, his daughter's 'artinatural' garden has been swept away and the lake naturalised by her son-in-law.* Ilchester Estates

Great High Wood back to life. Two long narrow lakes feed the cascades, the lower of which tumbles impressively again in its rock-faced channel (**26**). Eventually the hilltop circle will be cleared of its unfortunate conifers.[31]

Close up to the house, Susannah inherited the two hexagonal Tudor garden viewing turrets. One remains with the crisp, confidently moulded ogee arch which she set into the old tower (**colour plate 8**). It is directly modelled on an example illustrated in Batty Langley's *Ancient Architecture Restored and Improved*, published in 1741-2 and republished in 1747 as *Gothic Architecture*. The reworked, single-cell interior with its elegantly vaulted ceiling, flowing rib tracery and painted heraldry, is one of the most poetic examples of Langley's reactionary style anywhere in the country and, if it was of 1742 date, one of the very earliest.

Sadly, the garden which Susannah Horner laid out to be enjoyed from this Gothick bower was swept away in the 1760s when Lord Ilchester, her son-in-law, created a new lake with a grotto at its west end; this last survives in a gentle dilapidation of undecorated boulders. The design of the garden, however, is preserved in a plan, or rather half a plan, which survives (**27**).[32] Reminiscent in

26 *One of Horace Walpole's 'two beautiful cascades', created by Susannah Horner between the little lakes in the Great High Wood at Melbury, a 1743 revival of Bridgeman's formal gardens of the 1720s*

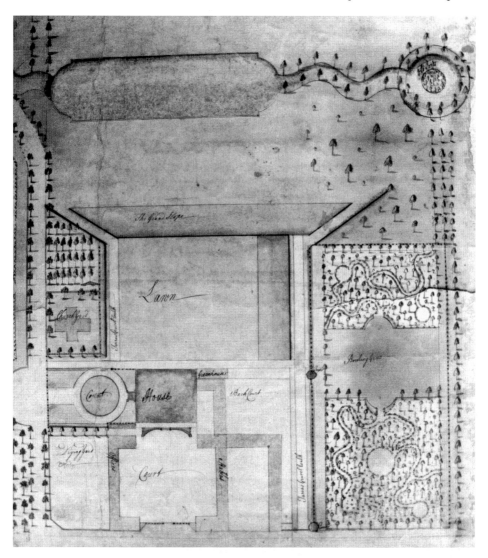

27 *The surviving half of a plan for an 'artinatural' garden in the style of Batty Langley, drawn and planted up at Melbury for Susannah Horner when she finally gained control of her father's estate in 1742. One of the two Tudor turrets shown on the upper garden wall remains.* Ilchester Estates

certain aspects of, for instance, the Wilderness at Frampton Court, her garden was half Baroque artifice and half Arcadian natural outline. It had a rectangular basin and that hallmark of the 'artinatural', a serpentine canal leading to a second basin with an island. Lower down the valley these waters flowed under Sir Thomas Strangways' grandiose six arches which would have accorded admirably with the charmingly absurd, unnatural appearance of the whole composition. Susannah's steward, George Donisthorpe, and her contractor, J.M. Kininmouth, a Sherborne nurseryman, put it together for her, but such was the tide of garden fashions, it would have a brief life of less than twenty years.

4

'The horrid graces of the Wilderness' – in the shadow of the 3rd Earl of Shaftesbury

Dorset is not rich in gardens of the vintage years of the eighteenth century when English garden design is usually considered to have been at its most innovative and influential. This is disappointing because the county should have had a head start in the movement towards setting eclectic garden buildings in such dispositions of idealised Nature as cried out to be painted or admired. The philosopher behind this visual revolution was a Dorset aristocrat, Anthony Ashley-Cooper, 3rd Earl of Shaftesbury; and its practical theorist and eager advocate of the new aesthetic was Alexander Pope, who experienced his most blinding revelation of its possibilities at Sherborne Castle.

In late June 1724, when he was already the most celebrated and influential poet in Britain, the inspired translator who had, with his *Iliad* of 1716, made Homer accessible to the English, Pope arrived in Dorset on one of his 'Rambles'. He had come to Sherborne's New Castle to stay with his friend Robert Digby, third son of William, the ruling 5th Lord Digby. Next morning the poet walked through the pleasant but unremarkable formal garden that William had laid out after 1698 between the New Castle and the ruins of the old. On that walk something in the accidental combination of formal features with a waterfall on the River Yeo and the Gothic ruins on the hill filled him with excited pleasure. His response was fascinatingly illogical and seminally eclectic. All that the scene needed to perfect it was, he claimed, a classical temple strategically sited on a nearby hill.

A letter which he wrote that night to Martha Blount reveals him as almost incoherent with this new landscape perception:

> The Gardens are so Irregular, that 'tis hard to give an exact idea of 'em but by a Plan. Their beauty rises from this Irregularity, for not only the Several parts of the Garden itself make the better Contraste by these sudden Rises, Falls, and Turns of ground; but the Views about it are lett in, & hang over the Walls, in very different figures and aspects.[1]

He was writing, whether he realised it or not, an obituary for the Franco-Dutch formal garden. The key capitalised word is 'Irregularity'. Yet ironically what had fired him was the union of a formal garden with a historic, Cromwell-slighted ruin; and his first reaction was to bring another, even less logical cultural icon, into the scene:

> a little Temple built on a neighbouring round Hill that is seen from all points of the Garden & is extremely pretty. It would finish some Walks, & particularly be a fine Termination to the River to be seen from the Entrance into that Deep Scene I have describ'd by the Cascade where it would appear as in the clouds, between the tops of some very lofty Trees that form an Arch before it, with a great Slope downward to the end of the said river.[2]

The temple would not be built; Robert Digby, the garden innovator in the Digby family, died two years later in 1726. What is important is the cultural sophistication in that eclectic response. Instead of gardening to demonstrate a macho superiority over Nature, with geometrical rows of disciplined plants, the new gardeners would be puppet masters, manipulating history and civilizations, setting a temple against a Castle ruin and then, as eclectic confidence grew, adding a Turkish tent, a Chinese pagoda, a hermit's cell,[3] coaxing an existing topography into greater dramatic beauty instead of flattening it with terraces. It was an advance in human confidence.

By using an early eighteenth-century estate map of Sherborne park (**28**)[4] every step of Pope's morning journey can be traced: a triangular wilderness, five terraces of topiary with honeysuckles, chestnut groves flanking a bowling green, a T-shaped canal widened at the midpoint of the down stroke into a semicircular basin, and then a second canalised reach of the Yeo leading to a small valley of magical incidents. In it there were concentrated 'a natural Cascade with never-ceasing murmurs', a circular Grove with 'the deepest Shade', Raleigh's own seat, to lend an historic frisson from an earlier poet, the Old Dinney bridge and 'a Rustick Seat of Stone, flagg'd and rough, with two Urns in the same rude taste upon pedestals'.[5] Towering above them on a fifty-foot bank were the ruins of the Old Castle. The place was, Pope wrote, 'inexpressibly awful & solemn', but being Pope, and writing before the romantic sensibility had matured, he proposed turning the ruins into a municipal park: 'Little paths of earth, or sand, might be made, up the half-tumbled walls; to guide from one View to another on the higher parts; & Seats placed here and there, to enjoy those views, which are more romantick than Imagination can form them'.[6] Those suggestions need to be remembered when any estimate is being made of Alexander Pope's aesthetic of landscape; he could be very kitsch.

It was those formal items, the canals and groves, that gave Pope 'these sudden Rises, Falls, and Turns of ground' that offered the 'Views . . . in very different figures and aspects', and they, unfortunately, have all gone, drowned in the inspired lake that Capability Brown would create in 1753-4.[7] So it is no longer possible to physically recreate Pope's experience. But that valley of evocative incidents is still almost intact, the cataract a little higher and noisier than in his day, and the 'Rustick Seat' replaced by 'Pope's Seat' (which he never sat in). It remains one of the county's golden garden experiences, almost a time trip.

There were two unexpected postscripts to Pope's episode: a visit by William Kent and a Shell House of Rococo perfection in Sherborne town which compensated for the New Castle's failure, in this period, to achieve any garden buildings. Kent's visit is mysterious and baffling. Pope admired Kent's work and the Digbys could easily have invited him down soon after Pope's stay to advise them on a temple. He did come to the New Castle, but he disliked the ruins of the old intensely and offered not a temple, but a design for a Gothick Seat (**29**). All of which, apparently, took place some years after he had died. The confusion arises from an undated letter from Robert Digby's nephew Edward, who succeeded as the 6th Lord in 1753. Writing to Lord Ilchester he complained:

> Mr Kent has been here ever since last Tuesday and does not talk of going away. He does nothing but advise me to pull down all the Ruins Old and New and says they are so ugly he hates to look at them.[8]

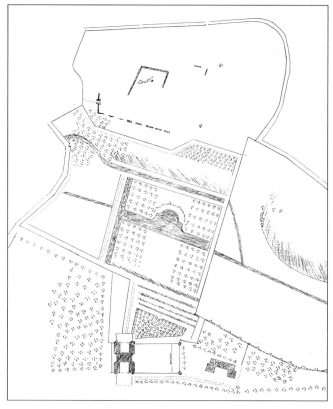

28 *A plan of the gardens at Sherborne Park showing the formal grounds between the Old Castle ruins and the New Castle now covered by the lake. On his 1724 visit Alexander Pope was delighted by their accidental complexities of vista.* Sherborne Castle Estates

29 *Pope urged a classical temple for Sherborne's grounds; William Kent, after a mysteriously undated visit, designed this Gothick Seat instead. Neither was built, the Digbys tended to please themselves.*
Sherborne Castle Estates

If Kent said this he was being ruthlessly honest. The ruins of the Old Castle at Sherborne are not at all picturesque. But when could it have happened if Kent died in 1748 and the 'New' ruin on the terrace below the 'Old' ones was not put up by a local man, Daniel Penny, until 1756-7? That Gothick Seat was drawn and is a handsome affair of deeply recessed ogee arches with flanking niches containing classical terms. In style it is close to Kent's work of the early 1730s at Esher Place in Surrey, but it never got beyond the drawing board.[9] Kent's response was, interestingly, far more in keeping with the site than Pope's.

The Shell House at Harper House, one of the boarding houses of Sherborne School, is equally mysterious. It was not only built but has survived in miraculous preservation, forgotten by all but a few housemasters of Sherborne School. Now that its presence is becoming more generally known in the town it is likely to become one of the most admired garden features in the county.[10] Recent inspired local research has thrown much more light on its origins.[11] While it belongs to the School, the Shell House actually appears to stand in the garden of the house next door, while its entrance looks down what was once the garden of another house down in Long Street. It appears to have been the polite focus of a walled garden attached to a house in Cheap Street as *The Western Flying Post and Sherborne & Yeovil Mercury* of 5 January 1801 advertises to let 'A very Roomy, Healthy, and Convenient DWELLING-HOUSE, situated in the most pleasant part of Cheap-street, in Sherborne, late the residence of Thomas Gollop Esq., and before him of Mr Samuel Foot, with the large walled in garden, hot-house, and shell-house adjoining, and at the upper end of the garden is a good stalled stable and granary.'[12]

The earliest reference we have to the building is the 1791 will of Thomas Gollop, which lists the Shell House as his property. It is assumed that he was too young to have been involved in its construction (he died in 1793 aged forty-seven), and that it was more likely to have been commissioned by the Sherborne solicitor, Samuel Foot who died in 1792 at the age of eighty-eight. None of the town records seems to mention it, yet it is an octagonal pleasure pavilion exquisitely decorated within, not with the usual amateur encrustation of shells and mineral specimens applied by local ladies, but by a professional craftsman possibly based in London, working around 1750 to a unified, carefully composed design.

The mere fact that the records are silent in a small town suggests something hidden, even perhaps improper. Its obscure setting in the garden wall accentuates this mysterious quality. This could have been an attraction in a *maison de plaisance* kept for a mistress by one of the town's respected professionals. Underneath the main chamber is a cellar which could have served as a cold bath for the men while the ladies chatted in the elegant room above. But that is speculation. One striking fact about the Shell House is how different it is from the apparently contemporary Shell Grotto at St Giles House. At Sherborne all the shells are small and native, there are no Jamaican exotics such as encrust Lady Shaftesbury's Grotto (**30**). But the tiny shells are set in shimmering patterns of diamonds and whorls on the seven wall panels and the eight roof sections (**colour plate 6**). They catch the light from the door, and the plaster into which they have been set so precisely is itself composed of crushed glass so that a subliminal glitter lies behind all the patterning.

Most remarkable of all, in their survival, are the floral swags and ribbons that play around the panels. They are composed of painted leather, copper wire and strips of lead, while the shell florets are composed individually and attached by lime putty onto roundels of cork.[13] At night and lit by candles the reflections must be numinous. Sometimes at this garden period it is not easy to distinguish the early Arcadian features from those of the later Rococo. But this Shell House with its c-scrolls of plaster, its shell basket and plaster birds is entirely Rococo in spirit, and a perfect definition of the style.[14]

Chronologically and by stylistic affinity the move from the Sherborne Shell House to the park of St Giles House, Wimborne St Giles is a natural one, yet it represents a complete change of mood. Apart from one roof section which has been dislodged, the Shell House is pristinely perfect. The grounds of St Giles, on the other hand, exist in hauntingly poetic decay, offering one of the most memorable garden experiences, not just in Dorset, but in England.[15] To walk around them is a psychic self-indulgence in melancholy and should be revelled in as such.

30 *Probably the most perfect unrestored Rococo garden building in Britain, the Shell House, an octagon of the 1750s, stands unremarked in the back gardens of Sherborne. Painted leather and lead twines in festoons around native English cockle shells*

First comes the wonderful Georgian and Ninian Comper church with the tombs of all the Shaftesburys, England's greatest political dynasty, the Ashley-Coopers, easily outpointing both the Cecils and the Cavendish-Bentincks. It is then necessary to absorb the dreary house. For St Giles' garden was conceived by the 4th Earl, out of the broodings of the pre-Romantic 'Philosopher' 3rd Earl, in an effort to escape the architectural mood of his own home. It was built as an expression of joyless Puritan Republicanism by the 1st Earl, the ex-Cromwellian and founder of the Whig Party. Some architectural historians, including myself, have praised its austere brick regularity, and certainly it was a hugely influential signpost in a negative direction. Across the rough grass from its bland regularities are the Jacobean stables that preceded it: infinitely more beautiful and positive, a home for horses opposite a gaol for aristocrats.

The house must be preserved as a monument to a direction which should never have been taken, away from the continental Baroque and subsequent Rococo, to utilitarian functional simplicity; as if the human spirit was ever

31 *Looking out from his Philosopher's Tower over Cranborne Chase, the 3rd Earl of Shaftesbury planned* The Moralists, *which he wrote in Naples in 1709, the most influential writing on garden aesthetics of the entire century*

intended to be enshrined in cost-cutting, disguised as good taste. Possibly it was the sheer tedium of the house that inspired the philosopher 3rd Earl to write in favour, not of regimented formal gardens, which would only have intensified the arid geometry of that house, but grounds of romantic escapism. He built the Philospher's Tower, a two-storey pavilion with a saucy domed roof, out on the edge of the park (**31**). 'Ye Fields and Woods', he wrote emotionally, 'my Refuge from the toilsom World of Business, receive me in your quiet Sanctuarys, and favour my Retreat and thoughtful Solitude.'[16] It was a gazebo, not for observing travellers, but for enjoying the rolling wooded slopes of Cranborne Chase. There he evolved an entirely new political iconography of landscape, praising not gardens in any accepted sense, but 'Things of a *natural* kind' and landscapes in a '*primitive State*'.[17] He would be, after Locke, the most widely read English philosopher of the new century, so rapturous writing like:

> Even the rude *Rocks*, the mossy *Caves*, the irregular unwrought
> *Grotto's* and broken *Falls* of Waters, with all the horrid graces of the
> *Wilderness* it-self, as representing NATURE more, will be the more
> engaging, and appear with a Magnificience beyond the formal
> Mockery of Princely Gardens[18]

impressed the educated classes of the entire country. Lancelot Brown's career
could hardly have been launched until the gentry had been brainwashed by
Lord Shaftesbury into accepting at least a sanitized version of 'the horrid graces
of the *Wilderness*'.[19]

His son, the 4th Earl, presided over St Giles' park for sixty years (1711-
1771), ample time to introduce any number of 'horrid graces'. Instead, what
he and his wife Susan created was one of the most committed Rococo parks
in the country (**32**). Much of it survives in an atmospheric overgrowth worthy
of the bayous of Louisiana and is recorded in an estate map of 1788 at the house
(**33**).[20] Even the surface of the carriage drive around the inner gardens is
Rococo and delicate in its finish: a finely pounded mosaic of tiny pebbles taken
from the western end of the Chesil Beach where it nears Bridport. Early in the
circuit a twin towered Castle gateway, finished in Rococo detail with hexagonal

32 *This 1774 view of the gardens at St Giles House illustrates the Rococo features which the 4th Earl of
Shaftesbury had laid out in the late 1740s. The boat on the left is emerging from the canal to the Grotto. A
Chinese Bridge with a Tea House arches over the lake, and the Great Arch is just visible between the trees
next to a row of marquees.* Bristol Reference Library: Central Library

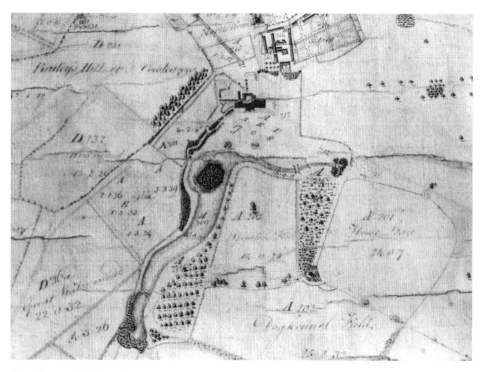

33 *The grounds of St Giles House in 1788 in their Rococo, pre-Brownian state, sinuous, full of incident but quite small. At the foot of the triangular wood is the 'round pavilion' noted by Pococke, at the top of it is the dark clump around the Grotto. The house is upper centre.* Lord Shaftesbury

glazing and draped in ivy, looms improbably out of the trees (**34**). This, referred to as 'The Great Arch', was being constructed by a mason called Barrett in August 1748.[21] On all sides there is water, the reedy lake with a modern bridge to its island on the right, while down on the left runs a fast stream from the moat by the Castle gateway. Soon the lake sends out a noisy cascade to join the stream and run away in a narrow canal. But to appreciate the didactic exuberance of a Rococo park in its prime, the description which an admiring Bishop Pococke wrote in 1754 deserves to be quoted in full:

> The gardens are very beautifully laid out, in a serpentine river, pieces of water, lawns &c., and very gracefully adorn'd with wood. One first comes to an island in which there is a castle, then near the water is a gateway, with a tower on each side, and passing between two waters there is a fine cascade from the one to the other, a thatch'd house, a round pavilion on a mount, Shake Spear's house, in which is a small statue of him, and his works in a glass case; and in all the houses and seats are books in hanging glass cases. There is a pavilion between the waters, and both a Chinese and stone bridge over them . . . There is a most beautiful grottto finished by Mr Castles of

Marybone; it consists of a winding walk and an anti-room. These are mostly made of rock spar, & c., adorn'd with moss. In the inner room is a great profusion of the most beautiful shells, petrifactions, and fine polished pebbles, and there is a chimney to it which is shut up with doors covered with shells, in such a manner that it does not appear. The park also is very delightful, and there is a building in it. The present Lord has no children.[22]

The term 'Rococo' is often applied loosely to any garden of the 1740-60 period, but at St Giles park it is entirely applicable. There is rocaille work on the heath-stone banding of the Great Arch and on the exterior of the triple chambers of the Grotto. This last is reputed to have cost the Earl £10,000 (**35**).[23] The technique used by Castles in creating stalactites, by working plaster around boughs fixed by hooks to the rafters and then applying shells and crystals to the

34 *Rococo-Gothick at its romantic best: the Great Arch in St Giles' park has rough polychrome masonry, hexagonal glazing, ivy and all 'the horrid graces of the* Wilderness' *as envisaged by the 3rd Earl and achieved by the 4th*

35 *The rugged masonry of the Grotto at St Giles is the true* rocaille *work of the Rococo: a deliberate contrast to the exquisite fineness of the interior. At few other English grottoes can the unrestored maturity of the buildings be enjoyed so completely*

plaster, can be observed in intriguing detail (**colour plate 7**). The best shells were supplied to the Earl as a favour by his near neighbour, Alderman William Beckford of Fonthill. Together with his agent, John Cope, the Alderman wrote several letters to the Earl during May and July 1749 about shipments of exotic shells from his Jamaican plantations.[24] This Grotto is a most valuable record because the Alderman's grottoes around the east side of the lake at Fonthill have long since lost their spars and their shells.

At St Giles' park it is still possible to see how delightfully the lake with its island and inlets would have worked, offering miniature voyages to picnics at castles, Chinese tea houses and at the Grotto itself (**36**). Handel was a frequent visitor to the house and took tea at the Grotto after one such voyage. Coming to this Grotto after the Shell House in Sherborne there is a striking contrast between the orderly calm of the Shell House and the bulging Baroque undulations and almost underwater organic life at St Giles. The craftsman at Sherborne could only employ tiny English cockles and winkles; at St Giles there were whole casks of Jamaican conches, 'Tamarinds', fan shells, corals and Venus' ear, smashed coloured wine glasses, quartz and felspar available for use. If it was all a far cry from the 3rd Earl's 'horrid graces', it was at least a joyous celebration of the natural world and an expanding tropical empire.

The gardens of Duntish Court, or Castle Hill as the house was known when Sir William Chambers first built it, were a more modest exercise, later

36 *In glorious stylistic confusion this 1774 illustration of Melbury House from Hutchins has a Chinese junk of the Rococo, sailing near Sir Thomas Strangways' Baroque bridge, below the delightfully inept classicism of Mr Watson's façade. A Tudor spy tower peeps up behind the house.* Bristol Reference Library: Central Library

in date, but in the same playful Rococo mood.[25] It may seem odd to associate the theorizing and scholarly Chambers with anything playful, but he did design the most Rococo creation in Britain, the Coronation State Coach in 1760, just before he designed Castle Hill in 1764. He was also responsible for the eclectic mix of exotic garden buildings at Kew, one of which, the celebrated Pagoda, survives.

Chambers' Castle Hill villa was demolished in 1965, to be replaced by a modern bungalow, and the gardens have been invaded by poker weed, an American shrub whose pink flowers are succeeded by hideous 'pokers' of poisonous green and purple berries. These apart, the grounds are among the most rewarding in the county. Immediately below the bungalow a big grove of wonderfully contorted yews stands at the head of a long weed-grown canal, much overshadowed by superb trees, a sweet chestnut and a plane being outstanding specimens. These, hanging over the broad grass walk along one side of the canal, create a moist jungle miasma about themselves and that, together with smoke wreathing from autumn bonfires, was a preparation on my visit for the oddities ahead.

High on the opposite bank, next to a modest cataract at the canal head, rise the humps of a perversely ugly slag and rough stone grotto in the Savage Picturesque style of the Fonthill grottoes. It is clearly by the same design team, the Lanes, father and son, Joseph and Josiah, of Tisbury in Wiltshire.[26]

Although they employ some spar at Duntish, the Grotto has none of the early shell-encrusted elegance of the Shell House at Sherborne or the Grotto at St Giles' park. What is interesting is that this Grotto was not intended for polite tea parties, but was built as a cold bath with side dressing alcoves.

The real excitement of Duntish, unnoticed until my visit, is the iconography of its Summerhouse (**2**). The bricky ugliness of this building has distracted visiting historians, including the RCHM inspectors,[27] from appreciating that here, by the application of rough logs, sliced laterally in half and applied loosely to the brick walls, Chambers, ever the tutor-instructor, was demonstrating for Fitz Foy, his employer, the nonsense of the theories of the Abbé Laugier's 1753 *Essai sur l'architecture*. Laugier had not only proposed that all classical architecture was an elaboration of the lintel–and-post structures of primitive wooden huts, but that modern classicism should restrict itself as far as possible to similar restraint, never using the Orders simply for ornament. In the first part of his projected *Treatise on Civil Architecture*, published in 1759 just before he designed Duntish, Chambers had argued strongly for such pedantry. Now his Summerhouse for Fitz Foy seems to mock Laugier, first by applying logs to the brick walls, completely unsound structurally speaking, to illustrate how lintels and posts would have worked. A double row of horizontal logs then demonstrates how, in the primitive Doric order, the mutule and taenia would have bounded the frieze (**37**). Short lengths of logs are placed where the triglyphs would have connected the two vertically.

37 *With chunks of log and rough flints Sir William Chambers mocks Laugier's theory of how triglyphs, mutule and taenia developed from primitive carpentry. This is a detail of his 1763 Summerhouse or 'Carpenter's Shop' at Duntish Court*

38 *A 1774 illustration from Hutchins of the pretty* ferme ornée *that Charles Brune improvised about 1750 in an otherwise dull country at Plumber, near Sturminster Newton.* Bristol Reference Library: Central Library

Tucked away now in damp, dark woodland and used, when I saw it, for workmen's lunch breaks, the Summerhouse is a valuable reminder of that decade when neo-classicism was beginning to oust both the Rococo and the Palladian from favour. It is also a reminder of the discoveries still to be made by detailed garden surveys of individual counties and offers a human note on Sir William's character. He had, after 1763, been obliged by his Scottish patron, the Earl of Abercorn, to apply Laugier's austere principles to the interior decoration of a new villa at Duddingston, Midlothian.[28] So at Duntish he may have been fighting back humorously rather than delivering a practical lecture. Fitz Foy, an irritatingly un-chronicled gentleman, must have enjoyed the joke.

So much of this engaging period survives at Duntish that it comes as a real disappointment, after studying the illustration in Hutchins of the perfect small Rococo garden at Plumber Manor, near Sturminster Newton, to find only the stream, the walled Kitchen Garden and the truncated façade of the house still in place (**38**). Hutchins describes Plumber as 'now a farm'.[29] This is no disparagement as Plumber was a gentleman's *ferme ornée*, improved about 1750 by Charles Brune in the manner of Philip Southcote's Wooburn Farm at Chertsey, Surrey, begun in 1734, and William Shenstone's The Leasowes, near Halesowen, north Worcestershire.[30] Crammed playfully together, between the house and a winding river crossed by a Chinese bridge, are a Gothick pavilion, a two-storey classical gazebo and some haphazard lengths of Chinese fencing (**39**). A Wilderness with a formal canal and a walled Kitchen Garden lie beside the house and the artist, William

39 *An example of the eclectic diversity essential to a true Rococo garden is displayed in Plumber's ornamental farm: a Chinese fretwork bridge and fence, an arcaded classical Pavilion and a Gothick Garden House on the far side of a little walled Wilderness.* Bristol Reference Library: Central Library

Tomkins, has drawn a typically bucolic couple, a milkmaid and a gardener, walking along admiring it all.[31]

Little else of this period has survived in Dorset's gardens. It is tempting to suppose that the county's gentry took the 3rd Earl of Shaftesbury's enthusiasm for the 'horrid graces of the *Wilderness*' more seriously than those of other counties out of loyalty to the Ashley-Coopers. Certainly the next chapter will reveal any number of parks remodelled in the handsome but uninteresting Brownian manner.

The grounds of Kingston Russell, as they existed in 1750, are a salutary reminder that, unlike gardens of the county aristocracy, as at Sherborne or St Giles House, the gardens around the manor house of the average Dorset squire were a pleasant, unpretentious muddle. Thanks to a dispute over land boundaries between John Mitchell Esquire of Kingston Russell and the Duke of Bedford, we have a detailed map, dated 1750 and drawn by J. Wynne, of the area 'adjoyning to Mr Mitchell's House'.[32] This calls for some analysis as it proves that the entrance and garden fronts of the house had been reversed.

The west front of the house had been completely refaced by Mitchell in about 1739 in a heavy sub-Hawksmoor classicism. That today is the entrance front, but Mitchell created it to face his garden, a long Bowling Green flanked on each side by yew hedges with no trace of a drive. The east front, an earlier Carolean composition, now the garden front, faced an entrance court and a public road with cottages.

South of the house was a large pleasure orchard divided into two halves by a 'Filibert Walk'. In the eastern half of the orchard was an irregular 'Grove of Box'. All the Kitchen Gardens, five enclosures in all, and the service area with stables, 'Privy' and a 'Dwelling House', were north of these areas and slightly above the principal house. The north wing of the house, which would be demolished in 1913 in the interests of symmetry, actually extended out over the road on posts, apparently to the annoyance of the Duke who believed, probably wrongly, that this was the original home of his Russell ancestors.[33]

What is interesting about these grounds is that, though the house had been recently brought up to date in a near Palladian style, the gardens could have been a homely layout of 1600. It will be interesting to see, in a later Edwardian chapter, how they fared in the twentieth century.

The grounds at Creech Grange appear to have been, in their 1750s prime, Arcadian rather than Rococo improvisations on an earlier formal layout. The canal has been noted in an earlier chapter and Norman Hayward, the present owner, informs me that he has found the footings of a small temple near the two irregular lakelets in the little Wilderness. The Creech Arch high up on the down south of the house was a token Gothick feature focused from the south front of the house by two large garden urns (**colour plate 5**). Another eclectic gesture was the removal in 1746 by Denis Bond, for placement in a chapel, of a Norman arch from the ruins of Bindon Abbey (or, by another account, from East Holme Priory). Nathaniel Bond built a dour little neo-Norman church around the Georgian chapel in 1849. Recently demolition of the church was proposed, but Mr Hayward, seeing shrewdly that the chapel had always been conceived as a garden feature, bought and saved it.

The rogue architect, William Benson, an enthusiast for Palladio, who persuaded King George I to sack Sir Christopher Wren and appoint him in his place as Surveyor of the Kings Works, is an unlikely figure to appear on a Dorset island. But Benson's Surveyorship lasted only fifteen months before he was sacked for corruption, and in 1724 he bought Brownsea Island in Poole Harbour from his brother,[34] intending to set up an experimental Botanical Garden there.[35] A year later he published an inaccurate translation of Virgil's *Georgics* and was trying to import, following Virgil's advice, Cytisus grass from Naples as a new cattle fodder. He had the support of the Cambridge Professor of Botany.

With Pliny's description of his seaside villa at Laurentinum in mind Benson built a 'Great Hall'[36] inside an existing Tudor blockhouse, and may have laid out some kind of garden there. Hutchins writes of it as a place 'where the proprietor sometimes resided for his diversion and where the late Prince of Wales refreshed himself, on a progress he made into this county'.[37] Wild fowling is more likely to have been Prince Frederick's mode of refreshment than a garden. Towards the end of his life Benson went mad, and when Sir Humphry Sturt of Crichel bought Brownsea in 1765 he found Benson's hall 'in a very ruinous state'.[38]

5

From garden to park –
the age of Brown

Blessed with a lively, naturally beautiful terrain, Dorset has more parks of this, usually rather dull if harmonious category, than any other. Landscape designers of the school of Lancelot Brown knew what their patrons required: well-drained slopes, a lake, good cover for pheasants and fast carriage drives.

No sooner had the Shaftesbury earls filled up their pleasure ground with eclectic diversions than they were laying out, far beyond the park bounds, a serpentine drive for scenic thrills in a fast carriage. Many sections of it can still be traced today, surrounding two entire parishes, Wimborne St Giles and Wimborne up Monkton. From the Roman road at the north-west to the present B3078 in the south-east it followed a ten mile circuit of intermittent tree belts, dashing down to the tip of the 4th Earl's lake, then swooping up Brockington Down, Tenantry Down and Harly Down, never too steeply for two horses to pull at a satisfying pace.

Technical improvements, well-tuned springing, had transformed lumbering conveyances for the infirm and old into objects of desire and prestige, spank-ingly elegant in line and colour. Such treasures were usually deployed on city streets rather than the appalling public roads. Private carriage drives, however, could be gently graded and carefully surfaced. Then a simple alternation of woodland and open vistas could, from a fast moving vehicle, produce a new, almost cinematic impression of light and shade. The male urge to move dangerously at speed could be satisfied, visitors could be given treats and, at the same time, the vast acreage of the estate could be demonstrated. The octagonal twin lodges at the village entry to St Giles' park are typical of the handsome but, where accommodation was concerned, grudging gate lodges of this period. Two rooms were all that was allowed to serve the estate family. Now they lie deserted, humanly inadequate despite their architectural charm.[1] It was all part of the widening gap between the rich and the poor.

Ranston House, on a mansion-crowded sector of the Iwerne valley, was built in 1758 by Thomas Ryves of Blandford. A standard Palladian style villa, it was set in an almost empty park of the period, relying heavily on the beautiful natural bowl of hills for its scenery and commanding it by a serpen-tine drive that was intact as late as the 1901 Ordnance Survey map of the estate. It still sets off from the house, alongside a brick walled garden and stable block, past an ugly rockery with a sinuous Japanese bronze of monsters to a little wood of beech and chestnut.[2] At this point there is the sound of falling water and that very eighteenth-century smell of drains running into an ornamental feature; the lake at Encombe produces the same effect. The drive crosses the Iwerne on a three-arched bridge, neatly elegant in the Palladian manner and built over a cataract that falls into a widening of the stream (**40**). From here, under the heavy shade of trees, there is a view back to the bridge and its white water. Hutchins' view shows that in 1774 the bridge was a park feature visible from the house.[3]

Then the drive, overgrown now, swings away west uphill to where there was still in 1901 a Summerhouse on the hill top: a picnic venue from which the whole park could be enjoyed before the party proceeded to inspect the tenants' cottages in Shroton village, returning via a picturesque Gothic lodge and a level drive to the house.

Ranston's drive was sedately charming. That laid out by John Pitt, in about 1770 around the far more dramatic valley at Encombe, Dorset's most secluded, poetic and entirely covetable property, must have provided an exhilarating and memorable carriage experience (**41**). The 1796 Faden map of the county which Pitt's son, John Morton Pitt, used in his 28 March 1798 'Report on the Dorset Coast',[4] shows a tremendous circuit running as far west as the park at Smedmore. From the high western Downs it swung down to the coast to

40 *The so-called 'Palladian Bridge' in Ranston park is not precisely to any of Palladio's designs, but it makes a handsome central feature on what was a Brownian-style carriage drive all round the park. There is a weir on the down river side*

41 *Encombe flourishing exactly as it was designed to function, hosting the 2002 Dorset Gardens Trust garden party. The right-hand bank of the lake looks natural, but is in fact a large earth dam, part of a Brownian-style layout*

feature a unique park event. The Encombe stream is channelled to the cliff edge and then bent at right-angles, so that it could be viewed from the drive, before falling seventy feet down onto the black rocks of the shore. The Pitts evidently had a taste for truly wild Nature.

After this high spot, the drive climbed up through woodland to Encombe Dairy and the Home Farm. The lower lake was not in existence in 1796 and, after the Dairy, the next event on the drive was the Cyclopean three-arched Grotto, a Savage Picturesque creation of roughly 1770 (**42**).[5] This is wonderfully threatening and romantic; one arch leads into a maze with a Druid's altar in a chamber cut under the drive. One way out of this led walkers down to the Dairy, another curls back to the starting point. So the mood of the Pitts' park was anything but classical. The serpentine continued up to the house, passing the lake, in itself a considerable engineering achievement, held up on its eastern side by an earth dam, planted with trees.

Lord Chancellor Eldon, who bought Encombe from the Pitts in 1807, staged a deliberate retreat back from the sea and too much savage drama to the Arcadian idyll more fashionable sixty years earlier. His is the Janus-faced Temple, Doric to the lake, Ionic to the stable yard behind where it houses a carriage shed (**43**). This most unusual economy of design acted almost as a limb to the low, wide-armed house. Both Eldon's Seat and the lean Obelisk, raised in 1835 to honour his brother Lord Stowell, are high up on the Downs,

42 *John Pitt favoured the Savage Picturesque garden style at Encombe in the 1770s. This entrance to his cyclopean Grotto leads to a Druid's altar in a chamber hollowed out under the carriage drive*

43 *Doric to the garden, but Ionic to the stable yard at Encombe, this Janus-faced Temple is an example of Lord Eldon's conservative taste in garden buildings. He bought the estate in 1807*

44 *This view across Capability Brown's lake at Sherborne proves William Kent's observation that the Old Castle ruins were inadequate. The small turret visible in the centre of the scene is a fake of 1756 by Daniel Penny*

inland and to the north. Pitt's serpentine was a rare garden feature because it was oriented towards the sea. In Eldon's time it began to fall into disuse and Dorset would have to wait for Highcliffe Castle before its gardens could look seawards again.

These serpentine belt drives are often associated with Capability Brown, but he did not invent them and none of his three commissions in the county, at Sherborne Castle, Highcliffe Castle or Milton Abbey, featured them. The Digbys of Sherborne, being themselves keen gardeners, never allowed Brown overall control in planning their park. He oversaw the creation of the lake between 1753 and 1754, handled a contract for his usual manicuring work close to the New Castle in 1776 and thereafter, as a valued family friend, advised on planting during visits every year until just before he died in 1783.

The lake virtually suggested itself during a flash flood of 1753 which demonstrated the potential beauty of such a sheet of water covering the low-lying areas of the park (**44**).[6] There was some trouble over rock works when a sluice and waterfall were being made on the site of Pope's 'natural Cascade with never-ceasing murmurs', but an underlying layer of Fuller's Earth clay meant that there was no need for expensive puddling, and the whole operation only cost £322.[7] What should not be underrated is the idyllic beauty of the resultant scene. Brown earned his nickname of 'Capability' because he had a perfect eye for any given topography and for what could be improvised around it. The New Castle now rises on a wooded peninsula like some English vision out of a Claude painting, and the views from the New Castle towards the Old are almost as fine. Further east, down the lake, that vision has been allowed to fade, but the shores are still lovely in neglect and the entire concept was inspired.[8]

Edward, 6th Lord Digby, died young and was succeeded in 1757 by his brother Henry who was such an ardent gardener that he planted shrubs in person, even during rainstorms.[9] It was Henry who had the idea of creating a *ferme ornée* at Pinford at the far eastern end of the lake to make a pleasure ground and a destination for boat trips. He was already widening the lake there as early as 1761. The graceful Pinford Bridge, of three arches with a balustraded parapet, was built in 1768-9 by William Privett to a design by Robert Digby, derived from a July 1767 design by Robert Adam (**45**).[10]

By 1774 the Digbys were ready for Brown's technical expertise to smooth out what had already been begun. The contract, signed in February 1776, was a classic instance of the Brownian treatment.[11] To leave the New Castle isolated on a vast green lawn the East Garden, parts of which with its terraces and twin pavilions may have dated back to Sir Walter Raleigh's time, was swept away leaving uninterrupted views from the house down to the far eastern end of the new lake. The stables were removed from that side of the Castle and hidden

45 *Robert Digby used a Robert Adam design for the 1768-9 Pinford Bridge at the east end of Sherborne's new lake. It was a landing point for visits to a* ferme ornée *and Brown had paid close attention to the planting of an island*

46 *The Adam-designed Greenhouse at Sherborne faces – incongruously – a Gothick Dairy of equally shallow mouldings by Capability Brown. The Digbys kept a tight control over planning*

away behind trees to the west. Three ha-has were dug to give the impression that the pleasure garden and the park were one unit. Brown was always ready to supply a park building if required and in 1780 a Gothick Dairy went up, followed in 1781 by the new 'greenhouse', an Adam-style building in complete eclectic contrast with the Dairy that faced it across a small grove of trees, now felled (**46**).[12]

A great tree planting programme was initiated to convert, by carefully colour graded tree clumps, the entire amphitheatre of land south of the Castle into one of Brown's ideal parkscapes. One typical clump included eighty oaks, nine elms, ten hornbeams and forty larch. Brown's suggested planting for the island near the Pinford Bridge was far more colourful and intimate: fifty laburnums, seventy-six quince, thirteen weeping willow with some hornbeam and alder.[13] A painting of about 1784 by Robert Sherburne shows the Pinford Bridge reflected in a clear reach of the lake with a clump of trees on the island behind it.[14] Most of this artificial elegance has now been lost.

An estate survey of 1796 shows the park clumped on both sides of the lake, but with the belt ride to the north running through unbroken woodland, clumsy local planning not at all in Brown's more subtle style of alternate open and closed vistas into the park.[15] There is a grand approach drive from the eastern Crackmore Gate, leading visitors from London in between the Flower de Luce gatepiers and over the Pinford Bridge. From that point there were tempting glimpses of the towers of the New Castle ahead and then a long easy drive with the lake to the right and tree crowned hills to the left. This was easily the grandest route into any of Dorset's parks, pushed through by Henry, Lord Digby, probably to Brown's advice.

Much of this survives today. The immediate surroundings of the New Castle are perfect and the ancient oaks in the park just south of the Pinford Bridge are splendidly bottled and senile, though there is little new planting here. What is regrettable, though it is easy to understand the financial pressures involved in running such an estate, is that the great amphitheatre of parkland to the south of the New Castle has been turned into a dreary, treeless agri-prairie, a parody of what Brown intended. The undulating 'Dry Land' north of the lake is in desperate need of a replanting of the clumps which once made such a flattering setting for the lake. Lastly, that arm of water which once led almost almost up to the *ferme ornée* at Pinford is now a muddy cattle pond and a bed of young willows. Between these two areas the aristocratic arches of the Pinford Bridge now look lost and mildly embarrassed.

A final verdict on Brown's work at Sherborne must be that he served the Digby family well, but that theirs were the basic landscape ideas which he then helped to carry through. Robert, later Admiral (after 1794) Digby, the third of the gardening brothers, transformed the bare valley below Minterne House, which he had bought in 1768, by deploying the Brownian formula: fishponds into lakes, cataracts for the little River Cerne, and shelter belts of trees to clothe the hillsides.[16] His brother, Henry, made the mistake, in that limited area between the New Castle and the lake shore at Sherborne, of building two oddly contrasted structures close together, an effect more quaint than inspired. Brown veiled their curious juxtapositioning with trees, which should be replaced. The same goes for the agri-prairie south of the New Castle. But at least something remarkable survives at Sherborne of what Brown and the Digbys intended.

The same cannot be said for Brown's work at Milton Abbey, the most over-praised tourist destination in the county. This is a park where great fortune and bad luck have run a joint course together. When half a cathedral church, a great Georgian house and a model village by Brown and Sir William Chambers are combined in an attractively wooded Dorset valley, it should be a blueprint for a masterpiece of the Picturesque. In sad reality not one of these items works well either in itself or together.

Hardly a single tree of Brown's landscaping, over consultations, in 1763 and 1773, survives.[17] After the sale of the estate in 1953 most of his woods and clumps were felled and now the Abbey and the house sit next to a street of second rate educational premises and a green desert of playing fields. The church, stripped and scraped bare of pinnacles, first by James Wyatt in 1789-91, then by George Gilbert Scott in 1865, desperately needed a sympathetic surround of mature trees, just as the house, an unhappy Gothick veiling of Palladian symmetries, required a relaxed garden at its front, not a cricket pitch.

The woods that remain, on the potentially fine setting of a union of two valleys, sit hard-edged and solid like a pudding basin haircut on the contour lines of the hills. In no way do they retain even a vestige of Brown's subtle planting. He must, however, take some blame for the lake south of the house. Either he puddled it inadequately or the chalk subsoil was impossibly porous. It shrank and makes no kind of impact upon the house or on the road leading to the house.

Up on the slope west of the lake is a post-1811 Gothic Temple, a pleasant folly but not one commandingly sited. The grass steps leading up over the road via a bridge to St Catherine's Chapel on the east side of the valley are an attractive curiosity of late nineteenth-century date (**47**), in no way related to Brown, though the pretty *cottage ornée* at their foot is of his time.

Whether Milton Abbas village counts as a garden feature is arguable. It has had an astonishingly favourable press. Nikolaus Pevsner and John Newman conclude their account with 'The view down the street here is magnificent',[18] while John Harris hails it as 'The most perfect of model villages', reflecting Sir William Chambers' 'humanitarian concern for the happiness and well-being of the working classes'.[19] Perhaps these verdicts date to the time when

47 *These late-nineteenth-century grass steps at Milton Abbey climb over a public road on their way up to St Catherine's Chapel*

48 *The monument in Milton Abbey to Joseph Damer, 1st Earl of Dorchester, and his Countess has an elegiac charm. In real life he was a ruthless garden creator who paid Brown in 1763-73 to drown a whole market town in order to float an inadequate lake*

flowering chestnut trees, planted between each semi-detached pair of thatched tenements, flattered their regular and entirely unpicturesque disposition down each side of the wide main street in the later manner of a 1930s council housing estate. This repetitive show, designed by Chambers, was laid out as late as 1780 by Brown, who had been paid £103 for a plan in 1773.[20] It was a poor substitute for the historic market town of Middleton, which once had six streets, clustered like another Tewkesbury, around the abbey church. Brown was the apparently willing instrument of the arrogant Joseph Damer, 1st Baron Milton and 1st Earl of Dorchester (**48**), in literally drowning Middleton with his lake. Milton Abbas remains today an indictment, both of the selfish philistinism of some eighteenth-century landscaping and of that acceptance of low standards of design which afflicted this country for twenty years after the Second World War.

Brown's third Dorset commission was actually in Hampshire, at Highcliffe on the coast to the east of Bournemouth, but in a part of that county which has now been included within Dorset's borders. Nothing survives of Brown's work there, which is a pity as it seems to have been quite unlike his usual landscaping. The 3rd Earl of Bute, who had been tutor to King George III and then one of his less successful Prime Ministers, had bought a house on the cliffs in 1773 as a second or holiday home. Robert Adam was employed to enlarge it with wings and to build lodges for the park which Brown was laying out.[21]

Lord Bute's principal seat was Luton Hoo in Bedfordshire, but he was so taken by the mild airs and sea bathing of the South Coast that he transferred many of the plants from his botanic garden at Luton to Highcliffe.[22] Brown created shelter belts to protect them, planting mostly conifers to suit the sandy soil. According to Repton he also created a 'bathing place', presumably at the foot of the fast crumbling cliffs and surely Brown's one and only seaside lido.[23]

Our only other authority for this intriguing seaside park is the Picturesque enthusiast and travel writer, William Gilpin. He first mentions it shortly after Bute's death in 1792, in one of his many letters, dated 2 July 1792, to the Bishop of Durham, Shute Barrington:

> Lord Bute's [-] house on the cliff here, and its appendages, will hardly, I suppose be long kept in the splendid manner in which it has been – Lymington market is at the time, I hear, plentifully supplied with every thing from it, that a garden can furnish.[24]

So Brown appears to have laid out a generous Kitchen Garden. But in another letter to the Bishop of 29 August 1795 Gilpin provides information of a more exotic nature:

> We have seen such an instance of selfishness at Highcliff as I never remember to have heard of. Lord Bute is supposed to have consumed little less than 100,000 on the house, and its various appendages. Scarce any body enjoyed it, but himself. His son, to whom he left it, had not the means to keep it up; and has been obliged to sell it for 1200. The purchaser has sold all the plant[ings] [in] the garden walls – the pavilions – the great water organ – and has severed the wings from the house – and reduced the whole to that original state, in which I remember it, when Lord Bute first began his improvements. Lord Shatsbury has bought the organ at a very low price, as it is a doubt, whether he can ever be able to erect it in perfection.[25]

Bute's third son, Lord Charles Stuart, was a professional soldier, by no means wealthy, and fully occupied with the French wars. But from the sale of the property he did retain a small farmhouse which, when it came into the posses-sion of his son, another Charles Stuart, became the core of Highcliffe Castle whose grounds will feature in the next chapter. For the present the problem is what kind of layout Brown can have provided for Lord Bute. The plantings in the garden walls must refer to those prized botanical specimens that Bute had brought down from Luton Hoo. So it cannot have been the conventional bare Brownian landscape with clumps of deciduous trees, but a garden enclosed by high walls and surrounded by conifers. It also had 'pavilions'; one small temple survived until at least 1942 when Christopher Hussey described the grounds.[26]

The puzzle is 'the great water organ'. This sounds like a Jacobean hydraulic garden toy, such as might have survived at Wilton as late as the end of the seventeenth century, certainly not as late as 1795. And did Lord Shaftesbury, the 5th Earl, ever manage to make it work again at St Giles House? There is no record, but there has to be the possibility that Capability Brown laid out an almost formal garden, described as 'like another Kew'.[27]

That was his last Dorset work, but the bare Brownian formula was applied often in the county by followers of Brown. Richard Woods (*c*.1716-93) was one such. He was called in by the Welds of Lulworth, on the recommendation of their fellow Catholic, Lord Arundell of Wardour Castle, Wiltshire, to advise on the slow, sad transition of their formal gardens into a conventional open park in the Brownian manner. This was in 1769 when he appears to have helped two local surveyors, John and Thomas Sparrow, to clump the park east and south of the Castle.[28] He planned an ice house and probably built two walled gardens. Purbeck is a notably under-watered area of the county and the Welds could never have created Woods' landscape favourites: a series of lakes giving the impression of a noble river, such as he had proposed for Wardour.

More Crichel, though a much lesser place than Milton Abbas, a mere village, suffered the same fate from aristocratic arrogance when Humphry Sturt the younger succeeded to the estate in 1770 and married a rich heiress. In that perverse, basically post-Shaftesburian aesthetic, he enlarged the pleasant Tudor house into a near palace, yet swept away the two-storey garden pavilion and terraced garden to leave his new façades looking lost and out of place on a broad green lawn above a long sickle-shaped lake. Hutchins illustrated it in 1774, just before its completion with a pretty Ranston-style bridge across the lake. By then More Crichel had been flattened for the sin of hugging its manor house too closely. The tenants were rehoused at New Town, south of the park, while their church remained isolated from its congregation and architecturally quite inappropriate near Sturt's grandiose, clumsily proportioned house.

As a reminder of how much this village vandalism was a matter of personal whim and ill nature, John Damer, brother of the Joseph Damer who destroyed Middleton, built his perfect Palladian villa, Came House, cosily within the existing village and churchyard of Winterborne Came, disturbing nothing. The house has a conventional park. All the broad Brownian sweep, that such a villa of 1754 required, is spread harmlessly with its fine beeches over both sides of the valley of the Winterbourne (**49**).

Aesthetic vandalism was not always involved. Sometimes, as at Melbury Sampford and Stock Gaylard, the villages merely melted away over the centuries, though in both cases the little churches survived. Stock House stands in a deer park of robust English oaks where the unvaried trees are relieved by just a token Gothick Kiosk on the edge of Brickles Wood (**50**). It has a thatched conical roof and inside a simple bench runs around the circle of walls,

49 *John Damer, Joseph Damer's brother, laid out an ideal landscape in the Brownian fashion on the north side of his Palladian villa at Winterborne Came. The informality of the grounds is intended to set off the formality of the house.* Bristol Reference Library: Central Library

50 *A sinisterly quaint little Gothick Kiosk at Stock Gaylard, among the oaks of the oldest of Dorset's four deer parks. There is a herd of Menil Fallow Deer, one of only three in the country*

as if preparing for a sylvan prayer meeting. The window towards the wood is blocked and the building has a faint air of M.R. James' *Ghost Stories of an Antiquary*: a park to savour, but not in the evening. As if reluctant to traipse so far out to it, the family converted their stone pigeon house into a Gothick pavilion, the dial of its wind gauge facing the stables to warn grooms what weather to expect.

At Melbury the 1st Lord Ilchester lost no time before sweeping away in 1762 his mother-in-law Susannah's old fashioned serpentine canal and island. In its place he built a massive earth dam to create a quite modest lake below the long lawns east of the house. At its upper end is a rough dysfunctional Grotto of coarse boulders; the Fox-Strangways, for all their vast estates and wealth, have never bred garden lovers like the Digbys. Consequently their park still retains much of the feeling of primaeval Dorset.

On its eastern borders, for a very short life span, was Woolcombe Hall[29] surrounded by the archetypal Brownian park, laid out at the height of the Brownian cult in 1782 for Edward Buckley by William Emes, one of Brown's ablest and most successful followers (**51**). Scarcely a trace of it remains and the Yeovil-Weymouth railway line passes through its site, but the fastidiously detailed plan deserves study for its clear demonstration of a Brownian park's aesthetic roots in the Rococo period. Every line of the layout, drives, lakes, clumps, coppices and boundary belts is a flowing curve. Trees screen the stables from the house; the Kitchen Garden is banished to the edge of the park and surrounded by sinuous glades. No vestige of a garden, formal or otherwise, has been allowed near the house, which stands in lonely isolation with only a semi-circle of fencing to keep cattle at a distance. Nature is in control, yet Nature is wholly tamed; that was the Brownian paradox.

As if the isolation was too much for its owners, Woolcombe Hall has vanished, but Dewlish House, a notably bland structure in that characterless Queen Anne style, neither Baroque nor Palladian, exists comfortably in a perfect Brownian valley. It was rebuilt in 1702 for Thomas Skinner, a Londoner, but the Michels, who bought it in 1756, will have been responsible for the austere simplicity of its setting. The main drive dips down from a by-lane without any fuss of gate lodges, passes at a discreet distance some retainers' cottages and the stables, before the house stages its appearance across immac-ulately plain parkland. The tree belts on both sides of the valley are retired to the skyline and just one arm of the essential lake shows up at the side of the house as a promise of Claudeian vistas beyond in this tasteful minimalism of distilled Dorset.

The principal drive of approach and that first glimpse of a house from a carriage was usually the chief concern of a Brownian park. At Stepleton House, near neighbour on the Iwerne to Ranston House, the tug of interests between an approach of convenience and one of boastful drama has ended in the triumph of convenience. Julines Beckford, brother of the great Alderman

William Beckford of Fonthill and father of Peter, the authority on hunting,[30] bought the house in 1745 and promptly began rebuilding it into a miniature version of Fonthill Splendens with a central block and flanking Palladian wings. It was not considered appropriate that such pomp should be viewed from its tradesman's entrance on the main Shaftesbury–Blandford road, so an absurd new drive was constructed from a relatively obscure lane at the farthest extremity of the small park. Twin classical box lodges guarded its entrance and, after a run through high woodland, the drive brought special visitors out at the edge of the valley with the house, looking larger than it really was, lying far below them.[31] There were wooded gardens behind it, the necessary open parkland in front, clumped with trees, and the Iwerne at the side widened by sluices to give at least the impression of a lake. Naturally no one wanted to use such a round about way in; the lodges are falling into decay and everyone still uses the tradesman's entrance, which divides, taking away the privacy of the house, by running alongside all its chief fronts.

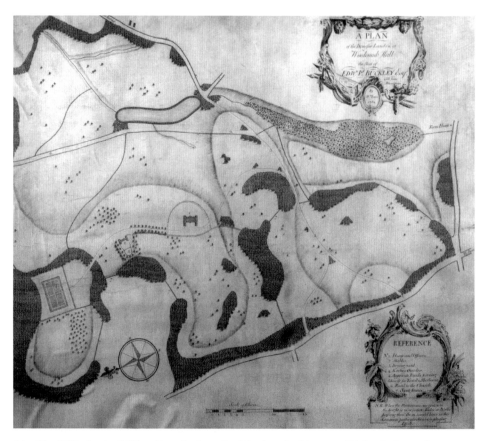

51 *The 1782 plan by William Emes for the park of the short-lived house at Woolcombe is a perfect compendium of flowing Rococo curves in its drives, lakes and woods; but in the Brownian manner the house stands in absolute isolation, unsupported by a garden.* Ilchester Estates

52 *This idyllic, apparently Brownian, landscape at Up Cerne was created by Reginald and Vera Broadhead after the Second World War, a mark of the enduring attraction of the 'Capability' formula*

Stepleton's village never recovered from the Black Death, but its church is still there intricately bound up in a hidden paradise of walled gardens, hedged enclosures and another lakelet of the Iwerne which belong to the next chapter. Mrs Coombs of Stepleton House acts as one, or possibly both, of the parish's two churchwardens.

Up Cerne's park, while entirely out of chronological sequence, deserves a place in this chapter because its owners, the Broadheads, Reginald and Vera, have done a 'Capability' since the Second World War by damming the Cerne to create a chain of four lakes, two of them with an island apiece (**52**). This has not only improved the view from their garden house immeasurably, but visually enriched the lane leading from the A352 to the village. These lakes, or, more accurately lakelets, are true Brownian constructs, not set Edwardian-wise in some semi-formal layout, but lying idyllically in plain meadow grass to transform the valley in a way that Brown would have admired.[32]

Last in this chapter must come a house of the Brownian decades which was never built, and a 'conceptual landscape' of those years which Brown would never have acknowledged as being a landscape at all. Thomas Hollis was a rich eccentric in the tradition of 'old Whigs' of the Commonwealth.[33] Suspected of being an atheist and a republican he was neither, rebuilding three churches around Halstock in north Dorset and being the valued friend of both the Pitts, elder and younger. He abstained from alcohol, butter, salt, milk and spices, spending his wealth on projects which would encourage liberty and science.

In 1770 he retired to his 3,000 acres in Halstock to be near the Pitt estate in Somerset. With no manor house to live in he took up residence in Urles Farm and a suite of rooms called 'Liberty Hall' in the Three Cups at Lyme

Regis, a town he loved. To spread his democratic notions he created a conceptual landscape, which he called 'patriotizing' his properties, renaming not only his farms, but every field on those farms after philosophers and virtuous politicians.[34] Liberty Farm, Marvell Farm, Locke Farm and Harvard Farm still retain his conceptual nomenclature.[35] Milton Farm seems to have changed its name. Woods and coppices were named after his black list: Powder Plott Coppice and Stuart Coppice. Liberty Farm had fields named after Confucius, Socrates, Plato, Xenophon, Aristotle and Pythagoras. Sidney Farm celebrated heroes of the Civil War: Lilburne Mead, Hambden Mead, Pym Mead and The Good Old Cause. Quite how a field called 'The Pope' got into Court Farm next to 'Cromwell' is not easy to follow.

Hollis died while out walking his conceptual landscape and 'in compliance with his own request or order was buried in one of his fields afterwards passed over by the plough'.[36] In an interesting reflection of the mild and tolerant tone of the times his obituary in the *Gentleman's Magazine* of January 1774 hailed him as a:

> Gentleman formed on the severe but exulted plan of Ancient Grace, in whom was united the humane and interested virtue of Brutus, and the active and determined spirit of Sidney; illustrious in his manner of using ample fortune, not by spending it on the parade of life, which he despised, but by assisting the deserving, and encouraging the Arts and Sciences, which he promoted with zeal and affection, knowing that love of them leads to moral and intellectual beauty.[37]

If he had died a few years later, when the French Revolution had alarmed the English ruling classes, it is unlikely that he would have been acclaimed so generously.

1 *To the rear of the hedge mountain at Bingham's Melcombe, Geoffrey Jellicoe disciplined the gardens into parallel allées, chiefly green upon green, though here edged narrowly with flowers. The Pigeon House acts as a focus point*

2 *With a more relaxed, even organic ingenuity, successive owners of Sydling Court have allowed their topiary to grow up, creating a series of accidental spaces between their green abstractions and the Kitchen Garden wall*

A PLAN of EASTBURY the Seat of the R.t Hon.ble GEORGE DODINGTON Esq.r

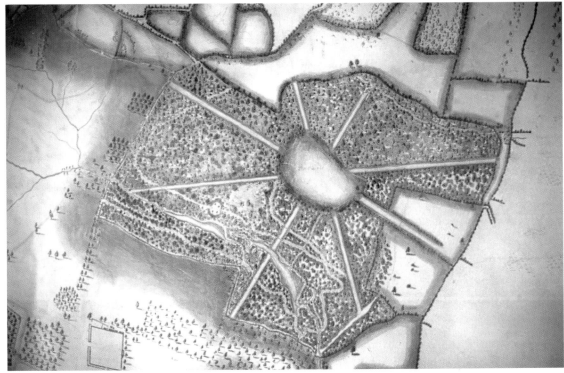

5 *One façade of Creech Grange commands a ruler-straight formal canal; this façade of 1738 looks uphill with the same direct geometry to an engagingly inaccurate Gothick arch. So the owner, Denis Bond, was on a garden cusp between formalism and the Rococo*

Opposite:
3 (Top) *Charles Bridgeman's design for the grounds of Eastbury proposes a lozenge garden within a roughly octagonal enclosure remarkable for its complete indifference to the downland topography on which it was to be laid out: not a masterpiece of sensitivity.* The Bodleian Library, University of Oxford (MS. Gough Drawings a.3, fol.10)

4 (Bottom) *The Great High Wood in Melbury Park as laid out, after 1742, by Susannah Horner, is so similar in design to Bridgeman's Spring Wood at Hackwood Park, Hampshire, as to suggest she was working to an old Bridgeman plan. The little lakes with their cascades survive.* Ilchester Estates

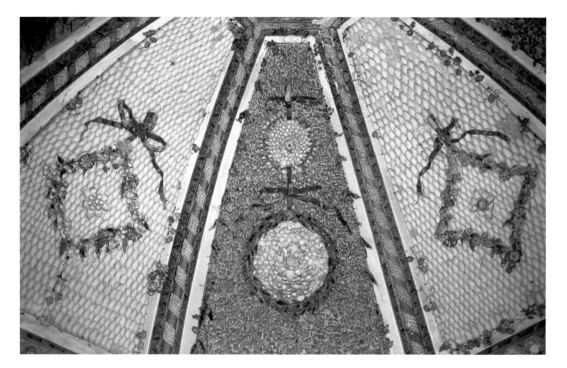

6 (Above) *Three of the eight roof panels of the Shell House in the grounds of Harper House, Sherborne, all feature the ribbons tied in bows that are the theme of this miraculously preserved Rococo garden pavilion*

7 (Left) *In complete contrast to the Sherborne Shell House's patterning in demure native shells, the Grotto at St Giles House is a riot of tropical shells from Jamaica with crystal-encrusted iron and plaster stalactites dangling at odd angles from an undulating ceiling surface*

8 (Opposite) *In her urgent post-1742 revision of Melbury's gardens into the 'Artinatural', Susannah Horner had this Batty Langley-style ogee arch applied to one of two Elizabethan garden turrets. Its interior has a delightfully inventive Gothick vault not taken from Langley's pattern book*

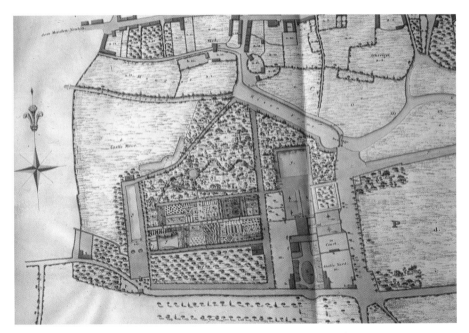

9 (Above) *In their pre-1778 condition the gardens of Frampton Court had, clustered about the intensely cultivated kitchen rectangle, straight walks, artinatural walks, a Wilderness and a whole chain of geometrically-shaped ornamental waters with several straight avenues*

10 (Below) *By 1836 the Brownian revolution in park design had wreaked havoc at Frampton. Gone are the straight walks and most of the ornamental waters. The Frome flows naturally in through open parkland with artfully clumped trees.* Dorset Record Office

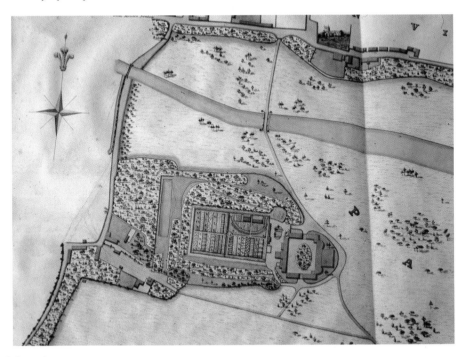

Opposite:
11 *The last survivor of Brownsea Castle's four defensive turrets has been turned into a Gazebo-Garden House with views over the original cannon platform and across the harbour to Poole*

12 *John Tasker's Chapel of 1786-7 for Lulworth Castle had, to humour George III who gave special permission for its construction, to be built to resemble a cross between a normal house and a garden pavilion*

13 *One of a typical pair of Humphry Repton water colours, intended to persuade the owner of Frome, or Stafford, House to improve his grounds to Repton's direction, this emphasises the squalor of the farmyard and the undrained condition of the fields*

14 *Once Repton has been given his way at Frome House the barn will go, revealing a bridge over an attractive stream and a lane leading to a picturesque church. Flower beds will occupy the foreground in Gardenesque richness and a walk will run between stream and wood.* Bristol University Special Collections

Opposite:
15 (Above) *The faintly artificial nature of the Regency Picturesque is apparent from this view of P.F. Robinson's Bridehead House and park. The lake has precise manicured edges and the house, in the newly fashionable vernacular, sits uneasily on smooth lawns*

16 (Below) *Surrounded with helpful geographical information carved into the limestone walls and backed by George Crickmay's Café-Castle on the hilltop, George Burt's Large Globe in Durlston Park was intended to prime a housing development that never happened.* Brian Earnshaw

17 *The 1920s swimming pool at Mapperton, a typical toy for the post-war generation, is backed by a seventeenth-century Garden House, which is three storeys tall on this side, but only one storey on its face to the upper Fountain Garden*

18 *It is easy to dismiss the Japanese Garden at Compton Acres as an English attempt at Japanese subtleties, but it is intensely beautiful in its own right, manipulating visitors into remarkable tactile experiences of stone and water. Native Japanese designers were bought over to create it*

19 *This is the putative 1907 Harold Peto Garden House on the terrace of Seaborough Court. Peto is known to have designed the grounds of Wayford Manor, a few miles over the Somerset border, and there were family connections between the two houses*

20 *During the brief occupancy (1910-14) of Parnham House by Dr Sauer, the previously relaxed Edwardian layout was regimented into order with obelisks and this grand south-facing terrace wall, its airy pavilion inspired by those at Montacute*

21 *Like some vision out of Monet, the old mill pool is the essential core of Springhead's garden. The walks which surround it, variously attributable to Harold Squire, Rolf Gardiner and Brenda Colvin, are merely its frame*

22 *A yaffle is the traditional name for a green woodpecker and when, in 1929, Cyril Carter, a director of Poole Pottery, commissioned Sir Edward Maufe to design Yaffle Hill, Maufe based the house on the bird's wings and this pool, in its confined garden, on the bird's body*

23 *This view of Chilcombe conveys something of the inspired confusion of features and themes: brick paths, rounded yews, intrusive potager vegetables, packed within the old garden walls of a yeoman's farmhouse. It is busy but never pretentious*

24 *Elizabeth Frink's menacing, naked Neanderthals stride towards the camera in Woolland's sculpture park, one item among bronze buffaloes, lazy hounds and Frink's trademark decapitated heads*

26 *The cobbled paving in the foreground of this view down the main axis at Bloxworth House is characteristic of Martin Lane-Fox's direction of the eye downwards. Whether the umbrella pines lining the canal will mature or prove an error remains to be seen*

27 *At Sticky Wicket Pam Lewis's artist's eye for subtle colour shading is always vulnerably involved with her feeling for a suburban cosiness of planting. A camera is not able to do full justice to the former; she plants phlox as Cézanne dabbed paint*

25 *(Opposite) Looking along a cross axis of Penelope Hobhouse's own garden at the Coach House, Bettiscombe, this view catches the extraordinary intrusion of stainless steel into the lower grounds, but misses the deliberate asymmetry of that bamboo clump in the canal*

28 *The author himself has been caught here in Lady Cranborne's practical joke. As visitors to the Lodge step uncertainly across a single plank bridge over a stream, they look up to stare into their own nervous alarm in this sculptured mirror set within the hedge. John Tradescant and even Mountain Jennings would have approved the device*

6

Picturesque to Gardenesque

A period of garden design that spans the move from the bare 'natural' land-scapes of Capability Brown to the ostentatious clutter of Victorian gardens is bound to be elusive in character. Humphry Repton launched out as a landscape designer in 1788 thinking he would take up where Brown, who had died in 1783, had left off. But by that time flower beds and an insidious subur-banism of petty garden furnishings – pergolas, urns, ornamental fencing and the artifice associated with the greenhouse-conservatory – were becoming popular. Cloyingly sentimental, Repton responded readily to this move, finding himself at the same time under attack from Uvedale Price and Richard Payne Knight, the advocates of a wild Savage Picturesque quite unlike Brown's manicured landscapes. An essentially weak, kindly man, Repton was never a true leader in garden fashions, but he was adept at communicating existing trends with his 'Red Books' and their charming 'before and after' water-colours. These showed the existing landscape of an estate and then, with a paper overlay pulled back, as it could be if Repton's suggested improvements were adopted.

Neither of the Red Books which he must have devised for his two Dorset consultations, Merly House, Canford Magna (1803) or Stafford House, West Stafford (1805) has survived.[1] Fortunately both the greater part of his text for Stafford House and the general illustration with its overlay (**colour plates 13** & **14**) were used to make a chapter in Repton's *Fragments on the Theory and Practice of Landscape Gardening*, his last book, published in 1816 and representing his final position on design. This reveals a Brownian landscaper in headlong retreat. Repton rejects with scorn the technique of 'lawning a hundred good acres of wheat' to produce a 'bald naked park, dotted with starving trees, or belted and clumped with spruce firs, and larches and Lombardy poplars'.[2] In its raw first state his illustration presents a view looking south-east from the house with a barn, a manure heap, hens, cows and ill-drained fields. When the overlay is pulled back, a Brownian process of draining has created a trimly banked stream, the winter-bourne, with a gravelled walk alongside and two wooden bridges. The barn has gone, the cattle are removed to the far side of the stream, and a three-arched bridge leads to a drive heading in the direction of the picturesque church and village. But to satisfy the flower bed enthusiasts an ornamental fence fringes the stream in the foreground, and roses, with peonies or some showy red flowers, are set in neat little beds beside the path.

It was entirely typical of Repton's frustrating career that this compromise scheme seems to have got no further than the design stage; though later a riverside walk was laid out, not along the winterbourne as he had urged, but along the larger River Frome. A Repton footnote on the winterbourne indicates how completely out of sympathy he was with the afficionados of the rough and rugged school of the Picturesque, however enraptured he pretended to be with 'Solitude, enbosomed in all the sublimity of umbrageous majesty.'[3] After commenting with surprise on the periodic flow of Dorset's chalk winter-bournes he urged, in finicky Gardenesque spirit: 'it will often be advisable to mow and rake the stream, which requires as much attention as a grass or gravel walk, not to appear slovenly and overgrown with weeds'.[4] The true beauty of the county's clear chalk streams being, of course, those weeds.

This is not, however, a chapter where much consistency of outlook is to be expected. It may help to remember that the literary contemporaries of this garden period were not only Wordsworth, with his delight in savage grandeur and deep feeling for the 'still, sad music of humanity', but Jane Austen, with a sensibility delicately attuned to the moral repsonsibilities of the gentry. Put the two together and the result could be Peter Frederick Robinson's Bridehead House and Little Bredy village. These two, when visited on a fine day, can easily be seen as Dorset's version of Shangri-La, a community so idyllic, so remote and, in the twenty-first century, so improbable that a visitor toys with fantasy notions about the place. Might its inhabitants age suddenly if they spend too long away from its magical climate, shopping in Weymouth or, worse still, Bournemouth, returning to their cottage homes bent, wrinkled and looking twenty years older, like the Tibetans of James Hilton's *Lost Horizon*?

The village bus shelter, proof that they must sometimes leave this rural perfec-tion, is the first indication that here the mature, High Tory Wordsworth's vision of a benign green England, where squire and tenant peasant live together in rural harmony has been realised, the absolute antithesis of that doomed and melan-choly countryside of Thomas Hardy's novels. Four deep alcoves run around the shelter under a pyramidal wooden roof. Inscribed around the eaves is:

> A shadow in the daytime from the heat and for a refuge and for a covert from storm and from ruin. Isaiah 4-6.

> A Gift to the People of Little Bredy from Philip and Margaret Williams for their Silver Wedding 1st October 1933.

The inspired Christian paternalism of the Williams dynasty had begun with a banking crisis in the City in 1825 when Robert Williams retired from his bank to make Bridehead the family's principal seat. His father, the first Robert Williams, Dorset born, had bought the estate in 1798. Work may have been begun by him, before his death in 1814, on Bridehead park and P.F. Robinson's house in an attractively loose-limbed and sprawling Picturesque Gothic (**colour plate 15**).[5] Pevsner characteristically sneered at its 'excruciating awkwardness',[6] but if he had read Robinson's *Rural Architecture* of 1822 he would have understood the architect's aim: a 'Gentleman's residence' designed in the 'Cottage style' to accord with the houses of the tenants in the village, an ideal social harmony, producing 'the appearance of a cluster of cottages . . . or rather that perhaps of the ancient Manor House (for it can hardly from its size be denominated a Cottage)'.[7]

This was a revolutionary movement away from classicism towards a Picturesque Tudor vernacular. The accepted date of construction is 1831-3,[8] and the inspiration for the aesthetic unity of house, park and village is usually credited to the evangelical revival of that period. It was then, however, that William Wordsworth was at the height of his influence, an idealistic Tory in his old age. The shaping of house, garden, lake and village to accord with that deep delved valley is as likely to have been inspired by the poet as by the pulpit.

A lane drops steeply down from the Williams' gifted shelter into the village, and Church Walk, a footpath on the right, sets the tone of Little Bredy: thatched, intimate little cottages, some semi, some detached, grey stone, postcard gardens and deliberate charm. There is an illustration in Repton's *Fragments* that catches their tone perfectly: 'Sunshine After Rain' (**53**).[9] Vines, gourds and roses climb a trellis, vases are perched in stands, a fountain plays by the stone urns, there is a table for implements, a rainbow arches behind the sugary perfection. Repton intended it as a vision for middle-class suburbia, but it looks forward to the cottage gardens of Little Bredy.

The walk ends in a field, with hillsides closing in and a waterfall tumbling noisily down from the hidden lake. 'But of all picturesque objects', Repton wrote, 'there is none so interesting as Water in rapid motion.'[10] Here a large earth dam has been built to create that effect and rocks are set convincingly for the water to fall down. Once up the steep grassy bank, at lake level and around a bend in the valley, the village has been left behind, though no intrusive barrier wall or lodge gates have been passed. It is here that Robinson's Picturesque pleasures pour in.

Immediately before the Bride begins its headlong artificial descent out of the lake it passes under a rough three-arched stone bridge almost spanning the drop (**54**). It is a livelier version of the fall and bridge at Ranston. In calm contrast the lake itself, of crystal clear, chalk filtered water, is neatly edged with a stone trim. At this stage of the Regency Picturesque there was no attempt to imitate Nature exactly, the artifice is enjoyed. The entire valley is, as Pevsner and Newman acknowledged, 'exquisite', but not grand. A giant Wellingtonia grows next to a superbly feathered beech on the far shore near to the 'excru-

53 *'Sunshine after Rain' from Humphry Repton's* Fragments *of 1816 offers a sugary preview of the nineteenth-century Gardenesque with flowers applied heavily to Italianate terracing and fountains.* Bristol University Special Collections

ciating' house, which is actually a pleasant asymmetrical composition in Regency Gothic by Robinson with later additions by Benjamin Ferrey.[11] On the near shore native sycamore and ash rise behind bamboo clumps, and there is a path leading up to a notice that all Dorset's landowners should learn off by heart, for the good of their souls: 'Visitors are Welcome' it reads, 'to enter and enjoy the Bridehead grounds for quiet recreation.' Who, after that squirearchic adjuration, could do anything other than recreate quietly along the bank, as the valley unfolds its impossibly perfect Arcady? Robinson's must have been the directing hand because there was once a half-timbered Boathouse and a Swiss Cottage: two of his favourite landscape devices. He may have been the one who persuaded the Williamses to give up far ranging outward views and site their house facing across the lake directly into the enclosing hillsides.

At an appropriate point a second notice reads: 'Private', and walkers, constrained by courtesy, must retire the way they came; this time, not by Church Walk, but by the true village street. Even the sheep dip here is an elegant circular pool, stone rimmed and edged with fern. There the water plays another trick, flowing underground a short space to brim out in the stream that will run alongside the street of cottage gardens. Once again Repton has given the hint:

> In all mountainous countries, it is common to place troughs to receive the water which flows from the neighbouring hills. These by the roadside, in drinking places for Cattle, form interesting circumstances in the Landscape peculiar to romantic scenery . . . a more striking example of the inexhaustible bounty of Providence.[12]

These cottages at Little Bredy never make the crude mistake Sir William Chambers made, sixty years earlier at Milton Abbas, of standardised, repetitious forms. Here the garden suburbs of the early twentieth century are being conceived with a coy variety of invention.[13] This battery of charm is what gives Little Bredy its improbable, dream-like character. The stream has one more duty to perform. Further down the valley is Bridehead's walled Kitchen Garden, there being no place for potatoes in that idyll by the lake. The path to it lies through an orchard and there the Bride is divided into rivulets to nourish vines and vegetables.

It is hard not to speculate, when all this aesthetic and social perfection has been left behind, what the fortunate villagers think about it all. Do they see themselves as playing out roles in some Archers-style soap opera? Does living in Eden ever turn sour?[14] Is there ever resentment at the contrast between big house and cottage, despite P.F. Robinson's good intentions? Are there Serpents in Eden? Probably not: the village has Dorset's most sublimely sited cricket pitch. Villagers who play cricket together could never be wicked together.

At Bridehead the Picturesque functioned socially as well as aesthetically. A few miles to the east along the coast at Highcliffe Castle the older, eighteenth-

54 *The Bride flows under this rustic bridge out of Bridehead's neatly stone-rimmed lake to fall down a picturesque artificial cascade of boulders to the garden village of Little Bredy, the epitome of P.F. Robinson's rural ideal*

century way of Picturesque thinking was being applied at exactly the same time, but by a diplomat and aristocrat intent upon combining, not nature with social benevolence, but nature with historic antiquities. Highcliffe's grounds had passed through an unusual but unfortunately short-lived reshaping during the eighteenth century. John Stuart, the 3rd Earl of Bute, had given Lancelot Brown the planting commission noticed in the previous chapter. After Bute's death in 1792 his son retained a small farmhouse on the estate, Bure Homage, later known as Bure Cottage, and when this passed to his son, the distinguished diplomat Charles Stuart, ennobled as Lord Stuart de Rothesay, it became the base for a remarkable transformation into what could be described as a Castle of Picturesque historicism. In these early years of the nineteenth century, the cult of the Picturesque was being shaped by conflicting new artistic and social directions. As Wordsworth and Austen were relevant to Bridehead's land-scaping, so those wealthy arch Francophiles, the Prince Regent and William Beckford, were influences upon Highcliffe, a French composite Castle with would-be Mediterranean grounds. When that is said, neglect, vandalism and greed have reduced those grounds to a shadow of what they were sixty years ago when Christopher Hussey illustrated them.[15] Even so, invaded by car-parks and crudely packaged for the tourist trade, they retain the most historic and arguably the most beautiful gazebo in Britain, still linked by its landscape garden to a sensational view of ilex grove, sea and island rocks.

Lord Stuart de Rothesay, the creator, or more accurately, the purchaser of this massive artefact, was one of those awesomely influential, quietly ruthless establishment figures who manipulate nations, armies and commerce to build great empires. It was Stuart's diplomatic skills that allowed Wellington to retain

Portugal in the Peninsular War as the base from which to drive the French out of Spain. His reward was the top diplomatic post of Ambassador to France in 1815. He was the man who bought Pauline Bonaparte's town house as the British Embassy, the elegant palace which we have retained ever since. As Minister to Brazil he was instrumental in abolishing the slave trade there; but throughout that glittering career he was obsessively buying historic furnishings and entire sections of stonework from French buildings of the Flamboyant Gothic period. His intention was to combine them into a house for his retirement, high on the crumbling cliff of Bournemouth. Even his choice of a title when George IV ennobled him was romantic and arrogant. The 'de' was bogus and Rothesay was a title traditionally reserved for a Prince of Wales.

During his second period as Ambassador to France (1828-31) he happened to be passing through Les Andelys on the Seine as they were demolishing its old manoir. It was in the room behind its radiantly ornate oriel window that the King of Navarre, Antoine de Bourbon, had died in 1562 as his son Henri, soon to become the first and best loved Bourbon King of France, knelt weeping beside him. Lord Stuart bought it on the spot and shipped it across the Channel to join the rest of his carved booty lying numbered on the lawn at Highcliffe. This was to be the focus and centre point of Highcliffe's entire garden front, skewing the whole Castle around at an angle, so that the oriel, acting like a magnificent gazebo on its first floor, should look directly down an avenue of the garden at that supremely picturesque seascape.

55 *This Gate Lodge of 1801 to Gaunt's House, Hinton Martell has all the coy, picture postcard rusticity that Repton and, after him, P.F. Robinson popularized*

Along all the rest of Highcliffe's sea front the gloomy grove of tall holm oaks, underplanted with Portuguese laurel and sea buckthorn, cuts out the potentially exhilarating views. At just that one focused point the Bourbon oriel commands a perfect composition of the Needles, the Wight and the ocean. It was a stroke of garden genius that Lord Stuart's contemporary, William Beckford, must have envied as, in his later years, he planted trees furiously in an effort to give his outrageous Fonthill Abbey the park setting it demanded. Lady Stuart de Rothesay survived her husband for twenty-one years and it was after visiting her there that August Hare wrote, 'I have left Highcliffe and the gates of Paradise seem closed.'[16]

Do not expect Paradise on a visit to the gardens today. Bournemouth had on its doorstep the perfect tourist attraction for sophisticated visitors, but every time the estate of Highcliffe could have been bought by the council they hesitated, and each time the park grew smaller and the state of the Castle deteriorated. Finally Christchurch Council rescued what remained. Now visitors will find Robert Adam's twin lodges of 1773 still handsomely cuboid, but with no drive to guard.[17] The tide of middle class housing has surged around them. Much of the holm oak grove between the Castle and the cliffs is a camouflaged car-park and its numinous presence is lost. The stone Conservatory is a room for the celebration of marriages and a new, mean wing houses a self-service restaurant. Despite these compromises, the oriel from Les Andelys still hangs splendidly over the south porch, its limestone crisply carved with floral quatrefoils and tiny saints under canopies. Down its avenue to the sea, far away like lost Lyonesse risen again from the waves, the last peninsula of Wight tapers away into the sharp outlines of the Needles. Few English vistas begin so richly or end so poetically. This is another of Dorset's villas that lie, like Pliny's Laurentinum, within sound of the waves. Lord Stuart, with his sound classical education, did not miss the parallel. On the parapet to the right of his oriel he had inscribed in Latin, though in Gothic lettering to accord with the architecture, Lucretius' lines: 'Sweet it is, when on the great sea the winds are buffeting the waves, to look from the land on someone else's desperate struggles.' A very eighteenth-century reaction to the elements.

What was quite contrary to eighteenth-century architectural and landscape practice was the stone Conservatory at Highcliffe. After the Bourbon oriel it is the most prominent feature of the garden front and very much a sign of the Gardenesque. In the previous century a greenhouse would have been a separate building, tucked away in a corner of the gardens, somewhere for visitors to be taken on a modest excursion, not an integral part of the house. Now, as the improved technology of glasshouses had come together with the returning emphasis upon flowers in the last half of the eighteenth century, the conservatory had edged its way into the grand enfilade of ground-floor entertainment rooms. Repton had not initiated the change but, as usual, he had formalised it convincingly and attractively in a watercolour ground plan of a house (**56**) where the sequence of rooms runs from 'Porch and green house', through 'Hall', 'Dining Room', 'Breakfast Room', 'Library or Living Room' (this last alternative a foreshadowing of twentieth-century practice) to 'Orangerie', 'Conservatory and Vinery' to the 'Aviary', and so into the garden.[18] The Repton ideal of house combining with its landscape via loggias on two levels and terracing with ornamental shrubs is illustrated in the 1861 edition of Hutchins at early nineteenth-century Springfield, near Poole (**57**).

A proposal such as this automatically left the standard Palladian country house in the standard Brownian landscape looking old-fashioned and, for purposes of horticultural display, dysfunctional. Colonel George Dawson-Damer of Came House, a mile or two south of Dorchester, was the fortunate possessor of an exquisitely light-hearted suite of Rococo-style entertainment rooms, but his Palladian house was set in a typical Brownian park noticed in the previous chapter. To correct this, the Colonel, who succeeded to Came in 1829, added a large domed Conservatory to the west side of the house. This is a wonderfully light-footed affair, fronted in stone but internally all glass and iron, the very essence of the Industrial Revolution, yet serving the elegant disciplines of classicism. At its heart is the domed octagon supported on eight pre-cast iron columns and its roof rises externally in two convex curves. With grapes ripening next to hot house blooms the Dawson-Damers could look out with relative satisfaction at the austere green landscape of their park. Over the last four years Mrs Sarah MacGregor has laid out a formal garden with a gravel path and round bushes leading up to the old, south entrance front and replaced the tennis court with a Kitchen Garden and a raised potager. The Conservatory, now called the Orangery, is well stocked with hot house exotics.

Came House is a mere three and a half miles from the sea, but for all the salt water influence, it could be fifty miles. Smedmore, three-quarters of a mile from the cliff edge, is more obviously windswept and involved. The Revd John Clavell of Smedmore appears to have had much the same drive towards a grandstand view of the ocean as Lord Stuart at Highcliffe Castle. He was an unmarried recluse whose only building on the estate, the Clavel Tower, a mile away from the house and perilously close to the cliff edge, should be described as an eccentric gesture towards the Picturesque. It was built in 1820, an unscholarly composite three storeys high with round-arched windows, an embattled parapet and an arcade of Tuscan columns around its base. This last gives it a frankly unattractive wedding cake profile quite inappropriate to the severe coastline which it commands so awkwardly. Now that it is in danger of falling over the cliff a wave of sentiment has washed over it, but from a strictly aesthetic judgement the coast would be more impressive without it.

Smedmore House has attracted more journalistic and literary descriptions than any other comparable house in the county. Sir William Clavell built in the 1630s 'a little newe House, and beautified it with pleasant gardens'.[19] These

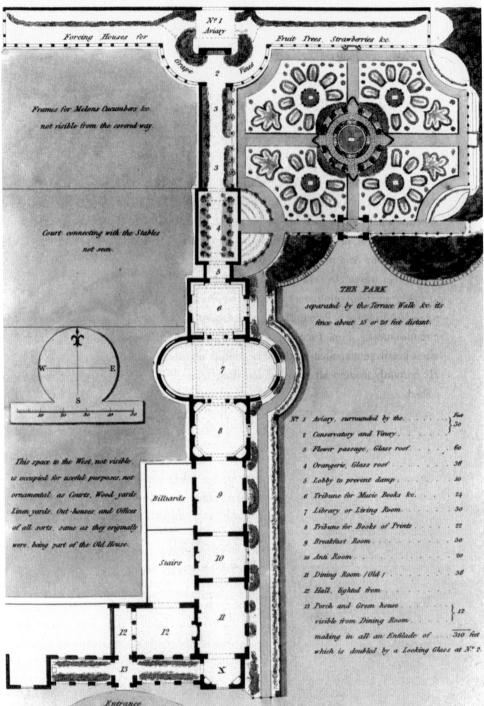

This Line is the flued Wall of the Hot Houses, and the South Wall of the Kitchen Garden.

Forcing Houses for

Nº 1
Aviary

Fruit Trees, Strawberries &c.

Grape   Vines

Frames for Melons Cucumbers &c.
not visible from the covered way.

Court connecting with the Stables
not seen.

THE PARK

separated by the Terrace Walk &c. its
fence about 15 or 20 feet distant.

This space to the West, not visible,
is occupied for useful purposes, not
ornamental, as Courts, Wood yards,
Linen yards, Out-houses, and Offices
of all sorts, same as they originally
were, being part of the Old House.

Billiards

Stairs

	Feet
Nº 1 Aviary, surrounded by the . . . . . . }	30
2 Conservatory and Vinery	
3 Flower passage, Glass roof	60
4 Orangerie, Glass roof	36
5 Lobby to prevent damp	20
6 Tribune for Music Books &c.	24
7 Library or Living Room	30
8 Tribune for Books of Prints	22
9 Breakfast Room	30
10 Anti Room	20
11 Dining Room (Old)	36
12 Hall, lighted from	
13 Porch and Green house . . . . . }	12
visible from Dining Room	

making in all an Enfilade of . . . 310 feet
which is doubled by a Looking Glass at Nº 2.

Entrance

56 *In this plan from his* Fragments *Repton demonstrated how a house, its conservatory and its Gardenesque grounds could be run together in one flowing sequence.* Bristol University Special Collections

57 *At Springfield, a house near Poole on the affluent Bournemouth side of Dorset, Repton's aims have been realised. Fountain, lawns and terraces lead easily into the generous verandah of the Italianate villa with a wide balcony above*

walled enclosures have survived the eighteenth-century reconstructions of the 'little newe House'. There are two small walled gardens behind the brewhouse and, to the side of the house, are two further walled enclosures, one long and narrow, the other a broad, level lawn, which has no trace of its seventeenth-century planting. This owes its bay trees and backing of hydrangeas to Sir Arthur Bryant who was a tenant for some ten years after the Second World War.[20] Now that the Mansells have returned to their property, all these gardens are richly colourful with that particular quality that flowers seem to take on when they are sheltered from sea winds and slightly under-watered. Two woodland areas flank the approach drive and the Grange Plantation with its cross walks could well be of early eighteenth-century date. The large walled Kitchen Garden behind the stables is eighteenth-century.

Beaminster Manor and the Old Rectory at Pulham both have minor Picturesque layouts. Within the confines of Beaminster town the Manor contrives to include a small lake whose waters tumble over a rocky cataract by a Grotto. Its gatepiers to the road are cannibalised pieces of Clifton Maybank and the garden does hanker after the Brownian dimensions by managing a sideways axis up to a small marker on White Sheet Hill. An entire narrow angle has been kept clear of housing development to preserve this Arcadian gesture.

The garden at Pulham Rectory was inevitably open to the whims and alterations of unrelated owners, and this shows. From 1797 to 1830 George Penfold was Rector, covering the Picturesque garden years quite neatly. Pulham was, by the accident of tithes and endowments, a rich living, so its rectors were Dorset squarsons, parson-squires. Facing the church the Rectory's front garden is a soberly modest little park entered between stone gatepiers in that lean Regency Gothic, affluent but restrained as the congregation would expect. To the rear of the brash, confidently inaccurate Gothic building the Rector gardened more like a squire than a churchman.

A broad lawn sweeps down to a ha-ha that makes the grounds seem larger than they are, in exactly the same way that the lawn at Duntish extends. A little Wilderness lies to the left with a rectangular pond. To the right is another pond, not quite big enough to be described as a lakelet and set too deep for it to work comfortably into a small Arcadian view. Beyond is the wreck of a formal yew avenue, miniature in scale.

The grounds at Pulham, so genteel and socially aspiring, will make an interesting contrast with those of Litton Cheney in the next chapter. The Rector there, probably less richly endowed with tithes, made no social gestures in his garden, but retained a farmyard to the rear of the house and built a swimming pool in his wood to serve the children of the preparatory school which he opened to increase his income.

7

Mainstream and rogue –
Victorian gardens

It must have become apparent from the previous chapter that, as the Regency ended in 1820 and the brief reigns of George IV and William IV followed, English garden design was drifting perilously towards maximum consumption of wealth and the mere display of expensive devices of horticultural one-upmanship. In 1890 for instance, Canford Manor, seat of the Guests, nouveau-riche steel barons of Merthyr Tydfil, had in its gardens a 250-foot-long, twenty-five-foot-high magnolia wall, a vinery, peach house, melon house and a fernery,[1] but not one ornamental garden temple or folly to give a focus point to its flat park. Drives led to three circles, one of statues, one of roses and one of trees at the centre of several avenues.[2] It did have a fine terrace with urns, but this looked self-regardingly back to the enormous Blore and Barry house across sunken gardens, there being nothing of note to look out to in the park. In the same spirit the park ignored the Stour, a fine river with a mill race, even though it bordered the grounds for half a mile. Variations on the themes of Nature were clearly not fashionable.

When Edward, Prince of Wales paid a state visit in 1890 it was January, but the local paper listed approvingly what Ivor Guest, 1st Lord Wimborne, could still offer:

> Early vines putting on their leaves and bunches of roses in full bloom, a large number of the best specimens of orchid in splendid bloom, calanthe with spikes over two feet long in flower, lilies of almost every variety, cyclamen, azaleas, cinnerarias, crotons, gardenias, and in fact all the choicest flowers that care and attention can make blossom at this time of year. The heavy bloom of the Marie Louise and Comte de Braize violets deserve special mention, the flowers being as large as small roses.[3]

That it should be considered desirable to produce violets as large as small roses says much about the spirit of mainstream Victorian gardening. Researchers of the Dorset Gardens Trust have come up with a fascinating alternative view of all this royal affluence in a news-sheet called *Truth*, a late Victorian forerunner of *Private Eye*.[4] According to that the royal visit was a disaster. Princess Alexandra and her daughters failed to turn up; Lord Wimborne was ill in bed throughout and Lord Randolph Churchill became poorly – he was a notoriously heavy drinker. Many of the guests failed to wear the mourning required for the recent death of a minor royal; the weather was bad and the pheasant shoot laid on for second class guests produced very few birds. It is to be hoped that the Prince enjoyed those outsize violets.

Fortunately both Canford and that other Dorset dinosaur of the High Victorian, Clayesmore, Alfred Waterhouse's shapeless monster built for the 2nd Lord Wolverton, were taken over by public schools in the twentieth century and have lost most of their municipal park-style features to playing fields. Canford has two imaginative modern gardens which will appear in a later chapter, and Clayesmore has a dark pool, once a boating lake, but now so overhung with trees and sinisterly reed-grown that it looks like the pool in 'Hylas and the Nymphs', that well-known painting by the other Waterhouse. Kingston Lacy has grounds which will qualify as mainstream Victorian, but only by virtue of the recent earnest stewardship of the National Trust, which has carried through some admirably accurate schemes of replanting. What is interesting about Kingston is that its gardens and park were touched by eclectic influences, Italian and Egyptian, but not in the way that an eighteenth-century park would have been affected. With less scholarship, an eighteenth-century garden designer would have created a very English Egyptian style garden or interpreted Italian villa gardens in an unmistakably English manner. The more conscientious, museum-minded Victorians at Kingston Lacy have not tried to assimilate their bought and brought-in pieces of Egyptian antiquity and contemporary Italian craftsmanship, but simply dropped them down as exhibits onto a lawn or a terrace.[5]

In fairness it has to be said that the house at Kingston presented a challenge. It was a plain brick box of Puritan Minimalism by Sir Roger Pratt, built by the Bankes family because their home, Corfe Castle, had been wrecked during the Civil War. Its seventeenth-century formal landscape has been noted in an earlier chapter, and in the eighteenth century this had been naturalised unskilfully to the Brownian pattern. The Victorian owners inherited, therefore, little of garden value, but failed to impose a decisive pattern on this mediocrity.

The key figure in this failure was William John Bankes, a man so cheerfully amoral and camp in his behaviour that Lord Byron, his contemporary at Cambridge, seems to have stood in awe of him. Bachelor, traveller and enthusiastic Egyptologist,[6] William would not succeed his father at Kingston until 1834, but already in 1821 he had brought over a damaged obelisk of 116 BC from the temple at Philae on the upper Nile, with some help from his friend the Duke of Wellington.[7] This obelisk would not be repaired and erected as a focus for views south from the garden front of the house until 1839. By that time the house would have been transformed into a compromise between a stone-clad Inigo Jones house of the Caroline period and Charles Barry's idea of an Italian Renaissance palazzo. It seems that Bankes intended to create an Italian garden to accord with Barry's façades. Barry had designed a handsome, reserved and entirely appropriate garden for the east front,[8] with a central pool between two lawned and quartered parterres; but then fate stepped in with a very Victorian moral episode.

Bankes was caught behaving improperly with a guardsman in Green Park. To avoid a scandalous trial he fled to lifelong exile on the Continent, retaining control of his wealth and his house. That was in 1841, so Barry's east garden was never laid out, but Bankes had already built a long broad terrace across the south front. He occupied the next fourteen empty years by commissioning modern Italian craftsmen to turn out the splendid *Rosso Veronese* lions,[9] massive stone wellheads and bronze sculptures of more active lions killing serpents (**58**). By a stream of letters to his sister Lady Falmouth he ordered the setting out of these on the new south terrace. Four of the wellheads are 1847-51 replicas, carved in Verona, copies of wellheads in Venetian palaces; two are genuine, detectable by their weathering. The Trust has followed William Bankes' directions and planted them with bay trees.

58 *From his enforced retreat to Italy, William John Bankes was able to control by letters the setting up of a gallery of contemporary Italian sculpture on his new south terrace at Kingston Lacy. He favoured wild animals rather than nymphs*

Gardens are not, however, best planned blind from a distance of many hundred miles; and that still left the broad undulating slopes of the park with only the Philae obelisk, an Egyptian tomb,[10] two earlier and smaller English obelisks[11] and William's long beech avenue out to Badbury Rings, quite unrelated to the house. William Bankes died in 1855, apparently after making several secret visits to see how well his instructions about picture hanging and furnishing had been carried out in the house.

Thereafter there was only some desultory planting of cedars and the creation of the Fernery. This last has not yet been dated, but with its brooding rocks and shadowy green paths it is quite out of character with the rest of the grounds. The reserved and sophisticated Walter Ralph Bankes, who ruled from 1869 to 1904, married Henrietta Fraser, after long hesitations, in his forty-fourth year and she took over garden policy at Kingston. She employed C.E. Ponting, the Salisbury diocesan architect, to lay out the 'Dutch Garden' on the east side of the house in a thoroughly old-fashioned carpet of coloured bedding – pink begonias and blue heliotrope edged with pansies or wallflowers – around golden yew bushes.[12] After her husband's death in 1904 she continued as the directing hand behind the estate until her death in 1953. When her son Ralph died in 1981, leaving the estate to the National Trust, he left the Trust some problems.

The art collection was so fine that the gift could hardly be refused, but the house was a compromise, neither seventeenth-century nor nineteenth-century in committed character and the gardens, though naturally well endowed, were dull. William Bankes' south terrace had, with the *Rosso Veronese* lions, a mildly interesting collection of nineteenth-century copies of Renaissance originals. The East Garden, given over to vegetables during the Second World War, was a blank and the Fernery was overgrown. There was no real alternative but to recreate a Victorian atmosphere. Henrietta's 1899 East Garden was faithfully replanted and now offers as good an example as any in the county for weighing the merits of the bright, neat, cheerful Gardenesque. The Fernery is an undoubted success, monochrome as opposed to the polychrome of the East Garden. Other additions, the equally polychrome and curiously isolated Sunk Garden, the Blind Wood and the Japanese Tea Garden are interesting events in no particular sequence, worthy attempts to entertain and justify the price of entry to otherwise unremarkable grounds. It is hard to avoid the conclusion that, William excepted, the Bankes family were a lacklustre dynasty. They never made sense with their avenues or their tree planting, the noble Lime Walk has, like the Beech Avenue, no relationship to the house, and the topography of the park cried out for a mid-eighteenth-century Arcadian treatment of temples and clumps.

Apart from pleasant municipal affairs with iron bandstands and iron clock towers at Sherborne and Dorchester there are no more mainstream Victorian gardens, unless 'mainstream' is extended to include 'parson's traditional', in which case the grounds of the Old Rectory at Litton Cheney just scrape by, even though so much of their social interest is of the twentieth century, while the Rector's glebe farm, tucked away behind the house, is Tudor.

The church of St Mary at Litton Cheney was, in the recent past, a rich and desirable living for its lucky rectors. For much of the nineteenth century it was held, in a neat piece of ecclesiastical nepotism, by the two Reverends Cox, father and son. Their attractive, unpretentious Rectory is perched on a shelf of land at the very edge of a precipitously wild, watery and wonderful wood. A few miles west along the coast the gardens at Abbotsbury are notably un-watered; the Old Rectory in contrast sits upon a positive sponge of springs. This is the ultimate 'green-welly' garden. Rivulets ooze out from under the house and dribble down through the harts tongue ferns and ivy of the dense tree growth below it. One concentration flows out into a Grotto of rocks, and before the waters leave the garden and its two mysterious pools they have already formed into a substantial stream that runs away through the village.

The front garden of the Old Rectory is a deceivingly tame frontispiece to this Dorset rainforest. A quaint thatched, hexagonal Summerhouse was built for it by the engraver Reynolds Stone during his occupancy from 1953 to 1979. He designed the Royal Arms for the old British passport and, with his wife Janet, entertained Benjamin Britten, Peter Pears, John Betjeman, Iris Murdoch and her husband John Bayley, and Sir Kenneth Clark of *Civilization*. Penelope Betjeman owed the letterhead of her Waterfowl Farm stationery to him,[13] and two of his slates, incised with elegant alphabets, hang on the walls of the Summerhouse. Those treetops surging on the south side of the drive appear to be kept at bay by neatly sheared, billowing box hedging, but if the narrow path downhill is followed a very wild wood soon takes over, diagonal pathways slither muddily sideways, stands of bamboo bristle up, butterbur, comfrey, lungwort and wild strawberries are underfoot. There is an intense New Zealand-like feeling of urgent growth and green fertility. Hugh and Carol Lindsay, the happy owners of this savage Eden for the last twenty-one years, keep hacking down the self-seeding sycamores and have managed, not only to keep the paths navigable, but also to plant more than a hundred exotic trees. The result is still pure Dorset.

At all points in the wood there is the sound of water and then, depending upon which path has been chosen, come the ponds. The uppermost is rectangular and rimmed with stone pavings, clear, quite deep enough to swim in for a few strokes before the overhanging trees and ivy touch the water; the lower pond is shallow, unthreatening and irregular, almost a delta of the rivulets. Inevitably the chief claim of the upper pond is that Iris Murdoch swam in it, and surely, though unrecorded, Peter Pears. What is never mentioned is that this most verdant, shadowy and romantic of swimming pools was originally not a mill pond, but a Victorian swimming bath built by the younger Revd Cox to entertain the boys of the little boarding school that he ran as an extra money

spinner in one back wing of the Rectory.[14] Did the children have to troop
down every morning for a healthy Victorian cold bath, or was the place
reserved as a treat for hot summer afternoons? It could never have looked as
evocative and beautiful in its rectangular Victorian geometry as it does now in
absolute overgrowth.

On the level ground above all this, the Lindsays have imaginatively transformed the Rector's glebe farm where he collected his tithes from the pros-
perous surrounding farms, into a farmyard garden. Where there were cobbles
now there is a lawn with yellow euphorbias and a laden quince tree. All the
buildings – tithe barn, stables, granary on staddle stones, pigsties and wooden
apple barn – are intact, but the double flowered *Rosa banksiae* and a big white
clematis scramble up their walls and up into the next door trees.[15] As a museum
piece, a relic of pre-Hardy Dorset, it is a most valuable group; as a garden it
has a deserted charm.

The county's real 'rogue' Victorians have an even more robust and
rewarding profile. Of the two real tearaways – Brownsea and Durlston –
Brownsea probably comes first chronologically, though none of the dating of
the gardens at the Castle is very precise. After the occupancy of the Sturts
none of the Island's owners stayed very long, but in 1852 or 1853 (accounts
vary), Colonel Waugh bought the place, convinced that the peculiar qualities
of its clay would make it a goldmine for fine pottery. Like Humphry Sturt in
the previous century he hurled money at Brownsea Castle, concealing the
Sturts' crude Gothic brickwork with Tudor cladding in Portland stone and
building a parish church, for his own convenience rather than for the potters
at the other end of the island. The clay did not fire as he had hoped and in
1857 he retired bankrupt. As a result there are today not one, but two,
Brownsea Islands.

One is for the ordinary day visitors who ferry over from Sandbanks, pay a
substantial landing fee and then have access to roughly half, the dull half, of the
island.[16] The other is for guests at the Castle, which is run as a hotel for the
staff of John Lewis. They voyage across Poole Harbour from Poole Quay in the
hotel's private boat and only they enjoy the strange fortified garden. When,
however, I made enquiries, I was most courteously invited to visit the hotel
and caught the boat, the 'Castello', which runs every day to prevent guests
from feeling too insular.[17] The twenty-minute trip threads the buoys and islands
of the shallow inland sea. Odd petrol stations, marine garages, float on the
waveless waters, yachts bob about, and sudden enormous lorry-carrying ferries
from France surge past on the narrow deep channel. The long pine-clad shore
of Brownsea Island drifts past, but the Castle shows up only at the very last
moment. There is a charming little harbour village in that primitive Gothick
battlemented detail that suggests a late eighteenth-century date. The hotel boat
ignores the National Trust quay, where commonplace day trippers land, and
heads for the twin octagonal towers of the Family Quay.

Between the Colonel's Tudor-style towers is the entrance to the Crystal Arcade: Dorset's least likely folly, a pink washed corridor, roofed in glass, its walls inset with the stones of Venice. There are massive blocks of armorial carving, the lion of St Mark, an angel and grotesques, all added to the Colonel's corridor by the next owner, the Hon. Augustus Cavendish-Bentinck after 1870. The colour pink imposes an instant lightness of heart, as was the intention, for the Arcade led not only to the pier but to a bathing place on the startlingly white sands of the shore. It was a charmingly ceremonial concept, worthy of Regency Brighton, a sculptural display en route to a dip in the sea.

With real garden drama the Crystal Arcade opens into the Walled Garden with the Castle towering up on the far side (**59**). One of the few pieces of evidence as to who did what here on Brownsea is an illustration in the 1774 edition of Hutchins (**60**). This shows the Castle as Humphry Sturt left it after an expenditure of £50,000 on the Island. Next to it is a fortified enclosure with four stubby corner turrets, all clearly intended for serious harbour defence, yet labelled 'Garden' with 'Greenhouse' and 'Hothouse in the Garden'. The 'Bathing or Boat House' stands outside the enclosure where the National Trust quay now lies, and the 'Platform for twelve 9 pounder cannon' is also outside the walls on the other side, commanding the hotel's bathing beach. There is a 'Pheasantry' and a 'Menagerie' placed up the hill behind the Castle next to a wooden dovecot.

59 *Humphry Sturt turrets and Colonel Waugh's Tudor windows overlook the fortified Walled Garden at Brownsea Castle. The urns, terracing and lush planting date to August Cavendish-Bentinck's late Victorian occupancy of the Castle.* Bristol Reference Library: Central Library

60 *Humphry Sturt of Crichel House poured money into Brownsea and this 1774 illustration from Hutchins records the result. In his time the Bathing and Boat House stood to the right of the Walled Garden with its Greenhouse and Hothouse.* Bristol Reference Library: Central Library

Brownsea is confusing because Colonel Waugh did so much yet left abruptly, a disappointed bankrupt with no time or patience for historic records.[18] There are photographs proving that in his brief occupancy this walled enclosure was almost half filled with a splendid Gothic Conservatory acting as a covered way from the Castle to the Arcade and then on to his bathing place beside the Family Quay.[19] In the 1881 *A Sketch of Brownsea Island* it appears that all those attractive Gothick quayside buildings were actually built by the Colonel, and the Conservatory is in exactly the same style. The Revd Theophilus Bennett, who wrote the book and who knew the Colonel personally, states confidently:

> Colonel Waugh projected and partly carried out great improvements. To the Castle he added a front in Tudor Gothic in Portland Stone and on the north side other buildings with towers and turrets to form a castellated group. Conservatories were so arranged as to form a covered passage to the water side.[20]

Why then should the Conservatory and the harbour houses have been built in a playful amateur Gothick spirit with no attempt at authenticity? The parish church of St Mary, another of the Colonel's good works, was designed in such a correct yet modest Perpendicular Gothic as to pass at first sight for a genuine medieval village church.

After the Colonel's financial troubles the Castle was some time before acquiring a new owner and it was in these years that the Conservatory fell into decay. Augustus Cavendish-Bentinck, the next proprietor, found two handsome wellheads of north Italian origin from the Colonel's time and aimed at a complete Italianate garden. He planted four Irish yews and rose bushes on the lower level and laid out a lawn with geometric flower beds around a central sundial on the upper.[21] Socially high powered house parties became the order of the day and something of the atmosphere of that period – exclusive, leisured and secure – lingers on under the Lewis lease, an unexpected survival. Only one of the Sturt's four defensive towers has survived (**colour plate 11**). It is in buff brick, their preferred material, with an ogee dome, and has been turned into a garden seat and Gazebo looking out onto a scene like a William Powell Frith painting updated and animated. In the foreground the guests of the hotel and their children play on the perfect white beach. Steps lead up to a tea terrace, the retaining wall of which supported the platform for the twelve 9 pounders. Beyond the terrace a long curving walk shaded by holm oaks and lapped by the sea runs at the foot of low wooded cliffs (**61**). Above is a second walk of beech trees bordered with hydrangeas and lawns. The charm of Brownsea is that gardens and sea lie together in neighbourly fashion with no apparent threat of storms, no intervening sand dunes or wind-blasted bushes. It is more like a scene on the Italian lakes than on the English Channel.

Durlston Park is in total contrast to Brownsea Island. People are allowed onto the Island grudgingly and for a fee. Durlston's cliff-top park was created explicitly to lure as many people in as possible, but they never came. In 1863 a local Swanage man, George Burt, who was prospering in the London constructional firm run by his uncle, John Mowlem, began buying up a narrow coastal strip of land between the little town of Swanage and Durlston Head. The site commanded splendid views out east to the Isle of Wight and Burt hoped to develop it as a high class housing estate, profiting from the rise in land values.[22]

Both Burt and his uncle started life as quarrymen and they are unlikely to have known how, a century earlier, the poet and Worcestershire squire,

61 *Holm Oaks shade this walk beside the pure white sands and almost waveless waters of the inland sea at Brownsea Castle*

William Shenstone of The Leasowes, attracted visitors to his moderately pretty property by creating a circuit of picturesque buildings and viewpoints, all sign-posted with improving inscriptions calculated to instil a feeling for the beauties of nature.[23] It was another retired London contractor, Thomas Docwra, who gave his friend John Mowlem the idea of buying cheaply an attractive neo-Gothic monument to the Duke of Wellington. This was being demolished to make room for developments at the south end of London Bridge, and Docwra suggested setting it up again on Swanage Harbour to raise the value of surrounding property. It still stands there, holding its own against an interesting new complex of flats.

Taken by the notion of improvements to raise property values, Burt and his uncle re-sited two Ionic columns from John Nash's Regent Street on Prince Albert Park. This was to draw potential house builders' attention in the Durlston direction. Then, with the help of the Weymouth architect George Crickmay, new roads were planned out along the cliff top and the site was advertised as 'New Swanage'. Thousands of trees and shrubs were planted on the bare wind-swept fields: tamarisks, rhododendrons, fuschias, Pampas grass, holly, yews and variegated laurels. Through them, the Isle of Wight Road, a carefully graded carriage drive, was laid along the top of the cliffs with several offshoots, all crying out for villas to be built along them. Lower down the cliff, reached by a zig-zag way, ran a picturesque path for walkers.

As a park destination Crickmay designed Durlston Castle, really no more than a restaurant, set high above a huge stone globe of the world. There were many little attractions on the route, exhortations to press on were carved in big block letters from chunks of local stone, many small side paths led to view-points with wooden seats and there was a tennis court with Burt's invention, a cross-shaped 'All the Year Round' seat, a Shakespeare Seat and a Walter Scott Seat, these last in solid stone.

Time has been both kind and unkind to Burt's project. Only a few villas close in to Swanage were ever built and the sea has crumbled the cliffs, destroying most of that picturesque lower path. It is still possible, despite many warning notices, to descend the Zig-Zag, but it leads only to a green shelf above a grim shore of boulders. The Isle of Wight Road on the other hand, still leads through constant shade of oaks and alders to Durlston Castle. It is no longer possible to play tennis, but the stone seats from which to watch the game look as if they will survive until Judgement Day. A metalled road has been driven through the fields to Durlston Castle and ends in a car-park, with the happy result that the old carriage road is left for walkers to enjoy with all those admonitory stones reading, 'Durlston Head And Castle', 'The Large Globe', 'Tilly Whim Caves And The Lighthouse'.

At Durlston Castle, which is Crickmay's odd cross between Queen Anne Revival and French Beaux Arts, the lapidary inscriptions become richly didactic. Along the side wall of the Castle they read: 'The Seas But Join The

Nations They Divide', and offer on a map of stone the distances from Durlston to London, Bristol, Honfleur and Boulogne. Down by the Large Globe (**frontispiece** & **colour plate 16**) where Britain's imperial possessions feature prominently, the messages turn into a storm of instruction: 'The Rate Of The Earth's Motion At The Equator Is About 1,040 Miles Per Hour' and 'The Common Black Swift Flies At The Rate Of 200 Miles Per Hour', with much further information on the Sun, the Moon and the Stars. A more solemn note of Pantheism is sounded with:

> Give Me The Ways Of Wandering Stars To Know
> The Depths Of Heaven Above And Earth Below
> O Thou Eternal One! Whose Presence Bright
> All Space Doth Occupy – All Motion Guide
> Let Nature Be Thy Teacher

Below the Globe, Burt planned a curved viewing terrace but to frustrate possible suicide attempts the Park authorities have concealed both the view and the drop over the cliffs with a tamarisk hedge. Burt, more shrewd, has inscribed on one stone block: 'Persons Anxious To Write Their Names Will/Please Do So On This Stone Only' and 'Persons' have obliged. On the next viewpoint, so near the cliff edge that the authorities have not been able to plant tamarisks, is a stone set in the wall (**62**) inscribed with Tennyson's:

> An Iron Coast And Angry Waves
> You Seem To Hear Them Rise And Fall
> And Roar Rock Thwarted In Their Bellowing Caves
> Beneath The Windy Wall
>
>   Above Sea 149 Ft

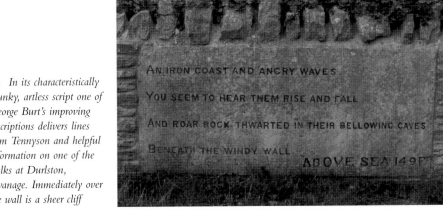

62 *In its characteristically chunky, artless script one of George Burt's improving inscriptions delivers lines from Tennyson and helpful information on one of the walks at Durlston, Swanage. Immediately over the wall is a sheer cliff*

After all these fascinating attempts by a post–Wordsworth philanthropist to convey the Sublime (and make money) there comes a sad anticlimax. The Gothic horror of the descent to Tilly Whim Cave has been closed to protect, so the authorities claim, a colony of bats, gregarious creatures who in reality seek out, in belfries and attics, human company. It is still possible to dare the cliff edge, resisting the attractions of suicide, and look down at the limestone ledges from which stones were lowered on whims (cranes) to waiting boats (**63**); but no longer possible to read Burt's last inscription from Prospero, chiselled into the rock face: 'The Cloud Capped Towers/The Gorgeous Palaces/The Solemn Temples'.

It is now time to view the lighthouse and read: 'Caution/It Is Very Dangerous/To Throw Stones'. On the way back there will be an opportunity to look inland for a change from the sea views and read one Burt stone that has not worked out as he intended. Low in the long grass the slab reads: 'Solent Road'. Up the gap in those well-planted woodlands, where Solent Road should have been lined with villas, are only a battered farm gate and a hedge of blackberry bushes. There should have been another stone, equally deeply inscribed with: 'The Best Laid Plans/Of Mice And Men/Gang Aft A-gley'.

After such an overtly commercial park, a garden of an ordinary Victorian ironmonger's family will end this chapter on a realistic downbeat. Behind the sixteenth-century Priest's House in Wimborne Minster is a complete town

63 *On the face of these cliffs at Tilly Whim, George Burt carved the last words of Prospero from the Tempest as the climax to his didactic garden. The cave leading down to it is now closed to the public due to an infestation of bats*

garden, one of those long thin burgage plots that were once standard behind the house fronts of every medieval town in the country. Time and the developers have swept away so many that it is easy to forget that town gardens were as important to the economy as cottage gardens and valuable indicators of the lifestyle and living standards of shopkeepers and the petit bourgeois.

It is unlikely that this was the garden of a priest in the Catholic sense, but it is at least 500 years old, though largely shaped from its time between 1872 and 1960 when it was the garden of the Coles family, who had the ironmonger's shop in the front downstairs room. Its last owner, Miss Coles, died in 1987, leaving not just her house and garden but the stock of her shop to the Minster Governors. Since that time some of the vegetable patches have, regrettably, been turned to lawns for the visitors. Working people in the past ate food, they did not sit around on lawns or spend their days picking and arranging flowers.

On first entry the garden works like a view down the wrong end of a telescope. One third of an acre in extent, but 100 yards long, it reaches down to the banks of the Wim, or Allen as the stream is now called. Consequently it seems very narrow, pent in between old brick walls and exactly divided by a long gravel path. Yet what is satisfying about this attenuated corridor is the variety of rooms and sub-areas it manages to create in its progress.

Immediately on the left, tucked in between a corner of the house and a wall, is the Garden Room, a miniature bark house, walled half in bark, half in tile, with a solid bench set back in the shadows. The garden faces east so this was not a seat designed for sun lovers. It overlooks the formal area of diminutive clipped yews, a small lawn and a border of flowers, all probably Edwardian in date as the yews are not old enough to be formal planting of the seventeenth or early eighteenth century. From this point on, the garden works around the markers of old fruit trees. A fallen but still flourishing black mulberry leans over the path, dropping its ink pellets; the museum has yet to decide whether it is 200 or 400 years old. One large quince was loaded when I was there with Yeats' 'Golden apples of the Sun'. Three clerodendrons were pouring out their intense perfume. Little lawns which should have been vegetable patches were littered with tempting windfalls of old, often rare, apple trees. One tiny side path led off left into a cul-de-sac of summer, with phlox and dahlias. At the far end near a conference pear was a walnut tree with the river, still running clear as Dorset streams tend to do, but spoilt on the opposite bank by a slab of the shopping centre.

At this limit of the garden a shelter has been roofed and floored self-consciously with tiles and tesserae from a Roman villa. There had been several other small sheds along the way. One holds the last stock of the Coles ironmongery, another a little tea house, contrived perhaps, but they give a sensible working feeling to these limited spaces. The garden conveys a lively insight into the twin functions – larder and pleasaunce – of a town garden, and its several enclosures are a reminder that, by date, it could be called Edwardian and it is not, therefore, so very remote from the grand Edwardian gentry gardens of the next chapter.

8

The lordly ones – gardens of the Edwardian summer

Parks of the Capability Brown era were created in response to rural economics, the desire to drive fast in well-sprung carriages and the urge to shoot large numbers of birds as conveniently as possible. Similarly, Victorian parks were laid out in order to express wealth and to display the horticultural treasures of an empire. So there has to be a reason why, from roughly 1880 onwards, parks declined in favour and gardens, which were comparatively modest in size but romantic, mood creating and historicist in associations, rose to fashion and popularity. It was a time of affluence for the upper classes, so economics are unlikely to account for the drawing in of resources. Ever since 1984, when Jane Abdy and Charlotte Gere published *The Souls*, a study of the aristocratic and moneyed circles that revolved around the limp figure of Arthur Balfour, there has been a tendency to explain the privacy afforded by the yew hedges, stone walls and elaborate garden pavilions that characterise Edwardian gardens by the desire to facilitate liasions and adulteries among the idle and exquisite rich. But this is unlikely to have been the overt policy of garden designers.

Botanical imperialism was one factor. The grounds of Minterne house neatly exemplify that devotion to exotic flowering bushes. Between 1838 and the mid-twentieth century, that narrow belt of fertile greensand running down due south from the house to the cascades and pools of the Cerne has been transformed into a flowery jungle of rare azalea, rhododendrons, magnolias and alien trees. All are planted along a triangle of paths down to the valley, up the stream and then back uphill to the level lawn immediately south of the house. It is a lavish and entirely un-English floral sequence that has been fostered by supportive planting and by investment in successive botanical expeditions, from Hawker's, back in the 1860s, through the Wilson, Rock, Forrest and Farrer expeditions of the early 1900s to Kingdon-Ward's in 1927.[1] The fluted Dawn Redwood was planted in 1949, only two years after that near fossil was discovered growing in China. But the Monterey Cypress has been here since 1838 and the Himalayan Marinda Spruce almost as long.

That avenue of Japanese Cherry had to be replanted in 1985, bush grown from the bottom to get the right feathery effect. Nothing at Minterne is hit-or-

miss. It is a reassuringly professional garden, the bushes on its well-ordered horticultural route march flower on time. The *Pink Pareverum* was just over on my late
April visit, and *Magnolia Soulangeana* was in full flower. Down at the valley
bottom the seductive chain of exquisitely contrived cascades, cunningly divided
by imported rocks into triple falls or tumbling coyly under rustic bridges (**64**),
was a relief from so many rhododendrons. The garden never ventures over Lady
Eleanor's Bridge, an Admiral Robert Digby creation of 1786-1802, into the park.
Isolated behind an iron fence from bucolic Dorset, Minterne does offer a great
and rewarding floral experience with scholarly information pinned to every other
shrub. It is not, however, a garden for surprises or discoveries, more for display.
Botanical scalp hunting was one factor leading to the Edwardian garden. Linked
with it, the rising power and influence of women must have been the other. It
is a safe generalisation that women like flowers and appreciate beauty on an
accessible domestic scale, that they are neither keen to shoot pheasants nor to
drive fast over an undemanding landscape. But why should Dorset, that retiring
and normally reactionary county of squires, have been in the forefront of the
movement towards these new gardens of historicist nostalgia? Athelhampton was
no tentative experiment in the style but a flamboyantly committed demonstration of architecture in the service of lawns, hedges, pools and flowers. It was
planned as a completely new garden by its designer, Francis Inigo Thomas and

64 *At the base of its triangular walk of exotic flowering bushes, planted in the late nineteenth century and
early twentieth century, the garden at Minterne touches down at Admiral Robert Digby's eighteenth-century
water garden of cascades, pools and ornamental bridges*

the owner, Alfred Cart de Lafontaine, in the winter of 1890. Built a year later, the garden was in place a whole year before 1892 when Sir Reginald Blomfield would publish his *The Formal Garden in England*. That book is usually seen as having launched the new style by its contempt for the designs of William Kent and Brown and by its advocacy of formal enclosed vistas, mounts, terraces and ornate garden buildings, together with simple flowers, herbs and topiary.[2]

Inigo Thomas was, however, actually at work in 1891 illustrating Blomfield's proposed book and in absolute sympathy with him; while Blomfield's polemics would express a reactionary mood in garden design that had been developing since at least 1882, when William Morris had written against gardens that tried to link up with the outside world of nature. Morris stated that a garden 'should look like a thing never to be seen except near a house. It should in fact look like a part of the house.'[3] Victoria's reign had already proved so successful that aesthetic patriotism was in the air. If there were to be garden buildings, why imitate Italy or France when the gardens of Queen Elizabeth were on hand as models?

The fact that Dorset was an intensely English county of squires, brimming with manor houses of the 1550-1650 period, many of them lapsed into farm-houses and going cheap, made it a natural questing area for de Lafontaine and by 1890 the railway system had made Dorset accessible for weekends. Moreton station is only a few miles away from Athelhampton, and soon the development of the motor car would bring the county even closer into the London orbit.

If Athelhampton is considered in the light of Inigo Thomas' later Dorset garden, Chantmarle of 1910, it is likely that de Lafontaine pressed his designer to be even more architectural in his framing of it than Inigo Thomas might instinctively have preferred to be. Chantmarle has no stone garden pavilions and responds sensitively to a very difficult topography. The garden at Athelhampton virtually ignores its parent house, turns its back upon a clear and beautiful chalk stream, the Piddle, with all its potential for water gardens, and moves in geometric formality from one stone-walled enclosure to another. As an amateur antiquary and the son of a French aristocrat, though born and educated in England, de Lafontaine is likely to have been prejudiced in favour of grand, formal axial layouts.

A clergyman's son, socially well connected, a cousin of a future Viceroy of India, Inigo Thomas had trained as an architect under G.F. Bodley. The future founder of the Guild of Handicraft, C.R. Ashbee, was a fellow pupil and a warm friend. A mood of self-indulgent decadence was beginning to characterise the last decade of the old Queen's reign: with the plays of Oscar Wilde and the poetry of Algernon Swinburne. A rhythmic indolence was in the air:

> And time remembered is grief forgotten,
> And frosts are slain and flowers begotten,
> And in green underwood and cover
> Blossom by blossom the spring begins.[4]

It was a time for overt, poetic beauty in garden design, and Inigo Thomas, who never married, fitted easily into a time of deference, gentlemanly elegance and richly ordered garden images, terrace above terrace, pavilion against pavilion. At Chantmarle he would be looking for that harmony with a site, that garden potential which Geoffrey Jellicoe would go all the way to Italy to discover in the Villa Lante and the Villa Gamberaia.[5] Here at Athelhampton, new to the game and obedient to his patron, he imposed a rhythm down three-and-a-half terraced stages, from an artificially raised platform to that unseen and ignored river, so he was manifestly not working in harmony with the site.

His garden lies oddly at the side of the house, to the south-east, making no attempt to regulate an awkward approach to the front door. Much later, de Lafontaine would call in a rival designer, Thomas Mawson, to attempt to correct the imbalance.[6] Athelhampton had been a courtyard house but it had lost two of the four sides in the mid-nineteenth century, leaving a v-shape of two exposed wings. Normally a high terrace with twin pavilions would lie at the back of a seventeenth-century manor house, but that was where the Piddle ran through a wild marsh, so Inigo Thomas raised his terrace at the front of the house, but well to the right. Below it three enclosures are set on a formal axis, visually they link today down a very narrow corridor of hedges, gates and fountains. In Inigo Thomas' day, when electric pumps were not available, fountains featured less and originally he worked on an axis of pools and sundials.

The first and most memorable enclosure is the Great Court (**65**), a garden sunk deep below its terrace whose wall trickles water out from lion mask mouths into a narrow pool at its base. At one end of the obelisk-studded wall is a House of Joy, French rather than English in the line of its roof. Over its door is a smiling summer mask of the West Wind. At the other end is the House of Sorrow and winter, with an East Wind mask of gloom and icicles, an iconography that savours of Oscar Wilde's *Salome*. Early photographs show the Great Court as Inigo Thomas intended it: twelve small yew bushes are set in demure punctuation around the central pool with a fair showing of flowers and roses in formal beds.[7] When the yews planted at Hampton Court for King William III grew lumbering and senile they were grubbed up and replanted from slips. Athelhampton has chosen another way. Twelve giant pyramids have totally outgrown Inigo Thomas' intentions, virtually filling up the space, now laid entirely to lawn. They are dramatic, even, in a comic style, they are magnificent, but they are not what Inigo Thomas first designed.

Down in the next stage, the Corona, the axis narrows theatrically, with obelisks on a circular wall picking up the theme of the obelisks on the terrace (**66**). Where, in de Lafontaine's time, there was blowsy profusion of growth, today the planting is low, a colour palette, seasonal and unsatisfying. At one time the yew hedges behind the pinnacled wall were, like the yew pyramids, growing enormous, but they have been cut back to the level of the pinnacle tops.[8] Roses and clematis riot appropriately over the walls. The axis is running south to north,

65 *In the Great Court of Athelhampton the yews have totally outgrown Inigo Thomas' original intentions of 1892, thereby creating the most visually memorable garden in the county*

but from the Corona an east door leads into the Lion's Mouth Garden, named after its wall fountain. Here the Arts and Crafts feeling of the garden is strongest: greenery, stone walls and trickling waters.

Returning to the main axis, the third enclosure, the Private Garden, was the first to be laid out and the least interesting. In no way private, it is simply a lawn with a long central canal. Unconvincingly Inigo Thomas claimed that there was another axis here, along the pond, through the house and out into a gap in the quadrant arms around the Pigeon House Court on the other side. But there is no visual link. He plays a similar invisible trick at Chantmarle; architectural training tends to make gardener designers feel guilty about their geometry and proportions. Inigo Thomas also maintained that his central south–north axis ran on to a summerhouse by the neglected Piddle. There in the last half section of the original grounds the 1892 design ethic has been lost. There is the inevitable White Garden on one side, roses on the other and much statuary, while the Piddle is completely underplayed. Most garden designers would have sold their souls for such a pure limpid stream, but if visitors press through discouraging hedges they will find a mildly interesting marshy tract of reeds and bushes, untamed and unintegrated. Yet this was the feature which demanded, probably back in Saxon times, the building of the house next to a watery larder of eels, fish and ducks.

Much has been added to the east of Inigo Thomas' axis in the twentieth century. Most effective because of its insistent feeling of enclosure, is a Cloister Garden of pleached lime trees around an octagonal pond. This was laid out by the Cooke family who have owned Athelhampton since 1957. Sir Robert Cooke, a hyperactive MP, created the Wealth Tax Walk, named after a Select Committee which he had chaired at Westminster. It lies on Inigo Thomas' mythical second axis, but to little effect. A Lime Walk, which runs parallel to the Great Court with the mad pyramids, works rather better, adding to the garden's original flow. With a touch of the absurd, in keeping with the pyramids, it ends with a glum statue of Queen Victoria in white marble stained by years of weather. She looks disapproving, both of the state of her robe and of her position in the shadow of the House of Sorrow. To balance her, the Cookes should buy a statue of her jolly son Edward VII and set it up on the sunny side of the House of Joy: that would be a truly Edwardian gesture.

66 *Architecture takes over from flowers and topiary in the Corona at Athelhampton, the middle unit in its brilliant three-part axis, Inigo Thomas' realisation of Sir Arthur Blomfield's seminal ideas*

After making such a bold statement at Athelhampton in 1892, Inigo
Thomas might have expected Dorset landowners to come clamouring for his
services. In fact he had to wait eighteen years for his next, or possibly his next
two commissions in 1910. Chantmarle is certainly his garden; Parnham is
attributed only on style. There was a real chance in 1904, when the 2nd Lord
Alington succeeded his father at Crichel House, that Dorset might be given an
imaginative new garden in the Edwardian manner by Harold Peto, the
architect turned garden designer, who already had to his credit the romantically beautiful gardens of Iford Manor and Wayford Manor, both in Somerset.

Crichel, however, has never been fortunate in its gardens. A fine terraced
layout of the seventeenth century, modestly appropriate to its house, was swept
away by the Brownian fashions for bare lawns and low bills for upkeep that
prevailed when Humphry Sturt was turning a modest house into a palace in
the years after 1772. There is no more potent evidence of the incongruity of
Brownian landscaping than the illustration in Hutchins' *History of Dorset* of the
great, bottom-heavy house, sitting in complete isolation on a green lawn, with
no more relationship to its environment than a circling drive and one unrelated
three-arched bridge over a lake. Yet Humphry Sturt's deep portico had created
an outside room which cried out for steps and a link with a garden.

After much hesitation, post-1904, and the construction of a wooden model
of a temple to judge its effect, Peto was allowed to lay out a garden on that
southern or portico side of the house (**67**). Generally described as an 'Italian
Garden', it was nothing of the kind.[9] Neurotically anxious to preserve the view

Crichel. The Italian Garden.

67 *After much hesitation and trials with a wooden model Lord Alington eventually allowed Harold Peto to lay
out this tame 'Italian' garden at Crichel House in 1906. It has since been swept away.* Private Collection

from his portico across the lake, Lord Alington only gave permission for a commonplace parterre of four lawns bordered with alternate high and low topiary bushes and centred by sunken flower beds. In the far south-eastern corner of this parterre a small circular columned and domed temple was finally approved and built. It overlooked the lake and stood at the end of a long avenue running back north, set with two semicircular stone seats and leading to a rose garden in Peto's dullest manner, an affair of trellises linked by wire supports for climbing roses. During the Second World War these two lacklustre gardens fell into decline and the Martens sensibly swept them away, retreating to garden behind the shelter of a walled enclosure.

Harold Peto, though a great and influential garden designer, was never fortunate in his Dorset patrons. Lord Alington foolishly kept him on a tight rein at Crichel and when he was commissioned in 1907 to work on the house and grounds of Seaborough, on the other side of the county, there are signs that the site defeated him. He had been working in 1902, just across the border at Wayford Manor in Somerset for his sister Helen Baker. Wayford was a pleasant late sixteenth-century house with an Elizabethan terraced garden and Peto had no trouble adding a round-arched loggia with two new terraces leading down to a wild garden.[10] When, however, he was called in to perform the same flattering transformation on Seaborough, he ran into problems. The arched loggia, which he built there in 1907 (**colour plate 19**), looks thoroughly intimidated by the violently muscular Gothic house of 1877 by T.H. Wyatt that stands aggressively next to it. Seaborough already had a stiff, balustraded double terrace in the Italian manner with long flights of steps down to a steep slope and a lake. In a half-hearted effort to soften these and perhaps distract from the axial emphasis, Peto (if it was he, the attribution has never been conclusively proven) added a flight of moon steps in the Lutyens manner and planted one side of the lower garden with a parterre. Then, wisely, he retired from unequal combat. Seaborough is a house of very strong character, not one for Souls.

The gardens of Anderson Manor, near Winterborne Tomson, fit embarrassingly into this imaginative sequence of 'Jacobean' gardens as envisaged and projected by Edwardian gentlemen. They were laid out by an Edwardian lady, Mrs Gordon Gratrix, in the ten years after she had bought that composed and confident 1622 brick manor house in 1902. The worrying quality of her gardens lies in their authenticity. Whereas most of these pre-1914 gardens – Athelhampton, Leweston, Parnham and the like – are imaginative improvisations on a roughly Jacobean theme, glorious stage sets for a posing twentieth-century gentry, Mrs Gratrix appears to have revived the gardens of Anderson as she revived the manor house itself, with a scrupulous care for the recreation of original features.

When she bought the Manor it had lapsed, like so many in the county, into a charmingly dilapidated farmhouse. But by the time she sold it to Colonel Tabor, just before the First World War broke out, the house was virtually back to its Jacobean condition, as its builder, John Tregonwell, would have recognised it. The gardens had been first carefully excavated and given a similar, archaeologically correct, treatment.[11] As a result they are today exactly what they were and, it has to be admitted, ever so slightly dull compared with the pavilions of Athelhampton and the canal of Chantmarle. The formal avenue approach from the south has been replanted and leads over the restored brick bridge across yet another Dorset winterbourne with brick gatepiers, stone ball finials and two sets of balustrades for dignity. Two endearingly huge yew balls have been allowed to brood on the brick forecourt along with wygeias. To the right of this court lies the formal garden centred tamely upon a small sundial, but enlivened with a fine diversity of box parterres and topiary: spirals, balls, deviant lumps and finally a 'Disney-esque' duck. A wisteria manages to self-support in no apparent context at the side. South of this collection and below it is a Ladies' Walk beside the dry winterbourne, overlooked at the south-east corner by a charming Jacobean-style Summerhouse built upon excavated foundations. To the north is a Bowling Green enclosure with a pleached lime avenue, almost concealing another pavilion built into the wall. This, one feels, is what Jacobean gardens were really like.

There is a way back across the Bowling Green and through the north wall and the limes to a big orchard and Kitchen Garden with more outsized yews, conical this time. A pleasant dreamy air, graciously unkempt, lies over both house and garden. Mrs Gratrix was clearly not interested in surprises or architectural overstatements.

The county was given its second truly Edwardian, rather than Jacobean, garden by Thomas Mawson who drove a most ambitious, almost urban, layout through woodland and a pre-existing garden. This was at Leweston Manor, now St Antony's girls' school. Mawson's grounds here, flawed in concept but fascinating and dramatic, interact with a mysterious earlier garden of unrecorded authorship. The whole complex layout deserves to be much better known, working as it does alongside the early Stuart church of the Holy Trinity and a classical house of about 1790, with a defiantly brash Art Deco interior of the late 1930s. Few country houses in Dorset can equal Leweston for variety of stylistic interest.

Mawson had designed his first garden in 1889 at Graythwaite Hall, Windermere and, though he opened a London office, he continued to be active in the north-western counties, Lord Leverhulme being his most influential patron. He had equal success as a town planner in the Beaux Arts style, with commissions in Canada and the States. His 1900 book, *The Art and Craft of Garden Making*, illustrated with his own gardens and plans, went through five editions, hugely irritating William Robinson, the champion of the, by then dated, mode of natural, relaxed gardens. Mawson was entirely of the school of Sir Reginald Blomfield and made no secret of his contempt for what he called 'the pedestrian imitation of Nature'.[12] His villain in garden history was 'Capability Brown, a man who was, for a long time, regarded as a genius'.[13] In our age of Brown idolatory it is a corrective to read Mawson's projection of Brown as the destroyer of good gardens.

Once he had become fashionable, Mawson writes, 'the tide had set in, and onward it ruthlessly swept, regardless of the labour of a past generation and recking little of the sanctifying hand of time'.[14]

Repton was different; 'while he professed to be a follower of Brown he was unquestionably ahead of him in intelligence and power to grasp the importance of the office of design'.[15] Mawson even quoted Repton's '10 Principles' in full to emphasise the role of artifice in good garden designing.[16] He was actually working on Leweston as the five editions of his book rolled out. There is one illustration of Leweston in his first edition and seven in his fifth of 1912. They explain most of the problems of Leweston in its present altered condition, but he never actually mentions the garden by name in his text, bound probably to silence by an agreement with a quarrelsome patron.

That was G. Hamilton Fletcher, who had bought Leweston in 1906. For forty years previously it had been tenanted successively by Sir Richard Glyn, Robert Whitehead and the Duke of Hamilton, all wealthy men, tempted presumably by its three Vinery Houses, Nectarine House, Peach House, Palm and Orchid House, rockery and fishpond: all the signs of a swagger gentleman's establishment.[17] One of these tenants had begun a perversely ambitious terrace garden, quite unconnected with the main house and intended, apparently, to look out to the north-west over the usual Victorian regiments of predictable flower beds; none of these, however, had been laid out. The sale particulars of 1906 were only able to describe:

> winding and shady walks that lead out on to A Stately Terrace with rare speciment trees interspersed with *Italian Statuary* including large and boldly sculptured stone flower vases, benches, troughs, a pair of Newfoundland dogs, a grazing sheep, a goat and a wild boar . . . beautifully executed and in excellent preservation.[18]

Remarkably all this statuary has survived. What is disturbing about the Menagerie Terrace is its incompletion. The best display of Victorian bought-in statuary in the county[19] commands, anticlimactically, a very ordinary field and a large water tower disguised as a windmill and now housing holiday accommodation. Someone, probably the Duke, ran out of either patience or money. At the end of this terrace steps lead back into a half circle of grass and rose beds which has been cut out from thick woodland. When Leweston first became a Catholic school for girls this became 'The Nuns' Garden', but the 1906 sale particulars prove that it was illogically sited in relation to the existing terrace scheme:

> The extension of the garden at this point would much enhance the enjoyment of this stately Terrace. Close by a Pergola leads to a large sculptured stone seat occupying a very secluded and sheltered position.[20]

The Pergola has gone, but the mysterious throne, supported on its arms by the owls of Athene, is still there in the shades. It was this odd semicircle in the woods that seems to have taken Mawson's perverse fancy as it is from this point that his axial layout, 'The Glade', of a grandeur which Mussolini would not have despised, takes off.

The international financier Wilhelm Kleinwort had been considering the purchase of Leweston himself in 1906, but when he heard from his agent that he had hesitated too long he predicted that Hamilton Fletcher, 'very probably will now proceed to spoil the place'.[21] That was an uncharitable judgement, but there do seem to have been indecisions and disagreements in the relations between Mawson and Hamilton Fletcher over the next few years. These make a tour of the grounds a puzzle, though a very rewarding one.

First on the left or east side of the house lies a banal, municipal-style rose garden, and this, according to the plans, is definitely Mawson's and unrelated to anything else. Next comes what is now a directionless, undulating vacancy of grass studded with trees and shrubs. As Mawson designed and laid out this sector of the gardens there was a large circular flower bed with rose pergolas backed with what the caption in his book calls 'A Small Range of Glasshouses', in reality a centrally domed conservatory with substantial side wings linking it to the house. On the far side of the circular garden, now quite lost, was Mawson's 'Fountain Pond', which has survived in an altered state. A semi-circle or exedra of box hedges has been carved into the edge of the woodlands (**68**). Six statues of cherubs, each representing one of the arts, stand on plinths around a paved area with a circular pond. A central opening in the hedges leads temptingly through into the woods, but disappointingly only to aimless winding paths. The feature has a delightfully mawkish sentimentality, but does that link it with the pre-1906 menagerie of goats and dogs on the terrace or could Mawson have perpetrated it? In 1908-10 he was laying out at Hoidöre, near Copenhagen for Queen Alexandra and her sister Marie, the dowager Empress of Russia, a garden of cloying sweetness, so the cherubs could easily be his invention. However, as illustrated in 1912,[22] this feature was entered between twin pillars of topiary, each topped with a topiary bird, and another bird, a bronze crane, stood in the middle of the pond. There is no sign of the cherubs, just one 'Acrolith', a favourite device of Mawson, a slim pedestal topped by a bust, stands centrally in the box hedge exedra. The cherubs of the arts must be Hamilton Fletcher's replacement for Mawson's underplayed Acrolith.

Then with a frightening statue of a huge wild pig, a replica of the Florentine Boar, the whole tenor of Leweston tightens up (**69**). The boar stands next to the Nun's Garden, Mawson's starting point for his serious work. From the boar on his high plinth a long straight avenue, 'The Glade', dark and unrelieved, cuts through the woods to two towering pylons and a brightness of clear sky. At the end of this gloomy walk there is a splendid sudden surprise opening out into a circular Belvedere that commands a great sweep of open Dorset fields and hills.[23]

68 *Thomas Mawson's Fountain Pond at Leweston Manor was originally backed by an exedra hedge centred by an 'Acrolith', a slim pedestal topped by a bust. The sentimental cherubs were added after 1912 by the owner, G. Hamilton Fletcher*

69 *It is evident from this view of The Glade at Leweston that its designer, Thomas Mawson, was at heart a town planner. Just visible at the far end of the vista are two pylons of near Fascist grandiosity. The Florentine Boar is part of a stone menagerie in these grounds*

The light after the darkness is a pleasure in itself, but there is much more. Twin four-bay classical garden houses (**70**) with seats and cupboards to store alfresco meals form a half-circle at the back of the Belvedere and a Venetian wellhead is set as its centpiece. To left and right alleyways between beech hedges lead to circular clearings, one with a statue of Ceres, the other with a statue-less plinth. From this last clearing, in a curious piece of parallel planning, another straight avenue runs alongside The Glade, but back to the Menagerie Terrace, at the far end of which, behind an enormous classical urn, there are steps down to the service area of the house. Both The Glade and the Belvedere are supposed to have been inspired by the Villa D'Este, but there is no evidence for this in Mawson's writing. While they do not make up a great or resolved garden, Mawson's additions are interestingly Fascist in feeling. As a part-time town planner he was naturally drawn to the bold through-ways and resounding vistas which have been the aim of so many European cities and parks ever since the first popular acclaim for Clementine Rome in the 1630s. Mawson and Inigo Thomas would do better on their second gardens in Dorset, though Mawson would have to wait until 1920 for his next chance.

Meanwhile, Francis Savile had bought Chantmarle in 1907[24] and called Inigo Thomas to rescue that golden stone house from a serious topographical problem: a railway line. Since his lavish architectural treatment of Athelhampton, Inigo

70 *The stone columns at Leweston introduce a dramatic circle of quadrant garden houses, a Venetian wellhead, side walks to statuary and views out across half Dorset: a great stroke of Mawson's stage management*

Thomas had been through the grim mill of war and become a serious and more sober designer. There is something engagingly quixotic about him. He actually rode around on a donkey when touring Italian gardens in the mid-1890s and then, when the Boer War began, he joined up in patriotic enthusiasm only to be captured and made a prisoner of war. That self-portrait in oils, painted in 1903, shows that he still retained the swagger of a moustached cavalry man, but his later garden style was less triumphalist, more mature and sensitive.[25]

Chantmarle is a most accomplished garden. Visitors to that remote house often remark on what a pity it is that the gardens should be neighboured so intimately with a railway line. The reality is that the railway was there, running from Yeovil to Weymouth, sixty years before the garden, and the garden owes its defining character to the way Inigo Thomas protected it from the railway. Nothing so formal as a drive with gate lodges leads down from Frome St Quintin to Chantmarle, but where a minor public road branches off there are two enchantingly sentimental thatched cottages in the Ann Hathaway tradition for servants of the house.[26] Then, where the road has to cross the railway, Inigo Thomas who, according to his friend Charles Ashbee, always remained a tremendous snob, has given the bridge a stone balustrading usually reserved for an ornamental bridge over a park lake. Even so the approach is underplayed. A side turning off the lane leads abruptly, but admittedly between towering ironwork gates and stone piers, into the forecourt of the mellow 1612 manor house.

The 1903 Ordnance Survey map shows Chantmarle in its pre-Inigo Thomas, farmhouse days, with just that short drive from the house to the lane. There was a pond and a copse on the hill rising to the west behind the house and, where the canal now runs north-south before the forecourt, there was a narrow ditch, originally the moat. Athelhampton had abounded in water, but Inigo Thomas had ignored it. At Chantmarle there was a tiny spring behind the house, but he harnessed it to create the new garden's proudest feature.

First he ran the streamlet down the side of his west-east descending axis of terraces through a sheltering belt of trees planted to give the grounds privacy and enclosure. At one point he dignified the diminutive trickle with a hump-backed bridge, balustraded like the railway bridge. As it fell into the old moat Inigo Thomas deepened that feature into a rectangular pool and widened the whole ditch out into a formidable, wide, ruler-straight canal running the entire length of the garden and forecourt to the lane (**71**). On the forecourt side a stone wall falls directly into the water, on the other an equally wide terrace of perfect turf runs almost flush with the water, with only a few inches of stone revetting between them. To complete this ravishing perspective of stone, dark water and grass, a sheer wall of yew rises on the other side of the terrace lawn. Below that, but unseen, a wild woodland garden pitches steeply down to the railway embankment which Inigo Thomas has thus excluded brilliantly from the house, while allowing it to direct the line of the garden's most memorable axial feature. At one point opposite the porch of the house a balcony is corbelled out over the water, picking up in subtle detail both the curve and the mouldings of the oriel window over the main door.

From time to time a fish leaps from the water and falls with a startling splash. For all its elegant simplicity the canal has the threatening quality of a drowning water, and at its far end, to stress that feeling, there is a lifebelt waiting. If ever there was a 'moat defensive to an house' it is this, but aesthetically defensive and enhancing. There is a breathtaking view along its whole length from the public lane. Two tall obelisks stand on plinths, one at either end of its backing wall, there is the corbelled-out balcony and then there are two smaller obelisks rising one on each side of a protruding bulge in the wall at an apparently random point. From the great green terrace their significance is a puzzle, but they flank a broad stone seat on the other side of the wall. This terminates and looks up the west-east axis of six lowering Irish yews and a flight of steps to the second of Inigo Thomas' two terraces. The upper third and fourth terraces were added after 1919 when Sir Charles St John Hornby, a barrister, bought the house and required tennis courts.

Descending the four terraces as they now lie, the uppermost is another wild garden with a small lake. A tall yew hedge with an exedra separates it from a spacious tennis lawn. Third in the chain is the Croquet Lawn, the highest of the terraces as Inigo Thomas originally planned them. It is lined with low box hedges, backed by eight Scots Pines, their inescapably savage profile curiously

71 *It is debatable whether Inigo Thomas or Mawson was the more inspired garden designer. At Chantmarle, after 1907, Thomas devised this vast moat with a lateral play of lawns and hedges in a successful bid to conceal the house from the railway line*

out of accord with the calm of every other feature in the grounds. Fronting this terrace is balustrading and a line of alternate blue and white agapanthus.

This is a key viewing point in the garden. Below it is the last and largest of the terraces, the South Garden, not overloaded with flowers, though its rear wall is lined with a conventional herbaceous border of phlox, monbretia, white daisies and yellow scabious. Its authority comes from the six yews and its four lawns focused upon a deeply sunken round fountain pool (**72**) with stone frogs, these last surely a Hornby intrusion. On the north side of the Croquet Lawn and well below it is the Courtyard Garden, simple again with another round pool and here a fountain of owls. At its side is a fuschia walk with a yew hedge on one side and, as he did so furtively at Athelhampton, Inigo Thomas has sneaked in another of those subliminal axes, this time from the oriel over the forecourt porch, back through the house and across the Courtyard Garden to the centre of a yew exedra.

Chantmarle's garden is so commandingly yet effortlessly gracious that it has been able, not only by clever barriers to exclude the railway line, but to cope, since 1950, with the house being turned into a police training college. To give the constabulary their due they tended the grounds with reverence and Inigo Thomas' twin axes have managed to front a proliferation of lecture rooms, gymnasium and accommodation blocks even subduing them with an aura more ducal than gentry. They flatter the pleasant rambling house into a

72 *At this point in the gardens of Chantmarle the lateral and longitudinal axes of the grounds come together with a punctuation of lily pond and giant yews. The lateral hedge along the moat is visible behind the yews*

grandeur it does not really deserve, and it is all done without a single garden building in the Athelhampton manner of his earlier work.

This is what makes the attribution to Inigo Thomas, of the gardens at Parnham, laid out in the 1910-13 period, so suspect.[27] Parnham is a large rambling house, early Tudor on its east-facing entrance front, a remodelling by John Nash of 1807-11 on its handsome, though not over-praised, south and western garden fronts. If Inigo Thomas could project Chantmarle to an English ideal perfection without pavilions, would he at the same time have framed casual, relaxed Parnham with such splendid but heavy-handed authority of stone? The scenario is even less plausible because he found Parnham already endowed with a mature and exceptionally atmospheric garden of yew-hedged enclosures, steps to sudden revelations and the spoils of a previous owner's Italian travels. For that must indeed have been the state of Parnham on the death, in 1910, of the art lover and philanthropist Vincent Joseph Robinson, a bachelor who had been tending the house and its grounds with affectionate and positive care ever since 1896, when he bought the place from the heirs of the Oglanders.

We would know nothing of this earlier Edwardian garden if it had not been fully recorded in a *Country Life* article of 29 August 1908. The eight photographs which illustrate that garden are a revelation and a puzzle. Apparently in 1896 Vincent Robinson had found an existing, and therefore possibly Jacobean, 'Ladies Garden' with well grown yew hedges. Whoever designed the other enclosures for him worked in the same style and by 1908 there was a Long Walk flanked with deep-buttressed recesses of yew hedge, each topped with balls of yew. This was entered through wrought iron gates between brick piers topped with urns. Small cherubs played trumpets on the scrollwork.

This remarkable garden was approached from the house down steps, framed by Nash's Gothic pinnacles, leading off an Arbour Terrace where a lion's head spouted water into a stone basin. Urns and sundials, marks of an undiscriminating collector, littered the walks. Could this Elizabethan-style garden have been an Inigo Thomas creation, laid out for Vincent Robinson as soon as he had completed Athelhampton? If it was, would Parnham's next owner, the mysterious Dr Hans Sauer, have called Inigo Thomas back again to destroy his own original creation? It seems most unlikely.

Dr Sauer's reshaped gardens at Parnham on the front and at the side of the house are obsessed or, if that is too mild a term, they are infested with obelisks, and these raise the nature and identity of Dr Sauer into question, for it was Dr Sauer who commissioned them all during the brief period 1910, or 1911 (accounts vary) to 1913 or 1914.[28]

Few of its owners seem to have been able to resist tinkering with Parnham inside and out and, to be fair to Dr Sauer, the skyline of the house must, long before his arrival, have bristled with dozens of saucy but entirely implausible 'Tudor' pinnacles added by the irrepressible Nash. Dr Sauer may have seen it as a house that required a more disciplined garden to pull it together. If that was his intention his success was complete. At some cost in charm and seclusion, Parnham demonstrates exactly why the 'Edwardian' garden treatment became so popular in those years: it works. Terraces, balustrades and, if possible, garden pavilions in the general airily elegant Montacute style are immediately flattering (**colour plate 20**). Houses, like pictures, benefit from a frame. But it would still be interesting to know Hans Sauer's nationality. His motto on a shield in the Great Hall is 'Never Vanquished', but he sold the house with suspicious speed in 1913-14, after a stay of only three or four years during which Robinson's romantic yew enclosures were grubbed up and a more open, 'lordly' and controlling garden was laid down all around the house.

There remains the intriguing possibility that Dr Sauer persuaded Inigo Thomas to revert to the style of architectural overlay he had produced at Athelhampton but virtually abandoned at Chantmarle. If Dr Sauer was an enthusiast for obelisks, Inigo Thomas, on his showing at the above mentioned gardens, was no reluctant convert. The result of their co-operation, if it ever took place, is immediately apparent in the forecourt of the house. At Chantmarle a visitor sidles past two obelisks into the forecourt with no preliminary warning views; at Parnham the E-shaped front is set behind a court enclosed by a balustraded wall with, on a rough count, twenty-two stone obelisks with balls on top and eight much larger square pillars, classical rather than Jacobean. As if that were inadequate punctuation, two tall classical columns set on high plinths stand inconsequentially on the carriage sweep, à propos of nothing.

The garden front stands upon a tremendously disciplining terrace, not quite so 'be-obelisked', though the obelisks here on the long balustraded wall are richer and grander than those on the entrance front. Pairs of them flank the steps down to the vast green lawns and there are shell niches in the wall underneath them. It is this wall that hints more than any other feature of Parnham's gardens that Inigo Thomas was the designer. By its height, length and fine stonework it is doing for Parnham what the canal wall did for Chantmarle. Its central steps break boldly forward and at each end, against beech trees on one side, dark yews on the other, round gazebos of spindly elegance carry wiry stone crowns up to finials. As garden houses they are useless, no protection even against a shower in April, and they are obviously deliberate copies of the gazebos at Montacute. That is evidence against an attribution to Inigo Thomas as he always preferred to design his own architecture, not copy from originals.

On the vast sweep of grass between the terrace and the woods, the conical yews of Parnham have never been allowed to grow gargantuan like those of Athelhampton. There are fifty of them and they impose their geometry precisely around one token central rill upon the close-cropped grass, making another point about Edwardian gardens: they may range out into several enclosures on more than one axis, but their beauty and their impact stems from their simplicity – dark green upon pale green against limestone. Owners of the house since Dr Sauer have experimented with abstract modern yew shapes on the terrace, but because they have kept to that dark-green-upon-light formula the garden can take them without a twinge. If Parnham has a weakness, it is its immediacy. Standing on that terrace everything is open to view. This is no garden of surprises; it has no melancholy corners of poetry; any member of The Souls coming here and hoping for sheltered yew arbours in which to conduct secret love affairs would leave frustrated after Sunday morning breakfast.

The First World War, which Dr Sauer may or may not have seen coming, did not put an end to 'Edwardian'-style gardens in this confidently reactionary county, though it did make a pause and modify their detailing. But before the society that launched them came near to committing suicide in Flanders, Dorset gentry produced two more of the 'lordly ones', at Waterston Manor and Kingston Russell. Neither was as grand as Inigo Thomas' pair of gardens, but both are well worth searching out. It was while visiting them that an explanation suggested itself for a slight sense of disappointment that had been troubling me in Dorset.

Coming to this county's Edwardian gardens after writing, in *Historic Gardens of Gloucestershire*, an enthusiastic chapter on that county's gardens of the same period, I was missing the excitement of the multiple enclosed, walled or yew-hedged gardens quite common in Gloucestershire. Dorset gardens were more open, and at Waterston I began to see why. All the great Gloucestershire gardens – Snowshill, Kiftsgate, Rodmarton, Hidcote – were grouped around houses of slight architectural distinction. Snowshill had charm but little more, the other three were fairly nondescript. Dorset, on the other hand, staggers under the weight of architectural jewels of artisan invention, most of them engagingly incorrect by strict classical definition, but positively oozing charm of detail and naïve composition. Pitched over to France they would automatically become a celebrated European tourist trail.

Was it possible that these Dorset manor houses had browbeaten the designers of their gardens, offered façades of such interest that the gardens fronting them had to be designed simply to set them off rather than as artistic ends in themselves? Waterston, for instance, has two façades of prime interest: a Jacobean south front riotous with restless invention and an east front with an imported classical frontispiece, dated 1586, of distinctive quality. So had their two gardens simply to act as subservient foils? This humble function may have meant that, when Percy Morley Horder came to plan Waterston's two main gardens in 1911, he could never propose creating walled courts to distract from the façades themselves. Privacies and areas of dramatic surprise were out. This is a factor to bear in mind when dealing with Dorset's other Edwardian layouts: some houses are just too good to be gardened inventively.

Waterston had long been a farmhouse and used as such by Hardy in *Far from the Madding Crowd*,[29] but in 1863 it suffered a bad fire which virtually gutted it. There was a sensitive rebuilding, but the 1901 Ordnance Survey map shows nothing more than one short drive from the road running directly to the usual carriage circle at the south front. There was perhaps a small lawn to the east, but no walks along the winterbourne. Morley Horder changed all that, scrapping the direct drive. In its place he laid out a new drive to the west front. This passed between bowl-clipped yew bushes through a gatehouse arch constructed from old service buildings. On its east face this gatehouse provided a deep garden alcove opening onto a new South Garden, but is it the garden or the undulations and balconied inventions of the Jacobean work that catch the attention? The garden offers no distractions beyond four sentinel yews, a small sundial and that deep alcove. There is too much stone paving, but a fine wrought-iron gate in the wall where the old drive entered gives some axial stress. Two Renaissance arches, which may have come from a loggia wrecked by the 1863 fire, now flank and emphasise the front. Hollyhocks, clematis, lilac, viburnum and potentilla make a pleasant old-fashioned show in front of the alcove.

Horder's only move towards enclosure lies on the east side of this south garden where a large stone flower basin is set up steps and backed by hedges. But then his real east garden is breathtakingly open, with a huge sweep of lawn sliced through centrally by a Lutyens-style stone rill for iris, now taken over by water lilies (**73**). When first laid out to Horder's design, the rill was lined on each side by flower beds with low stone walls dividing them from the lawns; then came further flower beds and young yew trees.[30] The effect must have been rich, linear and distracting; the far half of the lawn was intended for tennis courts. With much of this swept away the rill now runs from a glorious copper beech at the far end to two giant chess pieces of clipped yew at the foot of that celebrated classical frontispiece. Thomas Howard had brought it in before he succeeded to Bindon and Lulworth on the sudden death of his bad-tempered brother Henry. So all the drive of the garden is understandably directed to the house. On the far north side of the lawn is an avenue of pleached limes.

Beyond the limes a sunken garden does offer some measure of enclosed privacy. In its centre a moustached seventeenth-century herm stands on the slightly arid paving stones that Horder favoured. At the back of this area a shell niche has been inset within a tall yew hedge to hold the bust of a statesman who looks, as so many eighteenth-century busts do, like Pitt the Younger. Summer bedding with weeping floribunda roses makes a generally disordered show. To the side is an elegant conservatory and behind it runs the Piddle, fated here, as it soon will be at Athelhampton, to undeserved neglect. Once the Howards had created the great water garden at Bindon did the gentry of Dorset lose their taste for freshwater fish?

Last and, to be honest, least of the pre-War 'Edwardians', Kingston Russell scrapes by under that heading, though technically its garden belongs to George V's reign. It was rescued from decay by George Gribble in 1913, when an ash tree was growing out of its pediment.[31] A schizoid house, it has developed schizoid gardens. To the road and the west its face has a resigned classical

73 *The chess pawns of yew at Waterston Manor do not work as effectively as the pyramids of Athelhampton. Percy Morley Horder's Lutyens-style rill focuses well on Thomas Howard's 1586 centrepiece. Horder's original design had flower beds on each side of the rill*

melancholy; to its principal garden and the east its multi-windowed façade looks, to a superficial glance, like rich early Tudor, but in retardataire Dorset it is, apparently, post-1660 and Carolean. Mr Gribble's architect in the restoration of a deserted derelict that had lost its panelling and had its windows boarded up was Philip Tilden, and it was Tilden who designed the new gardens.[32]

He had little to go on except a broad straight terrace on the northern uphill side of the east garden. The 1888 Ordnance Survey map shows no gardens and where a gate lodge might have stood there was Long Bredy Farm and a track up to the house. This is puzzling as John Lothrop Motley, author of *The History of the Dutch Republic*, had died in Kingston Russell as recently as 1877. The presence of an American Minister to the Court of St James hardly suggests a derelict house. Hutchins, in his usually well-informed 1774 edition of his *History of Dorset*, seems not to have been aware of the existence of the house, which must have been a hundred years old by that time.[33] But in the later 1861 edition the house is described as 'a long ancient building, which was partly rebuilt by the grandfather of the present Sir John Mitchell, the offices and part of the gardens were formerly situated on the Duke of Bedford's lands, but were afterwards granted in fee to the Mitchells'.[34] This is a reference to the land dispute mentioned in an earlier chapter.

Whatever its real condition in 1913, Philip Tilden took that impressive terrace at the back of the house as a challenge and a marker. Above it, out of sight, he laid the Kitchen Garden; below it, where in the Carolean house there was the entrance courtyard, he chose, in the spirit of the fading Edwardian age, to go 'lordly' with a maze of Elizabethan-style yew hedges. But first and nearest to the house he set a lawn flanked by hornbeam hedges and, until recently, centred by a small round pool. Then the yews take over completely.

As Tilden first planned them they created a series of rooms, their walls clipped quite low along the relatively narrow central axis, but rising at their corners into taller, square bastions, eight squares in all. At the end of the axis stands a Summerhouse, a five-bay classical exedra twined about with wisteria. Overall the grounds lack the relief and shade of mature trees; there is something of a bare, seaside feeling about the garden. To that south or sea-side of the squares, where the ground drops, the hedges have been allowed to grow much taller and the individual enclosures are filled with flowers and linked under yew arches. It is in this southern section that the garden is most successful with its creation of surprise glimpses. Here in 1974 the Worthingtons built a bath house in 'Californian Classicism' with sliding doors, a round indoor pool and an outdoor pool surrounded by palms and yew hedges.[35] The central area is impressively regular, but the height of the hedges and the insistent squaring of their castle-like bastions neither reveals nor quite conceals the enclosed spaces. Halfway down the central axis there was a second round lily pond. This has gone, though it would have relieved the monotony, and the hedges have been ruthlessly cut back.

Several other owners have succeeded George Gribble the Reviver. They have tackled that sad-eyed entrance front. A very young beech avenue now leads from it to the road and a half circle of Irish yews stands respectfully, but as yet very under-sized, in front of that façade, so unexpectedly heavy for such a small house. Another avenue of young horse chestnuts, planted closely together, leads north up the hill, concealing the Kitchen Garden. George Gribble may only have had a heart to deal with his east garden. Then came war, when his son, Captain Julian Gribble, won a posthumous Victoria Cross in 1918 fighting on the Western Front. There would be more Edwardian-style gardens after the traumas of that conflict but planted, understandably, with less confidence and a certain stumbling.

9

Formalism or the grain of nature?
A conservative county between the wars

The First World War and the holocaust of the trenches of Flanders should have changed Dorset. Memorials in every village church prove that the price was paid, but, in garden terms, it is remarkable how little was altered. The garden history of the next twenty-one years would be, with minor exceptions, a holding operation rather than a surrender to Modernism. Planned as an elaborately formal, though imaginative, garden in 1914, the grounds of Kingston Maurward were laid out between 1918 and 1920 as if the war had never happened and the old landed order would endure, with a head gardener and six under-gardeners to every ten acres.

For a more revealing way into those timeless gardens than simply driving into the visitors' car-park, leave the car in Dorchester and cross the stile on the far side of Gray's Bridge on the Blandford road out of town. The 'Permissive Path', as it calls itself, runs beside the Frome under the by-pass bridge to where a metal and stone sluice diverts water out into a big water meadow. It is this sluice and another further back above Gray's Bridge that really give life and landscape qualities to the park at Kingston Maurward. All over the water meadow there are relics of Georgian hydraulics in decay: broken-arched brick vaults, little sluice gates, dykes, half-hidden channels and conduits. Before the engineering, this great level was a winter fen, marshy for half the year, dry reed beds for the remainder, and already the reeds are making a hesitant return. Investment by local landowners during the agricultural revolution created these water works and turned a fen into a verdant cow pasture like the one Thomas Hardy describes in *Jude*, employing a whole gang of dairy maids and bringing rich rentals for the Pitt family of Kingston Maurward. At the same time the two major sluices on the Frome diverted enough water to fill the lake and water features in the otherwise dry, chalk-soil gardens of their Baroque house.

At the far end of the meadow a notice unexpectedly cautions on 'Dangerous Currents'. This is where a narrow, but surprisingly deep and fast moving, arm of the Frome cut off from that upper sluice races noisily into the woods, just swimmable for a skilful sideways crawl and an obvious dare for the students of the Dorset Agricultural College who now occupy the house and keep its multiple gardens in perfect condition. The artificial stream hurries along beside the path under pipey hemlock growth and lush overhanging hedgerows to a bridge of four low arches. Then it disappears under bushes in Kingston Maurward park to swell the lake, all 8.634 acres of it, with five islets, the creation of John Pitt between 1774 and 1787 when the influence of Capability Brown was still paramount and natural-seeming parks with lake, woods and a temple were still the mode. Without this stream, so perfect for hyper-fast Pooh Sticks, the grounds of Kingston Maurward would lose half their charm.

The Pitts, who had built the house in 1720, sold up in 1845 and, after several shorter ownerships, the estate was bought in 1914, just as war broke, by Sir Cecil Hanbury, a very rich businessman who had made his fortune in the Far East through the very different water works and silk works of Shanghai. He and his wife were devoted gardeners. They owned the Villa La Mortola on the Italian Riviera and were anxious to try their hand at laying a new formal garden at Kingston. As soon as the war was over they began and, by 1920, had a most ambitious layout in place, part Edwardian in its multiple controlled areas and lavish topiary work, yet more open than the average pre-1914 garden, cascading down the hill above the lake with something of an Italian abandon.

While going through the usual motions of becoming, after three attempts, a Dorset MP, Sir Cecil continued to improve the grounds, laying a dramatic copper beech avenue out to the east, illogically orientated not on the house, but on an area of the gardens and because several of the garden's axes lie in arbitrary lines, it is not an easy garden to reconstruct in retrospect. Sir Cecil died in 1937 and then, when the Second World War came, Kingston Maurward drew a very short straw. It became an important base in the preparations for the D-Day landings: a petrol storage depot, criss-crossed by roads and burdened under forty-three concrete emplacements. How much of the ruined grounds survived when Dorset County Council bought the place in 1947 and the Agricultural College began a slow restoration is never clear, but the pattern of Sir Cecil's topiary has been faithfully followed. The principal programme of historic return was not set in motion until a new Head of Horticulture arrived in 1990, though there had been work earlier. This garden has to be seen as a 1990-95 revival of a 1918-20 design on a 1774-87 substructure, an intricate composite, but well worth the unravelling.

Because of its strange axes and at least eleven distinct gardens, Kingston should be navigated with a map and any written account is in danger of leaving the reader confused. As, however, that is the physical impact of a tour of the grounds, a guided description is worth attempting. Entrance now is not from the house as it was naturally in the Hanburys' day, but from the west through the fluffy toys and trinkets of the Visitor Centre, past a Shepherd's Hut full of baby chicks and by the side of a Guinea Pig Mountain, but there is nothing else stressful ahead. Two tall beech hedges close in, a necessary device to clear the visitor's eyes and prepare for garden theatre. It is the first of many controls in this excitingly proactive garden.

The hedges project not simply into a complex surprise view, but into the Red Garden, the true centre point, if such can be said to exist, in these ambitious grounds. It is here, out to the west of the house, that the twentieth-century features have developed, bordering, not embracing, the eighteenth-century Temple surviving down south by the lake. The Red Garden, with its lily pond, exquisitely planted like some self-conscious flower arrangement, is a paved court, more bronze than red. A refreshing side to these gardens is that, while there are flowers in profusion, they never dominate, except in the Penstemon Terrace to the east of the Red Garden and immediately below it. The College may have the most comprehensive collection of these temperamental flowers in England. Flowers otherwise are only the competent background to the firm shapes of hedges, avenues and steps.

There are three directions in which to look from this Red Garden and a shaded seat to sit in if it is already too much to take in. North over a beech hedge is Sir Cecil's avenue of copper beeches, now maturing. They lead the eye to Dorset hills at their most Arcadian, but lack a temple or tower to focus upon. South is the whole twentieth-century complex revealed arguably too early for surprises to unfold, but temptingly rich in detail. East, the view is up a perverse zig-zag path of steps climbing between box bushes to the Temple of the Four Winds (**74**): Ionic, monopteric and roofed with an open dome of black and gold metal. In 1938 Lady Hanbury shipped the round temple, which her husband had built up on this high mound, back to La Mortola, so it was a generous gesture of the College students to build this replacement in memory of Ralph Fitzau. A Christopher Fry note of whimsicality pervades this airy construct. 'Vous et nul autre. Jenny' is one inscription, and round the architrave 'Russia, Germany, England and Pakistan', an unexplained national grouping. Even the floor has an inscribed coat of arms.

Two intricate topiary areas lead steeply downhill. The more easterly of the two flows across the whole, wide, velvet carpet of the Croquet Lawn to the Terrace and the Crown Garden (**75**). Even from this distance it is possible to make out a diamond-shaped window cut into the yew wall of the Crown Garden to hint at further enclosures lower down towards the Laurel Lawn and the lake. This window is an original Hanbury feature recently restored. Immediately parallel to this axis and west of it is the firm topiary geometry of the second axis: Red Garden, Stumpery, Brick or Royal Garden and the long Herbaceous Border to the Laurel Lawn again. It must be one of the most engaging and bewildering yew mazes in Britain as, when a yew circle is grown inside a yew square, a number of tiny corner gardens are created. There is a Secret Garden somewhere and, while I have probably sat in it, nothing can be quite certain. It is all most inviting; like the interior of Buckingham Palace this garden has two grand sets of receptions rooms when lesser gardens make do with one. At most points it is easy to exchange one axis for another.

Four alcoves in the Brick Garden shelter statues borrowed from the Palace of Westminster, which seems unlikely ever to want them back. Charles II and

74 *Backed by a tremendous beech grove, the Temple of the Four Winds, a late twentieth-century addition to Kingston Maurward, rises above a perversely winding path and the strict geometry of the Red Garden's lily pool: one of many inventive axes in these grounds*

75 *In recesses of Kingston Maurward's topiary, Crown statues of Queen Anne and Henry III keep illogical company. This is a garden of rooms rather than vistas, with a remarkable permutation of routes and spaces recreated after wartime damage*

Queen Anne are reasonable enough in formal grounds, but why Henry III, who did nothing for fifty-six years except build half of Westminster Abbey, and Richard III who merely murdered his nephews? Kingston is full of such points of interest. A little to the side is a stone bench inscribed 'George Lawson. Sit down and enjoy my view' (of the lake). If it were necessary to choose a favourite among these topiary courts, the Croquet Lawn would be hard to beat. Its turf is perfect; behind it is a bank of pink cistus and that miniature hill with the round Temple between two glorious beech trees, a matchless neo-Georgian vignette.

The other half of the grounds represents a change in mood. There are no more geometric confinements. Below the house the lawns swoop smoothly down to the lake showing up the Thomas Archer proportions of its south front handsomely.[1] Their sweep is parted in the middle by a strange small grove described wishfully as the Japanese Garden, but a pale specimen when compared with the Japanese Garden at Compton Acres. There is water flowing here from that stream out in the water meadows, and a Modern Garden of mysterious green beauty could have been devised under the shady trees, but only two ugly Chusan palms, a pillar lantern and a snow-viewing lantern assert the Japanese claim. Probably I was there at the wrong time of year. A clerodendrum would have been scenting the air in August and arum lilies would have enlivened the bare earth back in July.

Down by the water is John Pitt's Lakeside Temple (**76**), built between 1774 and 1787. It composes well from the lakeside but not from any other angle. Arcadia is never invoked by bare brick side walls. By an avenue of stumpy oaks of recent planting the way leads to yet another of Kingston Maurward's surprises, a second manor house, this time a delicate Elizabethan toy of silver gables with a rubble stone rear. Beyond that, yet another major item, stands the 'Elizabethan Walled Garden', noble in size, but surely walled in Georgian, not Elizabethan, brick. Here the grudging, flinty soil has been coaxed into impressive lines of flowering hedges around a potager of flowers and vegetables designed to attract during three at least of the four seasons. A long greenhouse is Baudelairian with corrupt flower perfumes and overloaded citrus trees; no bush should be required to carry grapefruit, it looks like cruelty to plants.

There is an alternative route back to the Visitor's Centre via a Nature Trail on the far side of the lake, but the north bank has offered such variety that most visitors will want to enjoy it all a second time. This is one of the county's most rewarding gardens, a credit to all concerned with its revival. As a small suggestion: could the College some day take over the hydraulics of that water meadow and restore them to Georgian perfection? A Thomas Hardy Festival of Folk Dancing with students dressed as milkmaids milking long-horned cows might become a notable attraction. There could be services at Hardy's St Michael, Stinsford, to follow, Evensong with no organ, only the village band at full strength playing from the west gallery, 'Under the Greenwood Tree' would be returning in song.

76 *John Pitt's Lakeside Temple of 1774-87 at Kingston Maurward is consciously sited to be viewed from a boat on the lake*

Compton Acres is a garden almost the exact contemporary of Kingston Maurward, bought in 1914 for £220,000 together with a house, by Thomas William Simpson, an investor in the Indian Rubber Company, and planted from 1919 onwards. It comes, therefore, from the same sound Edwardian blood line, but has ended up composed more tightly, more typical, despite its overt populism, of the Edwardian archetype of enclosure leading off enclosure, than any of the true Edwardian gardens of the county. It should be visited with an open mind. People who will sneer at Sticky Wicket, Buckland Newton, covered in the following chapter, will incline to sneer at Compton Acres. The approach is not promising; Compton lies in the superior pine-clad suburbs of Bournemouth-Poole, the place where grey squirrels come to die happy. Its car-park is full of coaches with frail old pensioners climbing slowly in and out. From its first conception Thomas Simpson (who never lived in the house) must have intended to create a tourist draw rather than a private pleasure ground, consequently the themes of the various garden enclaves – Scottish, Egyptian, Italian, Spanish – are more brashly overt in character than those in a private garden might be.

After the usual 1939-45 wartime neglect, J.S. Beard, a London architect, restored the grounds to re-open them in May 1952. The Bradys bought the house and gardens in 1964 and today Compton continues in overwhelming floral good health. Half close the eyes to the massed tulips and primulas, follow the route proposed in the guide (there is no real alternative) and the last of Compton's ten or twelve distinct theme gardens, that of Japan, will more than compensate for anything overwrought along the way. That, at least, was a springtime reaction; in summer it is different, more subdued, heathery, less noisy with falling waters.

In common with gardens like Snowshill, Gloucestershire, of the same 1920s–1930s period, Compton inclines to little printed messages of encouragement. An early instance urges that: 'Achievement is but another milestone on the highway of progress. The end of the journey lies ever beyond.' A few yards further on it is a delight to have expectations fulfilled with: 'The kiss of the sun for pardon, the song of the birds for mirth/You are nearer God's heart in a garden than anywhere else on earth'.[2] Then things improve. After appetising glimpses of an Italian Garden through a grotto tunnel in a circular 'Roman Garden', a winding path leads past Matope terracotta lions to an authentic surprise panorama of a long canal with neat municipal bedding (**77**), terraces, balustrading and a Wildean plethora of erotic statuary, bare babies and naked bronze youths – the Athletes from Herculaneum – a display of nudity such as no twenty-first century garden would dare to feature.

A narrow 'Egyptian Garden' which follows is an unconvincing corridor of palms. It used to be a 'Palm Court with Wishing Well'. A tearoom is at hand to lay any desert dust and from that point onwards the themed spaces open up and improve. One advantage which Compton has over so many other Dorset gardens is an adequacy of big, shady trees; without them a visual and tactile

77 *Ancient Rome as Hollywood revised it has been conjured up here at Compton Acres, a garden planned to make money by delighting tourists with a sequence of international and historic reconstructions: a twentieth-century version of Rococo eclecticism*

aridity can easily set in. The Spanish Rock and Water Garden is not notably Iberian, but the waters play in complex patterns, more like narrow gauge railways, one above the other, than streams. 'Solitaire' by Tom Merrifield, an Australian sculptor, stands in the middle of one pool, a female nude to counterbalance the earlier blast of boys, and there is a Squirrel's Nutty Trail in a wooden arbour overlooking a deeply Bournemouth dell of pines and falling water. This is the 'Sub Tropical Glen' and to be avoided by anyone troubled by steps. There are seats everywhere with little summerhouses and the entire feeling of the 'Glen' is attractively geriatric.

The way out is via Zimbabwe. A long curving pathway between shrubs and hedges is called the Sensory Touch Sculpture Garden. Every few yards a large chunk of smoothly sculptured soapstone or African marble has been carved by artists of the Shona nation of Zimbabwe in stylized animals, birds and mushrooms. These are intended to be fondled and appreciated more by the hand than the eye. It is at this point that quite astonishingly beautiful, oddly un-English glimpses of Poole Harbour are framed between the pines, the water as blue around the islands as it would be in Greece. Brownsea Island with its Castle looks more like a book illustration than a real place.

Scotland interposes with the Heather Dell and two lead sculptures of an un-Scottish, distinctly French shepherd and shepherdess. A 'Memorial Garden', a stone-walled enclosure with inscribed benches, is hardly noticed because next lies the true masterpiece of Compton Acres, the Japanese Garden. This is one of those features where words literally fail. In mid-April, with few leaves on the trees and their linear elegance still clear, but with the azeleas in full flowering around the waterfall, the dark stream and the multiple stepping stones, it was quite extraordinarily beautiful, but in a complex, interactive way. The steps are so steep and the water around the stepping stones so dark that the garden paths impose a constant peril in the middle of flowering profusion. Every few steps create a distinct new vista of the red-roofed tea house (**colour plate 18**), the straw-woven summer pavilion, the granite pagoda or the sacred crane birds. And always that tumbling water at the head of the miniature valley exerts its visual control and music. A Torre Gate where a vicious bronze dragon stalks the bronze pigeon on its perch remains etched in the memory, but everything is exotic, carefully considered and, because Japanese gardeners were brought in to create it, relatively authentic.

From all those visual assaults the visitor moves on into the harsh reality of a gift shop. It is important not to be disenchanted with Compton Acres. It is as much a period piece of its times, that un-introspective, sometimes naïve, wholesome, obedient time between the wars as Bridehead is of the 1830s or Durlston of the 1870s.

There is one other Dorset garden which, like Compton Acres, lacks a big house to preside over it, and has been laid out primarily to attract paying visitors. This is Abbotsbury, a garden with no chronological right to feature in this chapter because its walled core was raised by Elizabeth Fox-Strangways, 1st Countess of

Ilchester, back in the 1760s, but it is so close in spirit to Compton Acres that it is appropriate to treat it here. Abbotsbury began to take its distinctive shape as a wood of exotic trees in the nineteenth century under the 4th and 5th Earls of Ilchester, reaching its prime in the Edwardian period under Joseph Benbow, the Head Gardener. Throughout that time it had a parent house, the weirdly styled Castle Strangways, the Ilchesters' holiday home almost on the beach at Chesil.[3] But in 1913 that burnt down, its replacement was structurally unsound and never occupied, so the gardens fell into a decline, hastened by the Second World War.

It was after 1968, when the aristocracy had recovered its nerve, that a process of restoration and replanting began, designed to make Abbotsbury, like Compton Acres, a profitable tourist attraction.[4] The interesting difference between the two is that, while Compton Acres depends upon clearly defined thematic areas – Roman, Spanish, Scottish, Japanese – defined by statuary and garden buildings, Abbotsbury plays to a more ecologically sophisticated taste, dependent largely on a succession of plant specimens. It makes its paying guests work harder.

At heart both Compton Acres and Abbotsbury are visitor centres with gardens attached. Their restaurants and gift shops open wide, welcoming arms. Abbotsbury, however, has, thanks chiefly to the 4th and 5th Lord Ilchesters, a treasury of botanical antiques, planted to rival the Digbys at Minterne. A false olive near the Upper Pond and a Monterey cypress are 4th Earl plantings, while a *Stranvaesia nussia* dates back to 1828, the time of the 3rd Earl; but are these rather esoteric, specialist's attractions?

It is a weakness of present-day Abbotsbury that visitors need to be directed around a complex circuit, otherwise they would wander aimlessly in a wood with few recognisable markers. As a garden it has no natural geography and only one artificially created view. Astonishingly it ignores the sea and Chesil Beach. But the visitor trail does begin brilliantly with *Pterocarya raxinifolia*, a hoary, rumpled Caucasian wingnut, a tree so likeable that it should be able, like one of Tolkien's Ents, to walk around the garden, pruning and weeding. A little stream trickles by it, a rare feature in this dry wood, and around the corner the Victorian Garden (**78**) bursts onto a visitor with a satisfying sub-tropical flourish.

This has a profile of soaring, gangling Chusan palms, a hundred years old, with fleshly leaved Ethiopian banana trees and a blaze of insect-shaped flowers in un-English, rich colours. If this Douanier Rousseau jungle is Abbotsbury's first introduction what riches are to follow? The answer is: nothing of quite the same distinction. After a repro-Gothic conservatory and a pets' graveyard the wood closes in. A Secret Walk delivers no secret, but a Himalayan Glade has a pretty red Summerhouse and a *Cupressus cashmeriana* that asks, almost like a cat, to be stroked for its soft foliage. The path winds back through a Bog Garden of menacing, thorny gunnera, still introverted and viewless, until the ground rises into the welcome open space of the Southern Hemisphere Garden.

Here, in August, a *Eucryphia nymonsay* was performing dramatically with showers of white convolvulus-shaped blossoms. This is how Abbotsbury tends

78 *Abbotsbury's garden circuit begins, like Compton Acres, with a themed creation, this distinctive Victorian Garden. Sub-tropical would be a more accurate description for its profile of Chusan palms and the chemical clash of its flower colours*

to be remembered, by a series of unusual trees with intensely academic names.[5] Above the *Eucryphia* are the Lily Ponds with a machine that, for 20p, delivers food to feed the fish. Gardens need punctuation of that homely nature. All along the wandering paths are little would-be interactive notices reading: 'Look out for the nuthatch', or 'Look out for the watervole'. These are superior to the pious moral adjurations at Compton Acres, but I never saw anything I was told to look out for. One red pheasant was, however, digging out a rabbit burrow.

Lacking a great house or a terrace overlooking the ocean, Abbotsbury is unlikely to attract romantic-minded, élitist garden fanciers. They will, however, love the grounds of Boveridge, high up on the Chase above Cranborne. These can be visited on an open day during the holidays of the school which occupies the house. Boveridge was Thomas Mawson's confident return to the county after more than a decade of successful practice, and Boveridge is a consummate professional achievement. Charles W. Gordon, a shipowner, had just bought in 1920 the stark, uncompromising Greek Revival house of grey stock brick, a home much in need of a flattering garden. There was already a terrace garden to the east and the approach was up a long drive from the south through stands of beech and conifers which, lacking either water, gate lodges or garden buildings, suggested more a heath than an English park. The immediate approach to the house was dramatic, with a broad turning circle, tree enclosed, and Regency stables lying on one side with an arched entrance facing the two-bay deep Doric portico of the house itself.

Mawson decided to use this circle as an approach to a new triple-terraced garden on the south side of the house. At the same time he enriched the existing east terrace with a broad lily pond. South and east terraces meet at right-angles, the composition satisfyingly set off by three magnificent mature trees: a cedar at the right-angle, a second cedar at the end of the east terrace and a fine beech at the end of the triple south terraces. To terminate the two uppermost south terraces Mawson laid out two circular clearings. The lower of the two terraces ended in a round yew hedge enclosure laid out with Getrude Jekyll's phlox beds. Sadly this has been grubbed up after overgrowing, as yews incline to do. That has left the long rose pergola, a Mawson favourite, on the terrace with no firm conclusion, only a circle of posts and ropes. The upper south terrace still works splendidly, sweeping on into woodland under an arch of creepers to a wide, round woodland lawn. Paths lead on from this formal feature, winding away into a wild garden.

Perhaps the real seduction of Boveridge's terraces is their exceptionally soft green turf, which makes simply walking them a sensuous pleasure; and there is never any sense that this is a school garden. Everything is manicured yet lush. The east terrace is axially divided at its centre point by that lily pond which, in keeping with the grounds, is so filled with lily pads that the water is barely visible.

Those south terraces are more complex by far. A wide lawn reaches from a loggia, raised to soften the profile of the house, to a stone paved walk. Then

comes the grass terrace which, with its exceptionally tall planting of herbaceous shrubs and flowers, is the real glory of the place. Below this is a terrace
that begins at its west end with a garden house, opens into a long lily canal in
the Lutyens manner (**79**), crossed by stepping stones, and continues in that rose
pergola. Both these terraces overlook a wide prospect of Dorset fields and
woodland. One step below them is a Bowling Green and lower again the
school's playing field, which Mawson intended for 'several tennis courts'.[6] For
sensitive children the school must be a most memorable setting for their
childhood: flowering terraces fading at each end into woods; the grounds still
overtly upper class and élitist in general feeling and in their detailed upkeep.

If any criticism is to be made it is to the way by which Mawson has led visitors
down into the south terraces from the carriage sweep. He begins in the grand
manner with gate piers, wrought ironwork and a long flight of steps. But these
lead in scenic bathos into the backside of that garden building facing the long
lily canal. Only when a corner has been turned do the terrace vistas begin to

79 *Thomas Mawson used the
Rill at Boveridge in his post-
1920s design, not to focus on
the house, which is frankly
plain, but to create the central of
three parallel lateral axes running
from an underplayed seat to a
woodland arena*

unroll. The rose pergola is in need of replanting and the lost Jekyll roundel is a disappointment, which could and should be replanted, otherwise Boveridge exudes tender care.

In his account of the place Mawson regretted the chalk soil as being hard to work and hostile to rhododendrons and azaleas. An alternative view is that one charm of the garden is the absence of hard, dark green rhododendron leaves, that and its reliance upon banks of tall sunflowers, hollyhocks and lobelias rather than yew hedges to delineate its limits. By 1920 were yew hedges going out of fashion? It is, as a result of its soil, a light, airy, singularly moist garden, a happy interlude in the dark woods. As Mawson remarked after his grumble over the chalk: 'My clients have continued to improve the quality of the soil and the lawns, which proves once more that gardens grow for those who love them.'[7] A very wholesome and comfortable doctrine, but is it true? Was Mawson right, or merely purveying encouragement to the hard working and hopeful who are struggling on poor soil with the wrong garden design in an inappropriate topography?

The question is highly relevant when posed in the Dorset gardens of the early 1920s, because it was in 1924 that Brenda Colvin, a trailblazer for the new generation of garden designers, was laying out the grounds of Steeple Manor in the Isle of Purbeck in that style of relaxed, apparently artless naturalism that would soon be making Mawson's formal terraces and geometrical rills look dated. While she was studying at Swanley Horticultural College in 1920, Ms Colvin and a group of like-minded students had rebelled against the teaching of one of Mawson's disciples.[8] Even Gertrude Jekyll's technique roused her suspicions as she found that Jekyll merely added colour to predetermined Lutyens gardens of basic formality.

At Steeple, one of her earliest commissions, Colvin was working her way towards subtle responses of planting, in both trees and flowers, to an existing landscape.[9] So infectious was her success that many of Steeple's garden features now read like clichés: stepping-stone paths across a lawn, large olive oil pots strategically sited, unmown grass where wild meadow flowers can flourish, trees grouped by species rather than mixed. At Steeple she had still not broken entirely away from formal beds of low box hedges planted in subtle colour symphonies after the Jekyll manner.[10] But the casual charm of Steeple's flowing lawns and bosky areas was undeniable, and it struck the perfect note for the post-war generation which found Kingston Maurward, Boveridge and Compton Acres old-fashioned and Edwardian.

Colvin was a friend of the Gardiners who settled in Springhead in 1931 and, while her exact influence on Springhead's planting has not been recorded, that garden's response to its topography seems to be Colvinian. A comparison between two gardens, Springhead and Mapperton, suggests that no amount of love and tender care will rescue a garden projected on the wrong concept; while a brilliant artistic response made, almost casually at Springhead, to a pre-existing environment and persevered with for only a few years, can result in a dream

garden. The painter Harold Squire was at Springhead in Fontmell Magna for a
bare five years, 1926–31, but these were the important Colvin years, while Ethel
Labouchere gardened to her dead husband's memory at Mapperton from 1925
until she died, aged ninety-five, thirty years later in 1955. Squire was working
with an artist's eye towards the new Post-Impressionist, post-Colvin idiom of
garden design; Labouchere, a typical Dorset landowner, aimed to impose her
formal order on the land. Both gardens had, as their initial canvas, a small valley,
so their respective achievements can be compared fairly.

Harold Squire was a minor artist on the fringes of the Bloomsbury Group.
He was born in Chile in 1881, came to England with his parents in 1891, studied
at the Slade under Stanhope Forbes and was a founder member of the London
Group, exhibiting in their first, March 1914, exhibition and in a 1928 retro-
spective.[11] He bought the derelict mill at Springhead in 1926, made a studio for
himself in its ample accommodation, painted furniture there and the walls of the
dining room in the manner of Duncan Grant and the Omega Workshop, but lost
all his money on the stock exchange and left, a ruined man, in 1931. Whether
Springhead had already achieved its Colvin-inspired accommodation with its
own topography by that time is not certain, but it seems likely.

Rolf and Mariabelle Gardiner took over the mill and the garden, running
it for many years as an idealistic centre for rural regeneration.[12] It was an
intriguing experiment, redolent of all the honest aspirations and symbolic
claptrap of the 1930s, that decade of the Fascist dictators. Rolf's uncle owned
the farmland around the Springhead Mill and Rolf's aim was to create self-
supporting communities of young people returning back to the land away from
the despair and unemployment of the big cities.

To achieve this he held 'Harvest Camps' at the Mill, each one for a group
of sixty-nine young men and women and lasting several weeks.[13] D.H.
Lawrence was one of Gardiner's supporters. 'We'll have to establish some spot
on earth, that will be the fissure into the underworld', Lawrence had written
to Gardiner on 3 December 1926, 'like the oracle at Delphos, where one can
always come to . . . Some place with a big barn and a bit of land . . . And then
one must set out and learn a deep discipline, and learn dances from all the
world.'[14] Springhead was to be that 'fissure into the underworld'.

The young campers dredged the mill pond and practised their crafts of
basket weaving, gardening and farming on the surrounding lands, planting
trees to successfully raise the water table. Rolf Gardiner planted three million
trees in all. Each morning they rose at 6.30am to 'the rhythmic beat of a
mellow gong' and ran barefoot, single file, snaking around the gardens, bushes
and flower beds in a circular sun dance.[15] Then they gathered around the
flagstaff to sing a hymn to the dawn while the cross of St George was raised.
Work in the morning was followed in the afternoon by study and folk dancing.
After an evening lecture everyone stood arm in arm by the torchlight to sing
the hymn of the Springhead Circle.[16]

It should all have been perfectly harmless and laudable, like youth hostelling. The trouble was that Rolf was blond, spoke fluent German, often wore lederhosen, and brought over each year a group from a German youth movement, which inevitably got taken over by the Nazi party. When war broke out in 1939 rumours went around that poor Gardiner had planted a wood in the shape of a swastika to guide German bombers and that Hitler intended him to be the first Gauleiter of Wessex. It was all lies and Gardiner continued after the war to work for VSO, the Soil Association and other worthy causes.

He died in 1971 and his daughter, Rosalind Richards, has dedicated herself to continuing his work in music and the arts, while restoring the garden to something of its original condition. So Springhead is not the usual Dorset manor house of semi-feudal domesticity and amiable, smelly Labradors. Water makes its first impact on the lane up from the village, a strong, clear stream running on the right but, on the turn into the mill yard, it has mysteriously vanished. There is just the yard, the substantial white-washed range of the mill blocking out the valley, and at right-angles to it the old miller's house. Behind single-storey ranges on the lower side of the courtyard are the organic herb gardens, with bed after bed of echinacea, set up by Neal's Yard in 1995 to take advantage of the extreme purity of the chalk-filtered water running a hundred yards from its source.

Like Mapperton, Springhead's garden launches itself with a surprise vista, with the difference that at Springhead you climb up into it, while at Mapperton, without warning, you drop down into it. Steps lead under an archway between mill and its mill house into a sudden roar of water pouring down into a chasm to turn unseen machinery. A few steps more and the long mill pond is at eye level, with all the inescapable Monet-esque associations. The narrow valley of the garden opens out, wooded to the left and at the water's head, open fields to the right (**colour plate 21**).

And that, in a sense, is Springhead: the roar of water, the water lilies and water weeds, the woods and the feeling of enclosure. The little white temple with its wrought iron dome and the flower beds are inessentials. All that Squire seems to have done was to slightly tame its rusticity by revetting the upper banks, where the spring heads pour out from sand under chalk, and by planting an orchard above the springs. Like Geoffrey Jellicoe garden designing at Shute, a few miles away in Wiltshire, Squire realised his good fortune in this charmed topography, and gardened simply to emphasise the bucolic composition. Jellicoe had the abundant head-waters of the River Nadder; Squire had the sources of the Fontmell Brook. Such profuse springs create their own miraculous atmosphere; a wise gardener merely dramatises them by overhanging bushes, a strategic bridge, some Shaftesbury greenstone for the margins; he or she goes along with the grain of Nature rather than competes against it.

Mariabelle Gardiner brought the temple Rotunda in sections from Venice; it is arguably more of a distraction from the valley than a focus point. Her daughter

Rosalind, with one part-time gardener to help (her mother had four full-time), has cleared the weeds and planted beds of annuals to pick up the terrace rhythm of the Celtic lynchet strips on the chalk down to the right. Across the mill pond from these, by the Rotunda, there is a yew arch and a bamboo clump, but do these matter? There is the usual scatter of choice flowers dear to garden journalists: Rosalind's favourite penstemon 'Sour Grapes', ghost bramble, veined cranesbill and astrantia. But when dark chocolate cosmos and zinnias invade that fernery at the head of the pond, where the waters visibly exude from the sandy soil, it is probably time to call a halt. Springhead is perfect as Squire and the Gardiners left it. He spent what artistic genius he had in the witty sprawling canvases applied to the walls of the mill house. A lesser Rex Whistler as far as paint went, he was a genius at leaving well alone where water, trees and grass went. Seventy years after his abrupt departure from the mill, and thanks to Rosalind Richards' weeding and tending, his garden creation not merely survives, but lives and is emotionally captivating.

Ethel Labouchere's Mapperton is fascinatingly different, the great roller-coaster ride of Dorset gardens. An essential stop on any tour of the county's ten finest gardens, it offers two tremendous *coups d'oeil*, disappoints after both of them, but leaves the visitor quietly drunk with experiences. First comes the entrance front of the manor with a *cour d'honneur*, chapel wing and an undemanding but adequate front garden of clematis and roses. Not many manor houses, in a county rich in them, can equal Mapperton's west front for self-conscious charm of barley-sugar finials, balustraded parapets and armorial display. But few manors with such a decorative front can have such a blank outlook over one single rising meadow. It cries out for skilful tree planting.

Expectations, therefore, have not been raised high and round the corner to the north they are kept low. There is just the plain expanse of the Summerhouse Lawn. On the 1903 Ordnance Survey map this is virtually all the garden at Mapperton, with a raised terrace overlooking the lawn on one side and the valley on the other, commanded close to the north-east corner of the house by twin garden pavilions in the seventeenth-century manner. Today the Lawn is hedged or walled on all sides, with the eponymous Summerhouse tucked away in the far corner, at the end of the original terrace, appearing at this distance neither classical and Arcadian nor vernacular and rustic.

Then comes the shock, arguably more acute and exhilarating than any other offered in the gardens of the county. With no warning the ground falls away into a narrow valley, some eighty feet deep and steeply sided. It is entirely filled with two aggressively ambitious formal gardens, the upper Fountain Garden, lined with brick walls pierced on either side by matching grottoes, the lower Daniell's Garden, tree-defined and set with two long basins of deep water. Both brim with the artifice of stone and clipped yew bushes, so densely arranged that the eye does not settle upon any individual point. But an irresistible impulse is created to get down into this isolated world and experience its crowded complexities; higher up the valley there is only an orchard; beyond there is no park, no setting, simply Dorset with cows. It is that which makes Mapperton so memorable and yet so uneasy in its relationships.

Below Daniell's Garden a curve of trees and wild garden leads seductively away out of sight behind the house, which is poised at the very edge of the drop in absolute visual command of it all. Between the two distinct gardens stands a strange building that features in most photographs of the place. This, because it is sited at a sharp drop in levels, is a single-storey vernacular late seventeenth-century garden house to the Fountain Court but a tall, gaunt tower to Daniell's Garden where it throbs with the pump that strives to aerate the brown waters of the swimming pool at its foot (**colour plate 17**). That odd double face is a reminder that, long before Ethel Labouchere laid these gardens out, there were already two levels and, from the 1903 OS map, a fish pond where the swimming pool now spoils the green harmony with its sinister soup-like depths and harsh concrete sides. All this present elaboration was a memorial. A tablet below a statue of a crouching panther in the upper garden reads: 'This garden is in memory of Charles Henry Labouchere who died in Holland 1916 made by Ethel his wife 1927', a strangely prosaic inscription: no rhetoric, no poetic prose, no explanation.

It was late to begin an Italianate garden in 1925 and the topography was challenging. There could be few surprise enclosures when everything was on view from that gap in the hedge of the Summerhouse Lawn. So, while the usual Edwardian devices of walls and yew hedges could have been deployed down below, it would all have to be conducted under the eyes of the house. Mapperton's garden is such a brave, risk-taking gesture that any criticisms of it sound carping and churlish; but once the descent into the Fountain Garden has been made it becomes obvious that there are flaws.

By 1925 Mrs Labouchere, a mid-Victorian by birth, had lived on into the Jazz Age of the Art Deco, with geometrical simplifications in the air. In advanced intellectual circles there was a conscious movement towards an International Modern style in houses and gardens, with both native and émigré architects and landscape designers working towards stripped-down, angular solutions: cuboid concrete-walled houses controlling hard, abstract landscapes. That stylistic shift becomes evident even before a descent into the formal valley. There is another gap in that Summerhouse Lawn yew hedge where the odd little building on its far north-eastern corner can be studied more closely. Already the designer is shying away nervously from conventional classical forms. The columns of the loggia have lumpish, token capitals of no order; tradition is on the slide. It dates from 1926, yet down the steps in the Fountain Garden the six-bay Orangery in perfectly correct Ionic order dates from much later, 1966-8.[17] This is because the lively-minded Ethel was dead by then, buried under a simple stone tomb slab, the only grave permitted in Mapperton churchyard. The MP for South Dorset, Victor Montagu, had bought Mapperton in 1955 and reverted (he was, of

80 *This view brings out the hyperactivity of Mapperton's Art Deco version on the original Edwardian theme. Begun in 1925, this upper Fountain Garden peppers the little valley with stone and topiary incidents but lacks a strong central feature*

course, a Conservative MP) to conventional classical forms. Neither of the two cave-like garden Grottoes had proved tempting for picnics – they are dank holes despite their chimneypieces – and his Orangery does give an authoritative note to the crowded garden. It is, however, built of artificial stone and its textures, linked to those of the ubiquitous crazy-paving and the outright ugly, over-sized central fountain, contribute to a certain sense of disappointment now that the details of the Fountain Garden can be absorbed (**80**).

There is much to admire: stylized Art Deco owls and eagles, little lead dolphin and satyr fountains trickling slight streams, terracotta urns of Bacchic revelry, two splendid, truly Art Deco crouching panthers by Cecil Thomas of 1928. Deco design is rarely naturalistic; but for all these the balance of stone and greenery is wrong. The former overbears the latter. That central fountain basin is far too large, with its crude acanthine angle brackets, for the pathetic squirt of the fountain itself. Water could have saved the garden even though green lawns have deserted it. The stone paths are too wide, the staccato of the multiple clipped yews could have been resolved into areas by yew hedges as they are in the lower garden. Essentially the garden, for all its 'Fountain' title, is dry. No water flows and shade is desperately needed, from trees not from the stone-columned pergola leading to the old garden house. Christopher Lloyd notes that Victor Montagu removed a pergola from the Orangery area and doubled the pergola by the Garden House.[18] At this point, where the two gardens unite, a great beech tree on the far side comes to the rescue, but for the Fountain Garden that is too late.

If lack of water damages the upper garden, too much rust-brown water spoils the lower. Its two basins both need fish, water weeds and lilies, the upper pool is not a tempting swimming bath and, if its function could be abandoned, then the swirling low yew hedges around a carved stone centrepiece would link the two pools together most attractively.

After these complaints and reservations it is a relief to climb up on the far side of Daniell's Garden to the Round Pool. Here there is clear water and ample shade, a return to the Edwardian element of enclosure. There is a host of hellebore for winter flowering and a perfect rural view out to the cows in the field and down to the Wild Garden and the Woodland Walk. Even here there are Art Deco touches in the triangular hoods over an inscription at the sides of the stone seat.

Mapperton's problem, and it undoubtedly has one, is that it was conceived with little thought for its setting. There was a big sale of the estate's farm properties in 1919, when Mrs Labouchere bought the place, so she probably lost control over the fields surrounding her valley.[19] Cow pastures are pleasantly bucolic, but they are not enough. Extensive tree planting is needed in those fields, some at least close in, to shade the walls of the Fountain Garden. The two skeletal trees on the skyline make gibbet silhouettes and they should be felled. For all her ninety-five years the Labouchere lady did not live long enough to settle her undoubted masterwork securely within its Dorset hills. Instead she dropped it down there, like a gift from a rather dry Italian heaven.

She was fighting a noble rearguard action, but no one in the county is as magnificently, self-confidently retardataire as the Pitt-Rivers of Hinton St Mary. If Dorset were a normal county, like Leicestershire or Bedfordshire, the garden which Mrs Labouchere threw down as a courageous gesture of defiance against her husband's death would be the end of the story. But Dorset is the last, shrewdly defended redoubt of the real upper classes, the old landed gentry, and a formal garden is a statement of order, of confidence in continuity. Planting a yew hedge exemplifies that confidence.

Yet for all its gloriously reactionary topography of great estates, mature parks and presiding manor houses, even Dorset has to stand respectfully back a pace from the garden and grounds of Hinton St Mary. They give the impression of some inner principality or fiefdom, a shade too intellectual and urbane for Dorset, too lively and yet too backward looking in garden terms even for this county. At Hinton the church clock does not stand at ten-to-three, but at roughly 1910, before the passing of Lloyd George's anti-aristocratic budget.

The lawns and avenues of the manor house have been planted over the last ten years by Anthony and Val Pitt-Rivers; the fountain in that square central basin leaps a confident fifteen feet or more, a treat after the miserable trickle in some other gardens. The tithe barn is a theatre, the garden to its rear is a place for drinks in the interval and analysis of the latest production. This is a living garden, not a mere area of antique nostalgia. But then Hinton St Mary is Pitt-Rivers land and there is nothing of the conservative squierarchy about that distinguished family, except, paradoxically, their preferences in garden design. The grounds of the manor lie high, windswept and open to wide views, but in plan and detail they are still being developed in an entirely Edwardian spirit.

Lieutenant General Augustus Pitt-Rivers, who inherited Rushmore House in 1880, together with a 25,000-acre estate on the Wiltshire-Dorset border, was not only an anthropologist, free thinker and scientific archaeologist, but an upper class gentleman who had absorbed Disraeli's dictum that, now we have given the working classes the vote, it would be to our advantage to educate them; hence his laying out of the Larmer Tree Gardens.[20] When the General came into his inheritance in 1880, an elderly couple, Mr and Mrs Harvey, had been living happily at Hinton St Mary as its tenants since 1858. In 1888 the General ordered them out and, despite Mr Harvey's pleas that he was eighty-seven years old and dying of bronchitis, while his wife was ill with sciatica and rheumatism, out they went.[21] Possibly the General was thinking of making the Manor his family's dower house, but by 1895 his eldest son Alexander was installed there. As an amateur architect, yet another of his roles, the General designed service buildings, including Hinton's estate office, which stands like a gate lodge at the back of the house, in an attractive Arts and Crafts timbered style.

The house itself, where Captain George Henry Lane Fox Pitt-Rivers settled in 1915, is a composite creation which, while looking acceptably Dorset and Tudor, has no feeling of age.[22] Immediately in front of it on a terrace, with big pots of agapanthus, are three parterres of box based on designs from its imported plasterwork ceilings. Then comes that exhilarating fountain with a wide open space of lawns and young trees. After so many mature grounds of the 1890–1914 period it is a revelation to find an Edwardian garden that is not hoary, mellow or overgrown, but still in its spritely adolescence with gardeners keeping everything shorn and trim.

One long axis leads first to a bronze Japanese lantern surrounded by beds of lavender and a box parterre; next comes a double avenue of young lime trees directed towards a wrought iron *claire voie*. A second axis of flower beds and yew bushes lies to the left of this and, to the left again, there is an enormous green lawn, with very few trees and opening up distracting vistas even further to the left. Hinton's is no one-shot garden; like Kingston Maurward it offers a superfluity of distractions to the eye. On the right-hand side there are the generous golden barns of the Manor's farm, now, in the family tradition of educational entertainment, converted into a theatre and refreshment rooms. A horse pond has been wittily gentrified into a stone basin with cherubs and other statues, and on one side of it, secluded by yew hedges, there is a seemingly inaccessible private garden. George Pitt-Rivers transformed this area, and his reward from the Establishment was to be interned as a Fascist during the Second World War, an episode which completely failed to subdue him. The theatre and the handsome stable buildings next to it lend the gardens a Glyndebourne air of artistic alertness quite alien to Dorset.

Returning to that axis of close-planted limes, there are two more gardens branching away unexpectedly from it. They have been cleverly managed and the general appearance of the grounds beyond that first fountain terrace is one of breezy openness. On the left is a sunken Lutyens-esque garden with a rill (**81**). Seven cypresses veil it, rather than cut it off from wide views over Cranborne Chase, and its lawn is firmly punctuated by young weeping pears of rounded outline and pale chalk-white leaves. On the other side of the axis, behind the theatre barn, is the lawn where drinks are taken in the interval. Captain George designed the rare Art Deco Garden Pavilion and belvedere in one corner. With its chunky stone detail it has the air of a strong gun emplacement covering the line of any potential enemy approach from the south-east and Bournemouth.

It is on the walk back from the *claire voie* gate that it becomes apparent that, while the manor house has this richly designed garden on its south side and a

81 *The latest of all Dorset's Edwardian-style gardens at Hinton St Mary is partly post-1950 in date, still maturing but confidently conservative. The trees flanking the cliché of the Rill Garden have startling chalky-white leaves*

pinnacled Jacobean-style wall with a door to the parish church on the west, it has no real entrance front, only a drive beside that estate office leading into a back yard on the north. It is a house that needs to be approached from its theatre, to the chink of the champagne glasses of special guests, drinking in that very private garden on the far side of the horse pond. There is, about the architecture and the gardens' styling, a conscious, conservative reaching back to tradition rather than forward to startling modernism; even the theatre seems more appropriate to revivals of Christopher Fry than those of Beckett or Pinter.

Over several of these inter-war gardens, Mapperton and Hinton in particular, the enjoyable Disney-esque directness of Art Deco designs is threatening to break through the older Edwardian classicism. It finally emerged, predictably in Poole, on Dorset's coast, near emancipated, Modernist Bournemouth. When compared with committed International Modernist sea-side design like Mendelsohn & Chermayeff's De La Warr Pavilion at Bexhill, Sir Edward Maufe's Yaffle Hill at Broadstone, Poole, may seem a mere dipping of the toe in the icy waters of Continental functionalism. Art Deco was, after all, only a warming up stage for true Modernism; but for Dorset in 1929, when Maufe planned it, and 1932 when he completed it with its garden, Yaffle Hill was the county's wild frontier.

A 'yaffle' is a green woodpecker, so called for its 'yaffling' cry, and the very name suggests reassuring, back-to-nature simplicities, a house that will sit easily into the pine-clad hills of the heath land behind Poole Harbour. Maufe was designing for Cyril Carter, one of the directors of the Poole Pottery, whose designs of gently stylized fruit and flowers applied in a soft pastel glaze to jugs and bowls belong more to the Art Deco 1920s than to the Modernist challenges of the 1930s.[23]

Yaffle Hill responds to that acceptable stylization; Maufe was a master of compromise. His two-winged house sits snugly on the south side of a hill. Round-arched veranda openings on its white walls lead into its garden, more Italianate than Corbusian, though there are first-floor roof balconies (**colour plate 22**). A pottery yaffle bird is set over its porch, the two diagonally set arms of the building are the yaffle's wings, and the central rectangular lily pool in the garden is the bird's body. To the left and right of the wing tips, a red oak is planted with a silver cedar where the head, or beak perhaps, might be. All these are Maufe's original planting in an otherwise plain, grass lawn garden, simple like the austere, but highly expensive, Travertine marble with stainless steel trimmings of the interior. Inexplicably, since yaffles fly with a distinctive flutter of green plumage, the roof tiles are not the usual Art Deco green, but a deep rich blue.

The waterfall in the front drive and the swimming pool with ornate pylons and a rockery are later, post-war additions by an enthusiastic Portuguese owner. One day it might be rewarding to pare Yaffle Hill and its garden back to its first Maufeian condition of white, green and blue sea-side Art Deco.

10

Later twentieth-century gardens

This is the area where a writer on gardens has to tread most warily. It is easy enough to criticize a garden by Sir William Chambers, safely dead some 200 years. But when writing about the work of someone who has been generous and brave enough to extend an invitation to visit, and spared the time to discuss his or her planning aims, it is very hard to write anything even mildly critical.

Initially then, let me put on record that, perhaps because an unusual number of wealthy, well-educated and often traditionally-minded people have chosen to garden in this exceptionally well-favoured county, Dorset has above the average of contemporary gardens fine enough to be described as historic. Even one of its public schools, Canford, has redeemed the Victorian mediocrity of its grounds with two inspired pieces of modernist invention. Its 1971 Arts Centre has a soaring two-storey window rising abruptly from a deep carp pool, with a small fountain playing in the reed bed of a wilfully asymmetrical side basin. Across the terrace fronting the school is a forecourt to the Music School where a Japanese-style garden of raked golden gravel, with classical pots sunk at perverse angles, lies next to another pool, shallow and rectangular this time, and sprouting a tiny grove of bamboos. This is a memorial garden created to celebrate the life and work of Anthony Brown, for many years the school's Master of Music, who died in 1977. For children to be visually challenged in this way is admirable, but every garden included in this chapter deserves to be admired, some naturally more than others. I am grateful to have been allowed to view them and, while they are not given here in any order of preference, four are, in my strictly personal judgements, towering successes and ornaments to the county. The others are merely beautiful; but to have visited any of them has been a pleasure and a privilege.

No apologies are required for opening with Sticky Wicket, four acres of intensely crafted land in the middle of Buckland Newton village. Forget the comical name, the faintly suburban bungalow and the awkward wedge-shaped site. Sticky Wicket does not pretend to offer an ordinary garden visit. It is a learning pilgrimage in aesthetic ecology. Pam Lewis who, with her husband Peter, has created this experience, is a serious, even a driven figure, with few smiles, little laughter, but most intent purpose. In so far as an ecological amateur can judge, her garden has proven her thesis, which is that land can become a safe haven for wild life while remaining beautiful and productive.[1] She has proved it, moreover, with consummate technical artistry. There is no other garden in Dorset, and that includes the wonderful, organically worked Kitchen Garden at Dean's Court, Wimborne Minster, so delicately interwoven with grasses, flowers, herbs, vegetables and trees. Its four acres are more like needlework embroidery than planting. At the same time, to prepare anyone thinking of making the pilgrimage, some of my gardening friends have mockingly, and with a certain unkind justice, described Sticky Wicket as 'twee'.

It does have any number of wicker baskets dangling from branches to offer bird food; there is a Witch's Den, a Shepherd's Hut and a Camomile Lawn (**82**). One whole section is devoted to frogs and all or most of the hens in the run next to the White Garden are white with little white bootees. Accept those elements as human interest, designed to tempt learner gardeners round the circuit. Then absorb what is really being demonstrated: an interaction of insect, reptile, animal, bird, wild and garden plants so subtle, so delicately balanced that, walking the new clay meadow, a visitor is on trust to tread within a narrow path cut by a hand-pushed lawn mower, and teeters along, desperate to conform.

In the ordinary common pasture next door is a huge green heap that they call 'Mount Wicket'. It is made up of the poisoned earth that was dug out from the meadow before it, to cleanse it of the top foot of chemically abused soil which the Lewises inherited when they moved here in 1986. Fertilisers and herbicides had made the land incapable of producing anything much besides a thatch of water sodden grass. Only when the poisoned layer was dumped on Mount Wicket could the ragged robin, dyer's greenweed, yellow rattle, birdsfoot trefoil and the orchids grow and flourish in a butterfly-friendly carpet. Only 2 per cent of England's native meadowland has survived in the textured condition of the tiny strip at Sticky Wicket; 98 per cent has been poisoned into becoming mere grass. But what else will cows eat except mere grass? The questions arise naturally; and that is exactly what Sticky Wicket is about. It challenges. Visitors begin to fight back, feeling perhaps a mean flutter of satisfaction at noticing that some of Pam and Peter's apple trees had a bad case of scab. Now, if only they had sprayed with chemicals. But people still go away disturbed, even upset, thinking actively about how our land has been treated over the last self-confident century.

The Lewises settled at Buckland Newton after half a lifetime as tenant farmers in Kent. For the last three months of 1986 they brooded over the condition of their four acres and on what was going on in the farm, cottage gardens and churchyard nearby. Their only true asset, they decided, was a flourishing hedge. This they proceeded to double in thickness with berry bushes to increase the foundation of native habitat.[2] Next they cut the four acres in half, leaving the far half as pasture and the nearer half around the house as a four-part garden. Visitors can follow a trail along those four parts. These, with the essential plant list, are the living text of Pam Lewis' artistic thesis: Frog Garden, Bird Garden, White Garden and Round Garden. In addition there is an orchard and a Kitchen Garden, but they are not main chapters in the thesis.

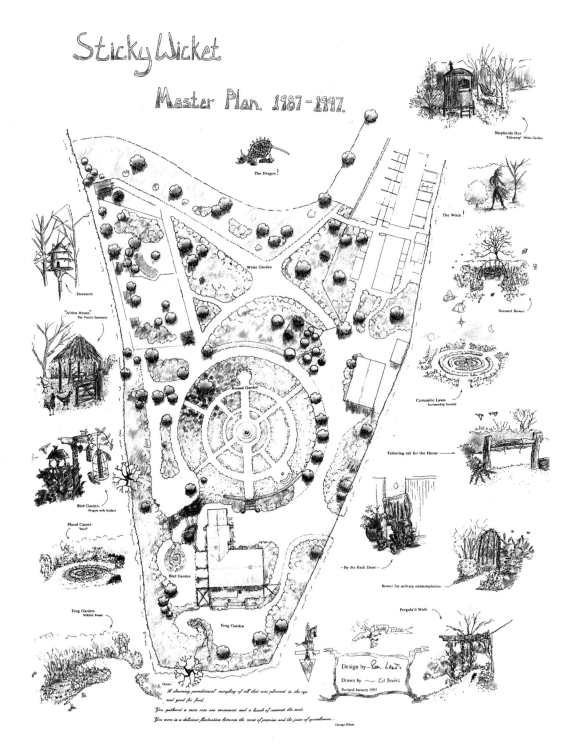

82 *Pam and Peter Lewis' achievement at Sticky Wicket has to be experienced in its subtlety and educational ingenuity, but this master plan gives some idea of their bold apotheosis of the suburban back garden into a revisionist Eden.* Pam & Peter Lewis

The Frog Garden is the least successful. It needs a larger, deeper pond, and its trick of turning a section of the lawn into a reproduction of the graveyard next door by little patches of gravel struck me as morbid and unauthentic. After this the tour becomes more impressive and, at times, brilliant. Near the house are the dangling wicker baskets placed so that the owners can enjoy bird life from their kitchen window. Here there is an intricate weaving of climbers, notably that pink, peony-like clematis around the wooden loggia. The *Aeonium schwarzkopff* with flat brown fingers growing eerily on brown arms looks as if it has dropped off a passing meteorite. Pam claims devotion to wild flowers, but her list of favourites, hung up in the conservatory, deserves quotation:

> *Prunus Padus* 'Colorata' with *Clematis Viticella* 'Purpurea Plena Elegans', *Papaver* 'Pattie's Plum', *Cimicifuga Atropurpurea* and the very dark C 'Brunette' and *Tricyrtis formosana*, *Miscanthus sinesis* 'Kleine Fontaine', *Angelica sylvestris purpurae*, *Angelica Gigas*, *Ligularis dentata* 'Desdemona', *Clerodendrum bungei*, *Centuara benoistii* and *Uncina rubra*.

Deep floral waters indeed and proof that Sticky Wicket is not all the simple life with primroses.

Each of the four gardens has a colour code: blue and yellow for the Frog, pink, red, purple and plum for the Bird; the White is self-evident, but goes with the most amazingly subtle ornamental grasses for seed (nothing at Sticky Wicket is ever dead-headed). Pam's favourite season is probably winter, when dead pods and kernels make a symphony of silhouettes and a banquet of fodder for wild creatures. Last and most sumptuously subtle is the Round Garden (**colour plate 27**), very flat and open in contrast to the wild bushy-ness of everywhere else. It centres upon that Camomile Lawn and its colours, 'from pastel pinks and lavender blues through to violet, magenta and crimson are spun softly together'.[3] If that sounds a trifle fey and pretentious, visit it in early August. The colours are matchless in their harmonies.[4] Even those who complain about the tweeness of it all will be awed by Pam's handling of a blue world of phlox. It is worth driving twenty miles to see that alone. This garden has a living message, and the more Dorset people visit Sticky Wicket to absorb that message of plant protecting plant, protecting wild creatures, creating subtle riches, then the wiser Dorset will become as a county, ecologically.

Sticky Wicket is a pioneering garden, Chilcombe is a perfect garden. That may sound an extreme claim, but Chilcombe's perfection lacks ambition. John Hubbard, the American artist who has created its perfection, was content to work strictly within the limited frame of a medium-sized walled garden that stood on an already perfect bucolic setting of steep, dry fields below a copse, with a farm and a tiny chapel very close on one side of it. At the head of the walled garden stands the house, little more than a big, bare-faced, grey farmhouse with a lawn on its garden front already beginning to slope downwards (**83**). It tips its

83 *A bare-faced farmhouse at Chilcombe presides over a walled garden of subtle diversity where every few steps brings a change of emphasis, the hint of a feature flowing immediately and at a new level into another, always bucolic, attraction: Sticky Wicket without the sermons*

visitors into Hubbard's infinite variety of flower, fruit, hedge, vegetable and lawns by either one of two fixed entry points; for Chilcombe in a kindly, unobtrusive way is a very controlled and controlling garden. One entry is between two giant black yews, grown almost into an arch. This leads into the main downhill axis. The second slips visitors in on the east side into a backstairs route to the vegetables, but with distraction upon distraction on the way there.

Two cross axes cut through the two downhill ways. One, reached almost immediately, is a green terrace below yew hedges and walls. The second, half way down, will function, as the garden is walked, as the master stroke, the spine, from which everything depends. It is a narrow grassy way between two tall hedges of complexly woven beech, yew, holly and hawthorn, authoritatively yet softly patterned, opening in the middle and at either end to release a visitor upwards to the house, downwards to the rough final wall.

Those disciplining features should create seven gardens at the most. In fact the number of gardens within their framework reaches twelve and then counting ends in despair: the variety is bewildering; formality has been encouraged to run wild. In no kind of sequence, for there is no sequence, pear trees and a jasmine pergola shoulder you the moment the top terrace is left (**colour plate 23**). There is a potager invaded by dahlias and ordered by five brick and stone paths in the Peto manner, pillars of Irish yew and bay, balls of box, box hedges, a lush orchard heavy with fruit, a sundial lawn, a bank 'where the wild thyme grows', a stone seat before a box triangle. All are scattered in miniature dimensions up and down the levels; and at every point, while there are distractions of flowers at ground level, floral climbers are brushing the face and taking the eyes upwards. Nothing is ever open for long. The garden revels in being enclosed, yet two doors in the grey walls demand to be opened. They lead immediately onto sheep and lambs, the one flock gathered in a dusty farmyard beneath hawthorn bushes, the other out in the headlong fields to the west. This is essentially a cottage garden on a grand scale, but with nothing inside it ever allowed to become large or dominant except that double hedge and the two yews at entry.

The difference between a garden that delights and one that merely pleases is hard to define. It has something to do with a concentration of resources, a unity of impressions, and then again a feeling of commitment to surroundings, if only, as at Chilcombe, in a high-walled determination to keep those sheep out. That walls do help a garden to build up a memorable atmosphere is proven at Stepleton, where the excluded are not sheep, but motorists. The inner gardens at Stepleton House are enclosed by those high and infuriating brick walls that create the infamous Stepleton Bends on the A350 between Blandford Forum and Shaftesbury, four blind right-angled turns, driven usually behind a convey of limping lorries. But I no longer curse the bends or the walls now that I know the gardens hiding within the walls and hedges that line the tradesman's entrance drive. A post-1753 Turnpike Trust created bends, walls and gardens by closing the old direct route in front of the house. The 1820 Turnpike Commission made a Visitation to try to straighten them out,[5] but Horace Beckford, son of Peter Beckford the great huntsman, talked them out of it, perhaps by leading them up the brick path to see what they would have been spoiling.

Once through the shrub barrier behind Stepleton House there is a brief note of Italian formality with herms and tall straight hedges. But then, possibly echoing the streets and enclosures of a little village that died after the 1348 Black Death, a tangle of smaller gardens opens up enticingly to the right.[6] All this was a wilderness before the present owners, Mr and Mrs Coombs, took over. Stepleton is not strictly a late twentieth-century garden so much as an inspired late twentieth-century restoration of a 200-year-old garden on a 1,000-year-old base.

First comes a prodigy of unthemed flower beds which can lead in characteristic Stepleton topographical perplexity, back into Peter Beckford's old stable yard, now green and not remotely horsey. Second on the right leads into the flowery graveyard of the Saxo-Norman church, St Mary's. Now a consecrated garden building, it has the tomb of Peter Beckford and a frighteningly ghostly relief of Martha Lindsay, an Edwardian lady who died of tuberculosis; Francis Sicard carved it. One more enclosed garden on the right with a modern wooden seat then, unexpectedly, the lake, a widening of the Iwerne crossed on a creaking, shaking, wooden causeway a mere inch or two above the water level.[7] The Coombs commissioned Alan Mitchell to replant the banks, and upriver to the north the trees close in with a varied profile of yews, bamboos, willow and purple leafed cherry. One small island has the statue of a nymph (**84**). Downstream the lake tails past a huge Asiatic plane tree into sunlight and the Brownian park noticed in an earlier chapter.

As the causeway ends, a little brick path leads the way; the Coombs found it hidden under bushes and it directs visitors, Wizard of Oz-style, to a gate in the first of the three walled gardens that create the Bends. The first is a vast Queen

Anne-style garden divided into quarters by trellises of roses that lead to a round pond circled by rose beds and centred upon a three-tiered fountain.[8] To the left is a walled orchard, to the right greenhouses and a walled potager with seven-foot -high thistles and a parterre of giant lettuce. Faintly from over the walls comes the sound of anguished car horns and urgent gear changing. By my count that makes at least seven gardens in one. Somewhere in the wood there was a tear-shaped lakelet, but that has reverted to shrubbery.

The gardens at Melplash Court and at the Priory Hotel in Wareham are beautiful and various yet both, in my subjective appraisal, lack that concentration and commitment.

Eyebrows may be raised at the inclusion of the gardens of a hotel in an 'historic' listing, but the gardens of the Priory Hotel featured on Wareham town plans of 1770 and 1820.[9] *Country Life* gave them three pages in 1976[10] and since that time the ambitious proprietors have added garden enclosure to garden enclosure until, now, the perfectly kept and precisely labelled grounds include

84 *This nymph at Stepleton House stands on a lake island which has matured into a peninsula. Mr and Mrs Coombs have refreshed and revitalised a garden here of so many parts and directionless charms that it is impossible to attribute it to any one century*

ten separate gardens laid out alongside the quays of the tidal River Frome. Only the Priory Hotel's gardens, in all Dorset, can rival the immaculate turf of Melplash Court. There is a broad main lawn down to the river, planted inconsequentially with two half-related trees, a large rounded bay, an apple tree in beds of cyclamen and one dazzling flower patch. To its west side and dispersed among pleasant service buildings are an Office Garden against the unattractive ruins of the Carthusian Priory, a Boathouse and a Cottage Garden. All are well planted; there is a low, complex cascade artificially inducted between the first two but no feeling of distinct identities, only that of one garden room succeeding to another.

Down river to the east the gardens are larger, ablaze on my visit with dahlias and again distinct from one another in their boundaries, yet each with much the same atmosphere of postcard prettiness. The two exceptions to this are the Fountain Garden of low clipped yew hedges, seventeenth-century in style though, like all the other ten gardens, post-1970 in date, and the New Pond Garden with its sizeable reach of water, commanding pampas grass and ruddy bronze ranks of hydrangeas.

This last garden is satisfying because there is an acknowledged relation to water in it, a shadowing of the river a few yards away, and that is where the Priory gardeners have missed their opportunity. With the moored ranks of pleasure craft, the broad, slow river with patient fishermen and the flat heath beyond, these gardens have a memorably picturesque setting, yet they tend to turn their backs on the river, or simply to ignore it. There may be reasons for this, but more trees along the banks, some dramatising of the riverside steps, even perhaps a bold inlet from the river, one or all of these would have given the gardens that commitment to its environment which could have become poetic. One rough, wild riverine area might have helped; even so the garden alone would make a stay there pleasurable.

Melplash Court is even harder to absorb as its gardens are laid out on three streams, a lake, a pond, a Tudor house and undulating ground. Yet because of that unreal perfection of its turf and the unfailing brightness of its flowers it remains linked in the memory with the very different, bankside Priory Hotel gardens. Early Ordnance Survey maps show two avenues radiating away to the north and the north-west from the house across the park, with lawns and a Kitchen Garden at the back. It was Lady Diana Tiarks who laid out the bones of the present garden between 1950 and 1975. During an interregnum following her death it lapsed, but the present owners have, since 1984, restored it to a rare perfection.

If a garden is large, and Melplash gives at least the illusion of being large, it helps to be directed occasionally, but Melplash rarely directs. There is a grand chestnut avenue, interplanted with young lime trees, leading to the gravelled forecourt. From there the natural direction seems to be clockwise, starting with a pets' cemetery, a mini holocaust of Lady Diana's dogs, the stones presided over by a large stone urn in a spreading laurel clump. Then the uncertainties set in. Up steps to the right are ironwork gates and gate piers, and at the corner a tastefully genteel Edwardian Summerhouse, but a high wall conceals the Croquet

Lawn, so two small streams, barely trickles in the smooth grass slopes, lead more temptingly down between camelia bushes to a marshy pool by a Regency water hopper. These grounds are alive with neat little bridges. Given a length of water Lady Diana's would throw a wooden bridge across it. By the hopper a slightly more formidable streamlet flows out of a primula-planted, bog garden, and on its opposite bank is the one truly defining boundary of this largely open area: a hillside of flowering shrubs and trees climbed by several flights of wooden steps.

Here the Melplash garden nearly comes together where these bridges and steps and streams lead to a bend in the valley that has been 'Japan-ised' with a Metasequoia, a stone-arched bridge and a stone lantern. Then it loses direction again and this time the culprit is a septic tank. It has been camouflaged so determinedly that the bulging yew bushes and flowering shrubs that surround it have become the dominating feature of that side of the little valley nearest the house. Logically the way forward should be downstream and onward to the lake;[11] but the septic tank shrubbery lures one up into the back of the Oriental Garden, which should sequentially have been approached from the side of the house.

An oriental gentleman stands enigmatically on an almost, but not quite, daringly geometric garden of grass and golden stone rectangles (**85**). Their abstraction does nothing for his figurative orientalism and the four columnar yews that dramatise this space are anything but oriental.[12] Now, however, over a fern wall and at eye level, the Croquet Lawn can be viewed from its rear. Here the Melplash turf reaches a velvet smoothness so sheer that individual grass blades are quite lost. On either side equally accomplished herbaceous borders present galardias and Michaelmas daisies. There are no surprises here, but Lady Diana's seat, a stone cabin with a stone table, has charm, and up steps, through that elegantly upper class insistence of wrought ironwork that enmeshes Melplash, is the three-star attraction of the grounds, the Walled Potager so bright and adventurous in its colour combinations of red rhubarb stalks, yellow daisies and clustered herbs, that it transcends the general affluent gentility of the place.

Neatness and tidiness in gardens is a subjective, personal quality. To me the lush growth and face-fondling bushes of Chilcombe were mature perfection, but I spoke with one Dorset gardener who thought it had passed its best. Melplash needs a truly 'wild' garden. That top pond near the forecourt could be assimilated, and then the whole potentially delightful sweep of the grounds could be given a fallow year with very little attention. It has one of the most handsome pigeon cotes in the county and that too could become a focus for imaginative treatment. Melplash is a demonstration of the perverse truth that brilliant flowers and a plushy greensward are virtually an irrelevance to making a memorable garden. A visit to Dean's Court, Wimborne Minster, would prove the point: rough grass and hardly a flower in sight, but such an atmosphere.

It may be a politically incorrect pronouncement, but women gardeners seem generally to have a much better eye for the beauty of the unkempt in gardens than men do. That compliment makes an ideal introduction to the gardens of

85 *An oriental priest stands with witty incongruity on a formal terrace of immaculate turf above the Japanese stream garden at Melpash Court*

the Coach House, Bettiscombe, for this is where Penelope Hobhouse, rightly styled 'the doyenne of Dorset gardeners', even though her move over from Somerset is fairly recent, has made what she says is going to be her last garden. It was Mrs Hobhouse who should originally have been writing this book, but she stepped aside and gave me the happy opportunity; so when I visited the Coach House one radiantly blue September morning I was properly deferential. She is one of this country's leading gardeners, equally influential in, and influenced by, America, where she has designed and regularly lectures.

Before even ringing the doorbell I had been bowled over by the astonishingly well-composed profile of Sliding Hill, which dominates her front garden to the north-east. Penelope has not attempted to compete with that view; all her north garden lawns, conical yews and four long hornbeam hedges are directed downhill towards it: a green frame lightened by stainless steel arches at its interconnections. These daring arches are intended to reflect the moonlight at night: an inspired notion which, however, I could not stay long enough to experience.

Exploration of the avenues would come later, in the meantime I was too early. Penelope was picking a vase-full of flowers, a concentration of the soft pinks, whites and yellows prevailing in the Walled Garden at the back of the house: a south-facing, enclosed private area that flows down to the sheer glass walls of the garden-sitting room. The walled garden is awesomely professional: a second Chilcombe in one sense, but rising upwards instead of falling downhill, and all to be taken in from the garden room rather than as a series of visual discoveries. It offers a symphony of subdued colours over an underlying discipline of gravel paths and topiary shapes and all, despite it being a mere nine years old, looking as if it has been maturing for fifty. The effect is almost wild, just gently restrained from a Havershamesque tangle. Along every path, branches or flower fronds brush the face. In October it must be threaded with drifting spiders' webs. At every yard there is an engaging incident: a towering silver thistle, a copper urn full of blue-lyme grass and geraniums, an arch of dangling dark pink roses that, on inspection, are not roses at all, a terracotta pot lurching sideways, giant fennel and elegant grasses browning down now to seed heads.

At the end of two seasons of intense Dorset garden visiting it was intriguing how echoes of other gardens came through; here was the foun-tainhead of ideas. The edges of the gravel paths were never visible for the perennials, nepeta and alchemilla, were on their self-seeding march. If autumn goes on too long, as our climate warms up, one morning they will be crowding against the great glass windows as Penelope eats her breakfast. But she will be ruthless. Already she has prepared her garden's doom watch. As she grows older and weeding becomes a chore she means to clear away the flowers and let the topiary, the yews, the box, the hornbeams and the *robinia pseudoacacias* take over. It will become an Italian garden of statuesque green shapes, a stoic vision out of Virgil. Then the shallow rectangle of water in the centre of it will become the relief and the keynote.

This has not been an easy garden to make. Water is scarce at the top and over-present in the stiff clays at the bottom where, on her avenues, hornbeam give up and alder has to take over. That explains why, in the front garden, there is no cascade running down to lighten the firm strokes of the hedges. Instead there is a canal, two-thirds of the way down, traversing the contours in a stainless steel basin, an east-west horizontal against the prevailing south-north verticals (**colour plate 25**). It is an uneasy feature and characteristically Penelope has flaunted its defiance of the axis by planting a cleverly composed group of gunnera and bamboo at just one end of the canal, a fierce asymmetry that challenges acceptance.

Behind these south-north hedges are hidden a billowing hedge of sweet peas and all the vegetable plots. Not for Penelope the artful potagers of Prince Charles at Highgrove or Rosemary Verey at Barnsley with their peony and peas confusion. Her front garden is single-mindedly for the view of Sliding Hill by day and mirrored moonshine by night. Real professionals have visions and project them. To the north her hedges will mature, to the south in that sunny walled garden the flowers will fade away, the topiary will take over and she, 'unburdened', like King Lear, will 'creep towards death'. A garden can and should reflect the human spirit of its creator.

I was expecting three stars from Bettiscombe in the lush remote west of the county. Bloxworth House by its mere name depressed the spirit, and from the map seemed to lie in that tedious heathland of east Dorset, which Thomas Hardy predictably took to his gloomy heart and that, in the twentieth century, has very appropriately been used for tanks to churn around on. To lower expectations even further, the Dorset Gardens Trust survey, an admirably thorough analysis by Mrs J. Bloxom, enclosed colour photographs taken as recently as March 1997. These showed the 1608 Jacobean brick house in near dereliction, rubbish and lank grass outside the late seventeenth-century Brewhouse and stumpy yew pyramids on threadbare lawns in the Courtyard Garden. To cap it all, Pevsner and Newman dismissed Bloxworth House as 'a somewhat nerveless building'.[13]

One of the golden surprises of my Dorset travels was to drive down from the hamlet of Newport, north of Bloxworth, into an enchanted hollow of order and garden inventions, where the manor house, a picture of careful restoration, stood demanding to be admired with a formal canal in front of it and terraces of gardens, pergolas and vernacular service buildings of ingeniously rusticated brick heaped up behind it. On the hill, fine trees were showing a mere hint of autumn colour around a brand new wooden garden pavilion. Best of all there was not a hint of that long-suffering scrubland that characterises the Dorset heaths. The hollow was lush, green, fertile and well wooded. Martin Lane-Fox, the new owner, like Penelope Hobhouse a professional garden designer, had clearly spent a fortune on the place and effected an amazing transformation.

The nature of that transformation began to take shape by the building next to the gravel sweep, a tall wooden granary, painted white. It has been fronted by a big square of golden gravel, hard-edged stuff; planted across it in regimented diagonal lines are hundreds of small lavender bushes, herbal geometry of a quite aggressive nature. Fronting the amiable, ambling brick façade of the house, where just five years ago the field grass came right up to the walls, is a terrace, golden gravel again, but bordered in with precise box hedges and planted with eight box pyramids. Most riveting of all is the long limestone-rimmed canal (**colour plate 26**) that now centres that relaxed elevation, slicing ruthlessly across a huge wild flower meadow away to the right under a line of trees. To make that alien canal even more disturbing it has been flanked with even more alien lines of umbrella pines, the Mediterranean in an overwhelmingly English meadow.

That was only the start of the work that Martin put into Bloxworth. The house, for all its decrepitude, was blessed with service buildings of rich character and real architectural distinction. Now they are set in gardens of equal distinction. In the cloister of the stable block, a big, full-length, blue swimming pool has been reduced to half the size, made clear and black, given two cascades and set around with poisonous, languorous trumpets of Datura flowers, while the cloister arches have been lined with chimneypots. The effect is water-loud, pleasantly claustrophobic, deliberately unsettling. Martin's influences are Harold Peto and Russell Page. The Peto effect comes over in an insistence upon structure through hard landscaping: pebbled, bricked or stony surrounds to as many features, bushes, flower beds, paths, as possible. The eye is always being caught downwards as one walks Bloxworth, down into a hard, coloured geometry that responds to the brick patterning of vernacular patterning around doors and windows.

While the front of the house is that simplicity of wild meadow and harsh canal, the back premises are a maze of levels, steps, terraces and sudden vistas. The Courtyard Garden to the rear has gone dry and is gravelled with paving stone paths and hesitant flowers. Up a flight of steps is a brick terrace patterned with grey stone diamonds, gravel filled. The young trees are rayed about with stone patterns (**86**). An arch through the Brewhouse leads to a striking stone classical bust on a pedestal. Highest of all is the Pumphouse Terrace where hornbeams are growing up two parallel trellis works, with a long lawn between brick paths leading to a wrought iron gate, a rare cliché. A white cherub throws up the black arch spaces of the Pumphouse admirably.

Nothing in this new Bloxworth is tentative. An obelisk stands at the edge of the wood to focus views from the drawing room. Stone steps lead up the hill to that new pavilion with its bird's eye views of all that has been achieved. The Walled Garden which, seven years ago, was mellow with creepers and had a big yew overhanging its walls, now stands like a glaring white rectangle meshed with

86 *Bloxworth House, in its recent transformation by Martin lane-Fox, is a garden where visitors are always looking down; partly because terrace succeeds terrace on a steep slope, partly because of the intense patterning at ground level, as here on the Upper Terrace*

wires for new climbers. The yew has gone and inside there is a tennis court and an unfinished mount with a stoneflagged cross laid flat upon its summit awaiting a statue or urn.

This is too early to pass judgement on the garden at Bloxworth. I suspect it may become one of the most praised gardens of the new century. A stony vision has been imposed upon it with breathtaking confidence and it delights as often as it surprises, which is very often indeed. That carpet of wild meadow flowers must be wonderful in high summer; in low autumn it was literally seedy. Pam Lewis of Sticky Wicket would have approved it as an abundant harvest ground for her wild creatures. Water has been handled in a masterly way at Bloxworth, clear and dark and full of lilies or, in the stable court, equally clear and dark but inviting as a cold plunge pool in the eighteenth-century manner. The Walled Garden will quieten down as the bright render is covered with flowering climbers. It was a privilege to see it in its raw adolescence. Dorset almost lost a remarkable house; now that house is secure in a garden of rare excellence.

Bloxworth could easily have been the hopeful, even triumphant conclusion to this final chapter. Instead here, to end, is one last historic garden that, if my information is correct, no one is likely to see again as the collection which made it so strange has been dispersed. Like some acclaimed Stratford production of *Richard III*, you had to catch it while the performance was on.

My visit to Woolland and the Elizabeth Frink sculpture park was part of a Thirties Society's Dorset outing. We had travelled from the Bliss house, Pen Pits in Penslewood, into that tight knot of downland that ties together into Bulbarrow Hill. The semi-circular three-storey house with its adjoining studio was some preparation for the strangeness of the statues, but not much. Bronze Indian buffalos lay thoughtfully or stood threateningly by a pool. On one flat area of mingled grass and paving stones patient bronze hounds were waiting. At right-angles to them on stone plinths was a row of fierce Frink heads, her trademark, loutish and uncouth, spattered with bird droppings, and on a bench a bronze man, more Neanderthal than Cro-Magnon, sat alert, prepared it seemed for a hostile confrontation. None of these were as worrying as the meeting, in a grassy glade between the huge stump of a severed beech tree and some slim conifers, with a group of white-faced, naked grey men, striding purposefully towards us like so many Stigs of the Dump, but to what purpose would never be revealed (**colour plate 24**).

It was all, as Frink would have wished, enigmatic and unresolved, not at all Dorset, but a learning experience in appreciation. After Woolland it was like meeting an old, rather formidable friend to come across another huge grey Frink head, lowering across the early spring flowers, in the gardens of Cranborne Manor. It seemed perfectly appropriate to a county of gardens which are always taking me by surprise, the playgrounds of a society whose social structures, reactions and relationships I have found every bit as enigmatic and, at times, as threatening as any of Elizabeth Frink's naked apemen.

Gazetteer

The following is a list of gardens of significant historic importance which are covered in this book and are open to the public.

Abbreviations

NT	National Trust
EH	English Heritage
P	Privately owned, but regularly open
NGS	Privately owned, but open occasionally as part of the National Gardens Scheme
H	Hotel
LA	Local Authority
AC	Agricultural College

Abbotsbury (P)

Athelhampton House, Puddletown (P)

Boveridge Park, Cranborne (NGS)

Bridehead, Little Bredy (P)

Brownsea Island, Poole Harbour (NT)

Compton Acres, Poole (P)

Cranborne Manor House (P)

Deans Court, Wimborne (NGS)

Durlston Country Park, Swanage (LA)

Forde Abbey, Chard (P)

Highcliffe Castle, Christchurch (LA)

Kingston Lacy, Wimborne (NT)

Kingston Maurward House, Dorchester (AC)

Lulworth Castle, East Lulworth (EH)

Mapperton, Beaminster (P)

Melplash Court (NGS)

Milton Abbey, Milton Abbas (S)

Minterne, Minterne Magna (P)

Old Rectory, Litton Cheney (NGS)

Old Rectory, Pulham (NGS)

Plumber Manor, Sturminster Newton (H)

Priest's House, Wimborne Minster (P)

The Priory, Wareham (H)

Sandford Orcas Manor House (P)

Sherborne Castle (P)

Sherborne Old Castle (EH)

Smedmore, Kimmeridge (NGS)

Springhead, Fontmell Magna (NGS)

Steeple Manor House, Wareham (NGS)

Sticky Wicket, Buckland Newton (P)

Wolfeton House, Charminster (P)

Notes

Introduction

1. In Sir Roy Strong's introduction to the issue: *Garden History*, vol.27, no.1 (Summer, 1999), p.7.
2. Dorset Record Office, D72/4 'Castle Hill Sale Particulars and Maps, 26 August 1845'. These particulars record that the main house was 'designed in 1764 by Sir William Chambers, the modern Vitruvius'. They record the 'Carpenter's Shop' as being to the rear of the house, the present location of the building.

1 A Renaissance garden for a Howard

1. *Royal commission on Historical Monuments: south-east Dorset (hereafter referred to as RCHM)*, vol.2, pt.2, (1970), p.408
2. For Lulworth see Jean Manco, David Greenhalf & Mark Girouard, 'Lulworth Castle in the seventeenth century', *Architectural History*, vol.33 (1990), pp.29–59; Jean Manco & Francis Kelly, 'Lulworth Castle from 1700', *Architectural History*, vol.34 (1991), pp.145–170.
3. Hutchins, *Dorset*, 1815, 1, p.130.
4. Dorset Record Office, D/WLC/E145.
5. As in the antiquary, John Carter's *The Ancient Architecture of England*, 1795–1814.
6. Conyers Read, *Lord Burghley and Queen Elizabeth*, 1960, p.123. For further information on Theobalds see Roy Strong, *The Renaissance Garden in England*, 1979, pp.51–6. For other Tudor and Elizabethan gardens see *Garden History*, vol.27, no.1 (Summer, 1999).
7. For Hatfield see Strong, *Renaissance Garden*, pp.103–10; the lozenge-shaped island is pl.59.
8. *Ibid.*, p.107.
9. Howard Colvin (ed.), *A History of the King's Works*, vol.4, pt.2, 1983, p.277, describing the gardens at Hatfield.
10. Strong, *Renaissance Garden*, p.53.
11. Some accounts mention a Calvary on the mount. That would have been a very Weldian garden feature.
12. Hutchins, *Dorset*, 1815, 1, p.130 quotes a report that in 1550 Lord Bindon's house had a chapel with vestments and an altar cloth for Catholic ritual.
13. Dorset Record Office, D/WLC/P76.
14. Dorset Record Office, D/WLC/P77.
15. Dorset Record Office, D/WLC/AF27–32.
16. Nikolaus Pevsner & John Newman, *The Buildings of England: Dorset*, 1972, p.94; the chapel is illustrated on pl.87.
17. Cresswell's plan is illustrated in Hutchins, *Dorset*, 1774, 1, between pages 176–7.
18. Dorset Record Office, D1/LX 8/2.
19. Compiled for the Dorset Gardens Trust in 1999 by Mrs Dowse & Mrs Andrews.

2 Jacobean enclosures and a Baroque precursor

1. The garden and house at Wilton are described in detail in Timothy Mowl & Brian Earnshaw, *Architecture Without Kings: The rise of puritan classicism under Cromwell* (Manchester, 1995), pp.31–47.
2. *The Camden Miscellany*, XVI (1936), pp.38–9; p.71. For a full quotation of Hammond's description of Lulworth see *Architectural History*, vol.33 (1990), p.50.
3. This is the façade of the grotto house, which was subsequently built as a front to a garden pavilion, now converted into a house, in a private part of Wilton's grounds. There are also several original statues, now in different locations around the estate; see John Bold, *Wilton House and English Palladianism*, 1988.
4. Dorset County Record Office, D/WLC/T5: purchase of lands adjoining Lulworth by Suffolk in April 1608.
5. *Historical Manuscripts Commission 9*: Salisbury (Cecil) MSS, vol.20 (1968), p.204.
6. Dorset Record Office, D/WLC/E99.
7. The local antiquary, Thomas Gerard of Trent, writing in about 1624. It is quoted in the Revd Coker, *A Particular Survey of the County of Dorset*, 1732, p.43.
8. Strong, *Renaissance Garden*, p.104.
9. Dorset Record Office, D/WLC/M71.
10. Dorset Record Office, D/WLC M71(3). My attention was drawn to this record in crabbed 'Secretary's' hand by Joan Berkeley, *Lulworth and the Welds* (Gillingham, 1971), p.28.
11. Dorset Record Office, D/WLC/T7.

12. For the prevalence of these forecourt gardens in the latter half of the seventeenth century see Timothy Mowl, 'John Drapentier's Views of the Gentry Gardens of Hertfordshire', *Garden History*, vol.29, 2 (Winter, 2001), pp.152-170.
13. Dorset Record Office, D/WLC/C4(b).
14. Published in Joseph Smith's *Nouveau Theatre de la Grande Bretagne*, 1726, vol.IV.
15. Buck's engraving was not published until 1774 in his *Antiquities*, vol.1, p.75.
16. The two maps, preserved at Hatfield, are discussed by Paula Henderson: 'Maps of Cranborne Manor in the Seventeenth Century', *Architectural History*, vol.44 (2001), pp.358-64.
17. *Dictionary of National Biography.*
18. When it came to be built the loggia was a mere three arches wide, but it would have suited the scale of the house better with the originally projected four.
19. Robert Cecil's private life is strangely unrecorded, but he spent three or four years in France when he could easily have made a tour of Italy.
20. Christopher Morris (ed.), *The illustrated Journeys of Celia Fiennes c.1682-c.1712*, 1982, pp.66-7.
21. Howard Colvin, *A Biographical Dictionary of British Architects 1600-1840*, 1995, p.298.
22. *Ibid.*, p.298.
23. Quoted in R.E.W. Maddison, *The Life of Robert Boyle*, 1969, p.55.
24. *Ibid.*, p.55.
25. The drawing is illustrated in Hutchins, *Dorset*, 1816, 3, p.676.
26. Hutchins, *Dorset*, 1816, 3, p.674.
27. *Ibid.*
28. Maddison, *Robert Boyle*, p.57.
29. For garden games and bowls in particular see Gervase Markham, *Countrey Contentments, or the Husbandman's Recreation*, 1633.
30. Hutchins, *Dorset*, 1816, 3, p.674.
31. For Raleigh's work at Sherborne see *RCHM: West Dorset*, 1952, pp.64-6. There are no estate records prior to the eighteenth century.
32. The opening lines of Sir Walter Raleigh's 'The Passionate Man's Pilgrimage – Supposed to be written by one at the point of death.'
33. Dorset Record Office, D/F5 1A/16: 'Maps of Melbury'.
34. Also for the greater part of the last 200 years Hammoon served as the local rectory.

3 Luxury and intolerable expense

1. John Harris & Gervase Jackson-Stops (eds), *Britannia Illustrata or Views of Several of the Queens Palaces also of the Principal Seats of the Nobility and Gentry of Great Britain*, 1707 (facsimile edition, 1984).
2. The book was aimed at sales in the French book market as an assertion of Great Britain's European cultural status.
3. From an advert in the *Post Boy* of 31 May 1710 it seems that Knyff required a subscription of £10 for each view taken.
4. All except the gatehouse, which has been re-erected on the Wareham road.
5. The Woodward plan is illustrated in Anthony Mitchell, *Kingston Lacy* (National Trust, 1998), p.83. The information on Sir Ralph's formal garden is taken from this source.
6. *Ibid.*, p.83.
7. The inscription reads in full: 'Under this roof, in the year MDCLXXXVI, a set of Patriotic Gentlemen of this neighbourhood concerted the Great Plan of the Glorious Revolution with the Immortal King William; to whom we owe our Deliverance from Popery and Slavery, the Expulsion of the Tyrant Race of the Stuarts the Restoration of our Liberty, the Security of our Property, and the Establishment of National Honour. Englishmen, remember this Glorious Era, and consider that your Liberties procured by the Vertues of your Ancestors must be maintained by yourselves.' See Jonathan Holt, *Discover Dorset: Follies* (Wimborne, 2000), p.24.
8. National Monuments Record: 'Oil Painting of Earlier House' (CC71/1292) and '18th Century Oil Painting, Charborough House' (CC77/1293).
9. A painting of Waddon before the fire is reproduced in *Country Life*, 14 November 1931.
10. See the aforementioned *Country Life* article for the piers before transformation.
11. Dorset Record Office, D/SHE 22.
12. From an uncatalogued plan of about 1651 in the Muniment Room of St Giles' House, Wimborne St Giles.
13. Dorset Record Office, D/WLC P84(F): 'A Plan of the Wilderness 28 August 1723'.
14. See John Harris, 'The Artinatural Style', in Charles Hind (ed.), *The Rococo in England*, 1986, pp.8-20.
15. Dorset Record Office, D/WLC P84(F): 'A draught for ye Greenhouse'.
16. Dorset Record Office, D/WLC P85(F). In addition to this there is, in D/WLC P84(F), an attractive undated design of four parterres arranged around a square garden house and linked to each other by steps, as if sited for a terrace. Again, as usual with Lulworth at this time, nothing was done.

17. Hutchins, *Dorset*, 3, 1813, p.272.
18. *Ibid*.
19. Sir James lived a few miles away at Thornhill Park, near Stalbridge, and could easily have obliged his Phelips neighbour with a design.
20. To be strictly accurate this is only an attribution to Archer, and the garden bench inside it has suspect late nineteenth-century Beaux Arts details.
21. The Hutchins view is illustrated in Legg, *Dorset Families*, p.133.
22. For an account of his work see Geoffrey & Susan Jellicoe, *The Landscape of Man*, 1975, plates 230-4. Jellicoe worked here in the late 1930s.
23. For Horton see Jonathan Holt, *Discover Dorset: Follies*, pp.34-5; also Gwyn Headley & Wim Meulenkamp, *Follies, Grottoes & Garden Buildings*, 1999, pp.205-6.
24. Bodleian Library, MS. Gough Drawings, a 3, f.10.
25. J. Cartwright (ed.), 'The Travels through England of Dr Richard Pococke 1750-57', *Camden Society*, 2 vols. (1888-9), 2, p.140.
26. From 'Autumn', lines 654-8.
27. For the Prideaux sketches see John Harris, 'The Prideux Collection of Topographical Drawings', *Architectural History*, vol.7 (1963), pp.19-108. See also Penelope Hobhouse, 'The Gardens of Forde Abbey', *Dorset Gardens Trust Newsletter*, no.17 (Summer, 2001), pp.11-14.
28. A letter of 14 July 1732 (British Library, Add. mss. 51386) from the Duchess to Susannah reveals that Susannah and her daughter Elizabeth had escaped the Horners and were indulging in a Grand Tour of Italy. The Duchess was scheming to marry off Elizabeth to Stephen Fox, the future Lord Ilchester. A few months later, on 1 March 1733, the bold women had got as far south as Naples where Susannah was worried about earthquakes. Stephen would marry Elizabeth in 1735.
29. Dorset Record Office, D/FS1 188: 'grubbing trees etc. in Great Aisle in the wood 80 feet width'.
30. Paget Toynbee (ed.), 'Horace Walpole's Journals of Visits to Country Seats etc.', The *Walpole Society*, vol.16 (1927-8), pp.9-80; p.48.
31. Among the many helpful informants met during the course of my researchs and garden walking, Andy Poore has been a quite outstanding guide and scholarly source.
32. Dorset Record Office, D/F5 1A/16: 'Maps of Melbury'.

4 'The horrid graces of the *Wilderness*'

1. George Sherburn (ed.), *The Correspondence of Alexander Pope*, 4 vols. (Oxford, 1956), 2, p.237.
2. *Ibid*., p.239.
3. Apparently the 'Rustick Seat' that Pope refers to was already known locally as 'The Hermit's Cell'. A cult in hermits goes back to the medieval period in England.; see Isabel Colegate, *A Pelican in the Wilderness: hermits, solitaries and recluses*, 2002.
4. The plan is unsigned and undated, but must date to before 1754 when the gardens were demolished during the creation of the lake. A further plan of 1733 by John Ladd shows the gardens, though in less detail. This last is illustrated in Janet Waymark, 'Sherborne, Dorset', *Garden History*, vol.29, no.1 (Summer, 2001), pp.64-81; figure 2. The layout of the formal garden is helpfully annotated in Peter E. Martin, 'Intimations of the New Gardening: Alexander Pope's Reaction to the "Uncommon" Landscape at Sherborne', *Garden History*, vol.4, no.1 (Spring, 1976), pp.57-87. Figure 1.
5. Sherburn, *Correspondence*, 2, p.238.
6. *Ibid*., pp.238-9.
7. Although Mrs Ann Smith, the Sherborne Curator and Archivist, tells me that remains of terraces can sometimes be detected near the lakeside below the New Castle, which Brown appears to have retained but smoothed out.
8. British Library, Add. MS. 51340. I am indebted to Ann Smith for this reference.
9. For Kent's garden buildings see John Dixon Hunt, *William Kent: Landscape Garden Designer*, 1987.
10. The Shell House is about to undergo restoration and is not accessible to the public.
11. I am most grateful to Anne Andrews for sharing her ongoing reseaches into the Shell House with me.
12. Information from Anne Andrews.
13. Parallels with Mrs Delany's 1740-50 grotto work and to the Shell House at Goodwood Park, Sussex (1730s) have been made by Christine Stones in an unpublished Archaeological Report on the building for the Bristol University MA in Garden History (2002). See also: Ruth Hayden, *Mrs Delany: Her life and her flowers*, 1980.
14. For the Rococo style see Timothy Mowl & Brian Earnshaw, *An Insular Rococo: Architecture, Politics and Society in Ireland and England 1720-1770*, 1999.
15. The gardens are strictly private and I am most grateful to Lord Shaftesbury for permission to walk the grounds and to Hazel Garrick for her help and advice with the archives.
16. *Characteristicks*, 1732, 3, p.344. Philocles has persuaded his friend Theocles to express in a mood of inspiration 'those Divine Thoughts which meet you ever in this Solitude'.

17. *Ibid.* 'We are on the most beautiful part of the Hill' Philocles exclaims, and Shaftesbury is clearly referring to the view across the Chase from the Philosopher's Tower. This small brick building was the source and fountain head from which eighteenth-century Deism and then the entire Romantic Movement flowed. In a well educated country it would be a place of national pilgrimage like Shakespeare's Birthplace.

18. *Ibid.*, p.388. One section of his *Characteristicks* is actually entitled: 'The Moralists, A Rhapsody'.

19. Interestingly there had been a Wilderness in the 1st Earl's park. It is shown on William Palmer's 1659 'A Description of the Manours of Wimborne St Giles & Wimborne All Saints', and on a 1672 plan, both preserved at the house. This last records four enclosures on the garden front: 'Garden', 'Court', 'Bowling greene' and 'Wilderness'.

20. 'A Map of the Manors & Parishes of Wimborne St Giles . . . the property of The Earl of Shaftesbury'.

21. F/C/1: Shaftesbury Papers 1237-1854 (4th Earl's Correspondence): 'Barretts Bill for the Castle in his Garden 64.11.0'. This was on the island and has now disappeared, but the companion archway is mentioned in the same accounts: 'To The Great Arch'. Other craftsmen noted are: William Knott, Matthew Ball and Morgan Singleton.

22. *Camden Society*, 2, pp.137-8.

23. Bea Howe, *Country Life*, 4 June 1959: 'A Shell Grotto Restored'.

24. F/C/1 Shaftesbury papers 1237-1845 (4th Earl's Correspondence): Letter from William Beckford of 25 May 1749: 'to send the Shells mentioned in your Memorandum'; Letter from William Beckford of 9 July 1749: '2 casks of Tamarinds on the Caesar, Templer', a third of the shells 'on the Happy Return'. For the grotto building connection between Beckford and the 4th Earl see Timothy Mowl, 'Inside Beckford's Landscape of the Mind', *Country Life*, 7 February 2002.

25. John Harris, *Sir William Chambers, Knight of the Polar Star*, 1970, dates Duntish to 1760, the date given uncertainly by Hutchins. It is more likely to have been designed, as the 1845 sale particulars record, in 1764, later, therefore, than Chambers' work at Duddingston House, Midlothian (1763-8). See my comments on the Summerhouse in the Introduction and later in this chapter.

26. For the Lanes' work at Fonthill see *Country Life*, 7 February 2002 and Timothy Mowl, *William Beckford: Composing for Mozart*, 1998, pp.35-6 and plates 5-7. See also Christopher Thacker, *Masters of the Grotto: Joseph and Josiah Lane* (Tisbury, 1976).

27. They devoted their attention to its rear fenestration, a survival of the Tudor house demolished by Chambers: see *RCHM: County of Dorset*, 3, part 1, p.50.

28. See Harris, *Chambers*, pp.206-7.

29. Hutchins, *Dorset*, 1774, 2, p.357.

30. For Southcote and Shenstone see Timothy Mowl, *Gentlemen and Players: Gardeners of the English Landscape* (Stroud, 2000), Chapter Ten.

31. The 1767 Tomkins oil painting from which the engraving for Hutchins was taken is preserved in the house. I am much indebted to Richard Prideaux-Brune for alerting me to the existence of the painting and for allowing me to reproduce an illustration of it on the back cover of this book. Tomkins was also commissioned to paint the Manor Farm at Winterborne Clenston and Sir George Morton's house at Milborne St Andrew, the latter featuring a formal canal; see *Country Life*, 26 July 1962.

32. Devon Record Office, Ph. 663/KR2.

33. See Oswald, *Dorset Houses*, pp.156-7 for this confusing and unresolved episode.

34. Dorset Record Office, D1/2693A: 1726 Petition from the Mayor of Poole recording that the Castle had been given in 1724 by Benjamin Benson to his brother William, 'who conveyed same into a dwelling house'.

35. See Anna Eavis, 'The Avarice and Ambition of William Benson', *Georgian Group Journal*, 2002, pp.8-37.

36. Hutchins, *Dorset*, 1774, 1, p.219.

37. *Ibid.*

38. Dorset Record Office, D263/E1: 'Certificate of Improvements by Sir Humphrey Sturt', dated 11 August 1817 and written by lawyers to justify a claim for compensation.

5 From garden to park

1. For gate lodges see Timothy Mowl & Brian Earnshaw, *Trumpet at a Distant Gate: The Lodge as Prelude to the Country House*, 1985.

2. The bronze was brought into the garden early in the twentieth century by the father of the present owner, Selina Gibson-Fleming.

3. The Hutchins engraving shows what could be a grotto on the approaches to the bridge from the wider park. If this was ever built it has since totally disappeared.

4. Dorset Record Office, D/C00.E, bundle 1. It was written in an attempt to persuade the Government to build a fort to defend Encombe from a possible French attack.

5. Its only dating is by a painting at the house which features men wearing the three-cornered hats which went out of fashion in about 1776.

6. Ann Smith, 'Sherborne Castle: from Tudor Lodge to Country House. New evidence from the archives', *The Local Historian*, vol.25, no.4 (November, 1995), pp.231-41; p.233.

7. The Agent, William Burnet, supervised the work during which two labourers drowned: Smith, *Local Historian*, p.233.

8. For views of the park and further information on Brown's work at Sherborne see Ann Smith, *Country Life*, 6 July 1995.

9. Smith, *Local Historian*, p.238 quoting Game Books for November 1766.

10. *Ibid.*, p.237.

11. Janet Waymark, 'Sherborne, Dorset', *Garden History*, vol.29, no.1 (Summer, 2001), pp.64-81; Appendix A, p.79 for a detailed account.

12. *Ibid.*, p.71.

13. *Ibid.*, Appendix B, pp.79-80.

14. *Ibid.*, plate VII. The artist was a natural son of Admiral Robert Digby who was creating a similar garden on a smaller scale at Minterne.

15. *Ibid.*, figures 9 & 12.

16. A map of 1767 (Winchester College Muniments, 21379) shows nothing but straight avenues south and, across the road, to the west. Another map (Dorset Record Office, D/ASH B P4: 'Plan of Admiral Digby's Leasehold Land' (no date), shows the same.

17. Dorothy Stroud, *Capability Brown*, 1950, p.81, dates Brown's first contract vaguely to 1763-70. It has not survived, but was for over £1,000 and included seeding the lawns with 1,120lbs of Dutch clover seed.

18. Pevsner & Newman, *Dorset*, p.294.

19. Harris, *Chambers*, p.61.

20. *Ibid.*, p.60, quoting a letter of 7 April 1773 from Chambers to Lord Damer: 'I have therefore sent a plan of a part of the intended Village & and Elevation'.

21. See Giles Worsley, 'Highcliffe Castle, Dorset', *Country Life*, 22 May 1986.

22. Roger Turner, *Capability Brown and the Eighteenth-Century Landscape*, 1985, p.178.

23. *Ibid.*, p.178.

24. Bodleian Library, Eng. Misc. d.579, f.48. I owe this and other references to the Gilpin-Barrington correspondence to Stephanie Macdonald.

25. *Ibid.*, ff.58-9.

26. *Country Life,* 24 April & 8 May 1942.

27. Turner, *Capability Brown*, p.178.

28. See Fiona Cowell, 'Richard Woods (?1716-93)', parts 1, 2 & 3, *Garden History*, vol.14, no.2 (Autumn, 1986), pp.85-119; vol.15, no.1 (Spring, 1987), pp.19-54; vol.15, no.2 (Autumn, 1987), pp.115-35. For his work at Lulworth see Spring, 1987, p.25.

29. The house, designed by John Crunden, is illustrated in the 1774 edition of Hutchins, but it was demolished before 1815.

30. He published the classic *Thoughts upon Hare and Fox Hunting* in 1781.

31. L. Smith in an unpublished 1989 dissertation on Stepleton for Bournemouth University attributes the lodges to Peter Beckford (p.46), and, therefore, all the Brownian improvements.

32. Rodney Legg, *Dorset Families* (Tiverton, 2002), p.140 claims that this involved demolishing redundant thatched cottages. I have not been able to verify this.

33. W.H. Bond, *Thomas Hollis, a Whig and his Books* (Cambridge, 1990). I am indebted to Dilly Hobson, who lives at Harvard Farm, and Patrick Eyres for information on Hollis.

34. *Ibid.*, p.153.

35. Dorset Record Office, D1/MO3: 'Plans of the Estate situate in the Parishes of Corscombe and Halstock in Dorsetshire belonging to Thomas Brand Hollis Esq. Of the Hyde, Essex. Surveyed by John Doyley, 1799.'

36. Dorset Record Office, PL 516: 'Hayman family memoir'.

37. For an account of Thomas Hollis' medals see Patrick Eyres' two articles: 'Patriotizing, Strenuously, the Whole Flower of his Life. The Political Agenda of Thomas Hollis' Medallic Programme', *The Medal*, no.36 (2000), pp.8-23, and 'Celebration and Dissent: Thomas Hollis, The Society of Arts, and Stowe Gardens', *The Medal*, no.38 (2001), pp.31-50.

6 Picturesque to Gardenesque

1. When Repton visited Stafford the place was called Frome House, 'A Seat of Nicholas Gould, Esq.': *Fragments on the Theory and Practice of Landscape Gardening*, 1816, Fragment XXI, pp.101-5. Repton's consultation probably dates to 1805 when Nicholas Gould came into the property; see *Country Life*, 22 & 29 March 1962.

2. *Ibid.*, p.104. Repton was conveniently forgetting that, in the first years of his practice at, for instance, Garnons and Stoke Edith in Herefordshire, he had suggested just such bald naked parks.

3. *Ibid.*, p.213.

4. *Ibid.*, p.105.

5. For this possibility see the Nicholas Pearson Associates survey of August 1994: 'Bridehead & Little Bredy: Historic Landscape Survey and Restoration Plan'. I am grateful to Sir Philip Williams for lending me his copy of the report.

6. Pevsner & Newman, *Dorset*, p.254; but to be fair they also write of an 'exquisite landscaped park'.

7. P.F. Robinson, *Rural Architecture; or a Series of Designs for Ornamental Cottage*s, 1828 edition, no pagination, notes to Design XIX and Design XX.

8. Colvin, *Biographical Dictionary*, p.828.

9. Repton, *Fragments*, p.100.

10. *Ibid.*, p.218. He ranked next to that, 'Steepness of ground' and 'abrupt rocks'.

11. Ferrey was working at Bridehead in 1850, extending the house: *RCHM: Dorset*, vol.1, p.37.

12. Repton, *Fragments*, p.219.

13. A more consciously picturesque example is the 1801 *cottage ornée* gate lodge to the demolished Gaunt's House, Hinton Martell (**55**).

14. See Hugh Montgomery Massingberd, 'Bridehead Visited', *The Field*, 23 March 1985.

15. *Country Life*, 24 April, 1 & 8 May 1942.

16. Quoted by Giles Worsley, *Country Life*, 22 May 1984, an article on the Castle which did much to stir the local council into a last minute rescue.

17. The 1872 Ordnance Survey map also shows Steamer Lodge to the west and Beacon Lodge to the east.

18. Repton, *Fragments*, Fragment 25, p.129.

19. The Revd. Mr Coker, *Survey of Dorsetshire*, 1730, p.46. Coker was in fact publishing a text written in 1625 by Thomas Gerard of Trent.

20. Pamela Street, *Arthur Bryant, Portrait of an Historian*, 1979 has a vivid account of Bryant's tenancy and his struggle to revive a property wrecked by the military during the war years.

7 Mainstream and rogue

1. *Journal of Horticulture and Cottage Gardener*, 20 August 1890.

2. Ordnance Survey Map, 1888. Only the Rosary survives.

3. *Dorset County Chronicle*, 23 January 1890.

4. *Truth*, Thursday 23 January 1890. The exceptionally thorough Dorset Gardens Trust researchers were Mr & Mrs Crisp.

5. In Victorian arboreta the trees are usually treated in the same way, as museum specimens unrelated to other trees or to the landscape.

6. See Patricia Usick, *Adventures in Egypt and Nubia: The Travels of William John Bankes*, 2002; see also Mitchell, *Kingston Lacy*, Chapter Four.

7. Mitchell, *Kingston Lacy*, p.86. Wellington loaned him a gun carriage for its transportation.

8. Barry's design is illustrated in Gervase Jackson-Stops, *An English Arcadia 1600-1900*, 1991, p.136.

9. He commissioned these in 1848 from Giuseppe Petrelli of Padua. For these and other sculpture on the terrace and the south lawn see Mitchell, *Kingston Lacy*, Chapter Nine.

10. A present of 1822 from the British Consul in Cairo.

11. The two obelisks (one survives) were placed in the Upper Park at some time between 1735 and 1774.

12. William Goldring of Kew was consulted for planting schemes from 1899 to 1906.

13. Bevis Hillier, *John Betjeman: New Fame, New Love*, 2002, p.468.

14. I owe my information on the younger Revd. Cox to Carol Lindsay.

15. See Susan Elderkin, 'Into the Woods', *Sunday Telegraph Magazine*, 6 December 1998, for the flowers and for the literary and social background.

16. A third of the island with its two lakes and its lagoon is a controlled Nature Reserve with limited access. See *Country Life*, 2 August 1962 for the hostility to any human enjoyment of the island.

17. I am most grateful to John D'Arcy for allowing me access to the Castle and Steve Teuber for a tour of the grounds.

18. An earlier owner, William Benson, went mad and burnt books and records on the Castle foreshore; see *Country Life*, 2 August 1962.

19. These photographs are in the Castle Muniment Room.

20. Bennett, *Brownsea Island*, 1881, p.7. In Bennett's time the Pheasantry of 1774 had become two cottages. He also mentions 'a charming grotto of shells', now lost.

21. These are illustrated in H. Avray Tipping, *English Gardens*, 1925, plates 93-6. In the 1920s the gardens at Brownsea were being worked on by the garden designer, George Dillistone of Tunbridge Wells; for Dillistone and his garden at Poole, see Graham Davies, 'The Restoration of the Garden at Scaplen's Court, Poole', *Dorset Gardens Trust Newsletter*, no.17 (Summer 2001), pp.18-19.

22. The Durlston experiment is admirably described by David Lambert, 'Durlston Park and Purbeck House: The

Public and Private Realms of George Burt, King of Swanage' and 'The Folly of Conservation: Conservation in Practice at Durlston Country Park, Tyneham and Lulworth Castle', *New Arcadian Journal*, 45/46 (1998), pp.15-25; pp.53-87.

8 The lordly ones

1. See *Country Life*, 21 & 28 February 1980; also Col. The Lord Digby, 'The History of the Minterne Rhododendron Garden', *The Rhododendron and Camellia Year Book* (RHS, 1956), pp.9-15.
2. Blomfield's book was preceded by John Sedding's *Garden-Craft Old and New* (1891), which also advocated a return to the simple planting and architectural confinements of Elizabethan and Jacobean gardens.
3. From 'Making the Best of it', in *Hopes and Fears for Art*, 1882; quoted in David Ottewill, *Edwardian Gardens*, 1989, p.29.
4. From the chorus from Swinburne's 'Atalanta in Calydon'.
5. Jellicoe published *Italian Gardens of the Rennaissance* in 1925; see Michael Spens, *Gardens of the Mind: The Genius of Geoffrey Jellicoe*, 1992, pp.31-47.
6. Thomas Mawson, *The Life and Work of an English Landscape Architect*, 1927, pp.85-6: 'my services were requested by Mr A C de Lafontaine . . . As he had already spent large sums upon the restoration of the old house and a formal garden on its south side, all excellently designed and executed, I could not help wondering why I had been consulted. My work was to replan the entrance and main drive, and the gardens north of the house and drive, and to find a site and plan for a new stable and garage. Some of this, I understand, was carried out, but my work was merely to supply plans'.
7. See *Country Life*, 2 September 1899
8. See *Country Life*, 1 December 1966. Early photographs in *Country Life* of two other Dorset gardens, Hanford House (22 April 1905) and Waterston Manor (12 February 1916), show how the original topiary of these Edwardian designs has now grown out of all proportion to their grounds.
9. See *Country Life*, 18 January 1908 & 30 May 1925.
10. For illustrations of Wayford see Ottewill, *Edwardian Garden*, pp.150-1.
11. The recreated gardens are lavishly illustrated in *Country Life*, 3 April 1915.
12. *The Art and Craft of Garden Making*, 1912 edition, p.6.
13. *Ibid.*
14. *Ibid.*
15. *Ibid.*, p.9.
16. *Ibid.*
17. Dorset Record Office, D/115.
18. *Ibid.*
19. With the possible exception of the south terrace at Kingston Lacy.
20. *Ibid.*
21. Dorset Record Office, D/115; written 28 July 1906 from his Swiss Kur-haus.
22. Mawson, *Art and Craft*, fig.238. I am grateful to Stephen Parker for bringing this fifth edition to my attention.
23. From the plan (fig.157) and an illustration (fig.184) in the 1912 edition it appears that we have lost two exedral seats facing each other across The Glade immediately before the pylons. Two loggias, one on each side of the Belvedere, illustrated on the plan (fig.157) are no longer there, if they were ever built.
24. Both Arthur Oswald, *Country Houses of Dorset*, and David Ottewill, *The Edwardian Garden*, 1989, give the purchase date as 1910, but the house was, in fact, bought by the Earl of Ilchester in 1898 and sold to F.E. Savile in 1907; see *Country Life*, 28 July 1950, correspondence.
25. For Thomas and the portrait see David Ottewill, *Edwardian Garden*, pp.13-21; pl.11.
26. Arthur Oswald, *Country Houses of Dorset*, states that these were designed after 1919 for C.H. St John Hornby by Alfred Powell (p.99).
27. This is, admittedly, a tentative attribution by Ottewill, *Edwardian Garden*, p.18, n.95: 'This work bears the stamp of Inigo Thomas but has not been investigated by the author.'
28. Pevsner, *Buildings of England*, Oswald, *Country Houses of Dorset* and Legg, *Dorset Families*, give 1911; Ottewill, *Edwardian Garden*, gives 1910.
29. He called it 'Weatherbury' and it was Bathsheba Everdene's inheritance.
30. See *Country Life*, 12 February 1916.
31. See *The Field*, 20 May 1984.
32. See Oswald, *Country Houses of Dorset*, p.157; pls.178-9; also *Country Life*, 16 November 1951.
33. Hutchins appears to believe that the ancestral home of the Russell Dukes of Bedford was at Kingston Russell Farm about a mile to the north (1774 edition, vol.1, p.298).
34. Hutchins, *Dorset*, 1863, 2, pp.191-2.
35. *The Field*, 20 May 1984.

9 Formalism or the grain of nature?

1. The original red brick house was encased in Portland stone ashlar in 1794; it is attributed to Archer by John Newman & Nikolaus Pevsner, *Buildings of England: Dorset*, pp.247-8.
2. Dorothy Frances Gurney, 'God's Garden', 1913.
3. It is illustrated in Hutchins, *Dorset*, 1774 edition, but without a comment, as if Hutchins disapproved of its crude Gothick styling.
4. Lady Teresa Agnew, born a Fox-Strangways, and her first husband, Lord Galway, initiated this recovery.
5. Perceiving this weakness, the Curator, Stephen Griffith, has shrewdly set his light designer, John Newton, to devise a light show which lends the various trees as almost architectural solidity of form. Could sound be added to light? See Stephen Anderton's article, 'Very Caravaggio', in *The Times*, 2 November 2002, Weekend/Gardening.
6. Mawson, *Life and Work*, p.322.
7. *Ibid.*, p.322.
8. For Colvin I am indebted to Trish Gibson's unpublished Bristol University MA Dissertation: 'Brenda Colvin – Unsung Pioneer of Modern Landscape Design' (2002).
9. Steeple Manor was Colvin's job number 50, carried out for the Swanns; information from Hal Moggridge.
10. In private correspondence (4 September 2002) Hal Moggridge records that the garden 'has been sensitively restored by its present owners including replanting so like Brenda's work that it is hard to believe that it is not her own; it is as if she returned in person at a later date to complete the planting.'
11. See Denys J. Wilcox, *The London Group 1913-39: The Artists and their Works* (Aldershot, 1995).
12. Brenda Colvin was a close friend of the Gardiners and although she was not formally commissioned to work at Springhead, she is likely to have given advice on the planting. I am grateful to Hal Moggridge for this suggestion.
13. Information on the Trust's activities is taken from 'Utopia Britannica – Organic Nationalism', *www.utopia-britannica.org.uk/pages/Springhead.htm*. I owe this reference to Trish Gibson.
14. *Ibid.*, p.1.
15. *Ibid.*, pp.1-2.
16.. D.H. Lawrence would have loved the homoerotic pantheism, but then so, one suspects, would Himmler's SS.
17. This is built of reconstituted 'Minsterstone' replacing an earlier building on the site shown on the 1903 OS map.
18. See *Country Life*, 6 January 1994.
19. Dorset Record Office, D/795/17.
20. For further information on the Larmer Tree Gardens see Lt.-Gen. Pitt-Rivers, *A Short Guide to the Larmer Grounds, Rushmore; King John's House; and The Museum at Farnham, Dorset* (Farnham, *c.*1907); also Legg, *Dorset Families*, p.117.
21. See Mark Bowden, *Pitt-Rivers*, 1991, for the letters of this heartless correspondence.
22. However the RCHM dates the recessed hall portion to the thirteenth century: see *County of Dorset*, vol.3, part 1, p.115.
23. See *The Architect & Building News*, 8 January 1932.

10 Later twentieth-century gardens

1. Pam Lewis claims as her figure of influence John Brookes, under whom she studied, and the gardener-writers Peter Seymour, Christopher Lloyd, Marjory Fish and Vita Sackville-West.
2. Professor Chris Baines influenced Pam profoundly with the need to provide sanctuaries for our displaced farmland wildlife.
3. Taken from one of a series of rustic display boards that guide the visitor around the garden.
4. Nori and Sandra Pope of Hadspen House inspired Pam to use plants in a 'painterly' way.
5. R. Good, *Dorset Paths*, 1966, p.96.
6. R. Good in his *The Lost Villages of Dorset*, 1979, finds no evidence for village life after that date, yet the Rectory survived at least until the 1885 Ordnance Survey map.
7. The lake was in existence as early as Isaac Taylor's 1765 Map of Dorset.
8. This is a recreation by the Coombs of what is shown on the 1888 Ordnance Survey map. The map also records a central pond in the potager.
9. Dorset Record Office, D/RWR/E53 and *The Proceedings of the Dorset Archaeological Society*, vol.64, p.93.
10. *Country Life*, 4 March 1976. The article was written as a tribute to John Greenwood, a retired vice chairman of Boots the Chemists, who, together with his wife, laid the foundations of the garden from 1953. He died in 1975.
11. There is no sign of this feature on the 1890 OS map, only a 'Spring'.
12. The statue is without provenance and could be a Japanese priest to accord with the garden down in the valley behind it.
13. Pevsner & Newman, *Dorset*, p.103

Index